# The historian and film

*edited by* **PAUL SMITH**
*Lecturer in History*
*King's College, London*

**CAMBRIDGE UNIVERSITY PRESS**

*Cambridge*
*London   New York   Melbourne*

CAMBRIDGE UNIVERSITY PRESS
Cambridge, New York, Melbourne, Madrid, Cape Town, Singapore, São Paulo, Delhi

Cambridge University Press
The Edinburgh Building, Cambridge CB2 8RU, UK

Published in the United States of America by Cambridge University Press, New York

www.cambridge.org
Information on this title: www.cambridge.org/9780521209922

First published 1976
This digitally printed version 2008

*A catalogue record for this publication is available from the British Library*

*Library of Congress Cataloguing in Publication data*
Main entry under title:
The Historian and Film
    Bibliography: p. 186
    Includes index.
    1. History – Study and teaching – Audio-visual aids –
Addresses, essays, lectures. 2. Moving pictures in historiography
– Addresses, essays, lectures. 3. Historical films – Addresses,
essays, lectures.
I. Smith, Paul, 1937–
D16.255.A8H57     907′.2     75–19577

ISBN 978-0-521-20992-2 hardback
ISBN 978-0-521-08939-5 paperback

# Contents

# Preface

The amount of work now being done by historians on and with film and the absence of a substantial survey of the field in English have together made the moment ripe for the production of this book. It aims to say something about almost all the major aspects of historians' interest in film: considerations of size and in one or two cases the absence of a suitably qualified contributor have prevented its coverage from being quite complete.

I have to thank the contributors for giving me a much less harassing passage than falls to the lot of many editors, the staff of the Cambridge University Press for their invaluable encouragement and aid in the project, and my wife, who knows more about all this than I do.

The book has no dedication, but if it did it should perhaps be to the growing band of historians, archivists and others from several countries who, in 'film and history' meetings over the last few years, have enlarged not merely their understanding but also their circle of friends.

Paul Smith

*King's College, London*
*August 1975*

# The contributors

Paul Smith is Lecturer in History at King's College, University of London

Lisa Pontecorvo is a film researcher and member of the B.B.C. television Open University arts production team

Clive Coultass is Keeper of the Department of Film at the Imperial War Museum, London

William Hughes is Professor of History and Lecturer in Film at Essex Community College, Baltimore, Md., U.S.A.

Marc Ferro is Directeur d'études at the Ecole Pratique des Hautes Etudes and Maître de conférences at the Ecole Polytechnique

Nicholas Pronay is Lecturer in History at the University of Leeds

Rolf Schuursma is Assistant Managing Director (documentation and distribution) of the Stichting Film en Wetenschap, Utrecht

John Grenville is Professor of Modern History at the University of Birmingham

Arthur Marwick is Professor of History at the Open University

Bryan Haworth is Principal Lecturer in History at Padgate College of Education

Donald Watt is Professor of International History at the London School of Economics and Political Science, University of London

Jerry Kuehl is a producer with Thames Television, London

# Introduction

PAUL SMITH

'Of the scholars, nothing is to be expected, I am afraid', wrote Sir Arthur Elton, a pioneer of the documentary film, pleading in a much-quoted article of 1955 for greater recognition of the value of film as a source material for history.[1] It was true that up to that time professional historians, in Britain at least, had shown small interest in the utilisation of film, either in research or in teaching. Yet even in 1955 Elton's words disregarded some significant developments. If in the early days of film it had tended to be those involved in the craft of film-making themselves, like the American W.K.L. Dickson or the Pole Matuszewski, who called attention to its potential historical importance, there had none the less been considerable discussion of the matter by scholars between the wars within the International Congress of Historical Sciences and elsewhere, and a distinguished Cambridge historian, George Kitson Clark, had been among those who, in 1948, founded the British Universities Film Council to promote the use of film in higher education. Moreover, had Elton's vision extended to Germany, the gloom generated by the British situation would have been lightened. Not for the first time in the history of historiography, the Anglo-Saxons were lagging behind. In Göttingen, serious work on film regarded as a historical document had been in progress since 1949 under the aegis of such figures as Professors Walther Hubatsch, Percy Ernst Schramm and Wilhelm Treue. The 'Referat für zeitgeschichtliche Filmforschung und Filmdokumentation' established in 1953 at the Institut für den Wissenschaftlichen Film in Göttingen, working in close co-operation with the Bundesarchiv in Koblenz, was already beginning to produce edited film documents of contemporary German history for research and teaching purposes.[2] History was catching up with the moving picture.

It was, however, not until the sixties that the use of film (which term is taken to include television) in historical studies could be seen to be advancing on a broad international front. The status of film as evidence was becoming accepted: already in 1961 the French historian Charles Samaran felt it appropriate to include in his massive manual, *L'Histoire et ses méthodes*, important sections on film sources from the pen of Georges Sadoul. Increasingly, film was coming to be used in teaching, though often only in an elementary way, as incidental illustration. Historians were even embarking on making their own films for teaching purposes. In 1966 Dr R.L. Schuursma, then head of the Sound Archive at the Historical Institute of the University of Utrecht, was responsible, in

1

collaboration with the Stichting Film en Wetenschap, Utrecht, for the production of a film on the life of the Dutch Fascist leader Anton Mussert, soon to
be followed by another on the battle of Arnhem. Britain was not far behind in
this field, for in 1968 Professor John Grenville and Nicholas Pronay produced at
the University of Leeds *The Munich Crisis*, and initiated the British Inter-
University History Film Consortium to promote further ventures. In many ways,
1968 was a year of take-off for the application of film in historical studies, not
least because of the increasing publicity given to the subject among historians
and others and the establishment of contact between those who had hitherto
tended to work in isolation. An important step was taken in April 1968 when
the Slade Film Department at University College, London, already much
involved under Professor Thorold Dickinson in showing film material to history
students, organised, in conjunction with the British Universities Film Council, a
conference on 'Film and the Historian', whose published proceedings, together
with the first (February 1968) issue of the Council's new journal, *University
Vision*, devoted entirely to film and history, were to play a substantial role in
stimulating and guiding interest in the field. The Slade Film Department went on
to secure support from the Social Science Research Council to compile a register
of film material in Britain of use to history and the social sciences. At the same
time Marc Ferro, who had already been involved, with the collaboration of other
French historians, in two major productions for French television, *La Grande
Guerre* and *1917*, published in *Annales* (23, 1968), in the section devoted to
'Débats et combats', an urgent call for greater attention by historians to the
documents which film placed at their disposal. And in Göttingen the group of
young historians, educationists and social scientists which had formed in 1964
as the Studienkreis Geschichte und Publizistik, under the wing of the Institut
für den Wissenschaftlichen Film, was holding a working meeting on contemporary film and television documents in research and higher education from which
resulted the publication in 1970, under the editorship of Günter Moltmann and
Karl Reimers, of a collection of studies entitled *Zeitgeschichte im Film- und
Tondokument*, still the most substantial work in its sphere.

Even in the short perspective of seven years from which I am writing now,
1968 seems an age of cheerful innocence. So much has been done since then, in
many parts of Europe and North America, as to defy a brief summary. Work has
progressed steadily on all three main fronts, investigation of film as source
material, use of film in teaching, and making of films for academic purposes,
with concomitant publication both in print and on film. A string of international
conferences in London, Utrecht, Göttingen and elsewhere has helped to maintain contacts and sometimes to promote mutual comprehension, not only among
historians and other scholars, but also between academics as a whole and those
professionally involved with film, as producers, directors and archivists. There
have inevitably been committees, too. In Britain, the University Historians' Film
Committee set up at the 1968 conference has to a large extent been content to

see the work of liaison and information performed by the British Universities Film Council, through its network of representatives in universities and other institutions of higher education, and its publications, including a regular newsletter and journal. The Film Committee established by the Historical Association, much concerned with school- as well as university-level work, has now gone out of existence. In the U.S.A., the Historians' Film Committee formed in 1970 maintains in *Film and History* the only periodical devoted to the subject.

On the whole, organisation among those engaged in exploring the use of film in historical studies has remained loose and informal, and this has perhaps helped them to avoid the excessive self-consciousness, search for dogma and tedious proselytising that would have vested their co-operative efforts with all the panoply of a movement. None the less, from the point of view of historical scholarship, there might appear to be something odd in meetings, publications and committees devoted to the utilisation of film. Historians normally interest themselves in history, rather than in particular media of record and communication. There are no groups, to the writer's knowledge, devoted to the study of print and history, or even of newspapers and history. Concentration on film as such can produce curious results, as in those faintly unreal sessions at film and history conferences when the natural professional instinct of at least a part of the audience to discuss a historical topic in the round, from the standpoint of all available evidence, is frustrated by the necessity to restrict consideration to those aspects which are illuminated by one, not always central, source. What is needed in the long run is, of course, the full integration of film into the range of resources at the historian's disposal, so that its use, where appropriate, is a matter of course, not needing special remark. But it is precisely in order to make the use of film commonplace that it has been necessary to give it special emphasis and study. Awareness of film and willingness to take it seriously were not widespread even among contemporary historians in the sixties: hence the need to devote to it an attention that may sometimes have seemed to border on the eccentric.

The situation has changed a good deal in recent years. Film is now becoming fully assimilated into the accepted corpus of historical source materials and means of instruction. The experience of the graduate student at Columbia University in the early sixties who was reproved by his professor for using so dubious a source as film and advised by a sympathetic instructor to establish himself academically before dabbling further with it is less and less likely to be duplicated.[3] Yet there remain a good many historians of the modern period who are insufficiently acquainted with film's possible uses or who are diffident in face of the practical and theoretical problems which those uses may pose. As the acceptance of film grows, in fact, the need to devote careful investigation to its nature, content and mode of use increases rather than decreases.

There is much ignorance about what sort of material is available, what it can provide, and how it can be employed both in research and in teaching. At present, the search for guidance has to be conducted through many scattered

3

publications, not all of them easily accessible, as a glance at the bibliography of this book will show. There is no wide-ranging handbook in English comparable to Moltmann and Reimers, itself confined to German and Austrian experience. This volume attempts to supply some part of the deficiency. It does not set out to provide a complete manual of the use of film by historians, desirable though such a production will be in due time, or to offer a series of definitive pronouncements about the areas with which it deals. The field is too new, its exploitation still too experimental and unskilled, to make such aims feasible at the moment. What we have tried to do here is rather to provide a survey of the actual and potential uses of film material in historical research, teaching and presentation, reporting on the position that has been reached and indicating the problems and possibilities with whose resolution and exploration we shall be concerned in the future. No line has been laid down to which contributors have been required to conform; their diversity of opinion reflects, as is proper, the state of the subject.

The book seeks first to outline the nature and range of the material available and to look at its preservation and provision to users through the film archives and other collections; second, to consider film as a historical document and the types of evidence that can be derived from it; third, to see film as a historical factor, developing within and operating upon a particular historical context, by means of a case study of the newsreel; fourth, to discuss the use of film as a teaching instrument and as a medium for the interpretation and presentation of history both to students and to a wider public. A select bibliography offers a guide to further study, and a list of addresses of organisations is appended to help those seeking practical information and assistance. It is the hope of its authors that the book will not only aid and encourage those students of history who feel that film may be of value to them but help to stimulate the further work on film resources and the methodology of film's use which is needed.

Perhaps, also, it will do something to persuade those who remained unconvinced of film's relevance to serious historical study to think again. Even if the necessity to argue the case for taking film seriously is much less acute than it was ten years ago, it has not altogether vanished. Given that the film in the modern sense made its début in 1895, it has taken historians a long time to come to terms with it either as a source or as a possible medium of interpretation and instruction, and the prejudices, suspicions and difficulties which have held them back have not yet been entirely removed.

Possibly the deepest root of historians' reserve has been the unthinking but not unnatural identification of film with 'films' or 'the pictures', understood in the sense of the production of the commercial cinema and classed simply as a medium of trivial and ephemeral popular entertainment. Film thus regarded has retained the taint of its café and fairground origins, of being in Georges Duhamel's phrase 'une machine d'abêtissement et de dissolution, un passe-temps d'illettrés, de créatures misérables abusées par leur besogne'.[4] Traditional history

4

has tended to be snobbish about materials, arranging them roughly in the order of the social strata which produced them. Archivists codify historians' prejudices, and the following, from the classification scheme of a German archivist arranging papers in Strasbourg in the early 1940s, is symptomatic of the status assigned by old-style history to film: 'G I Höhere Kunst (auch Theater); G II Kleinkunst: Theater, Lichtspiele, Zirkusse usw'. Even the gradual conversion of cinema from a resort of the masses to a pastime of intellectuals has not altogether wiped out this stigma or succeeded in transferring it to television. And if the historian is now less likely to dismiss the film as 'mere popular entertainment' and more likely to be a devotee of it himself, that perhaps only increases his reluctance, now that it has become a source of pleasure, to make it yet another object of work.

A second reason for neglect of film has undoubtedly been the conservatism which affects all professions, in which acquired wisdom may find itself consorting uncomfortably with sloth and narrow-mindedness. A third has more to do with limits of time and mental endurance: the contemporary historian, overwhelmed by the mass of written and printed materials for the study of the twentieth century, may well shy at the thought of taking on another large area of unfamiliar character. It is an area, too, and here lies a fourth reason, in which he may find it practically difficult to operate. Not only may he need to master new techniques of analysis and perhaps of presentation, but he will have to face possibly substantial problems of availability of material and of the time, money and facilities required to utilise it. Finally, and very important, there have been serious doubts about whether film could yield results of a value proportionate to the trouble invested in using it. As a source, it has often been pointed out, film is subject to grave disadvantages, considered from the point of view of factual record. It reaches the observer almost always in highly edited form, from raw material representing in itself only a very partial and selective view. It can quite easily be faked, or put together in such a way as to distort reality, give a tendentious picture, and practise upon the emotions of the spectator. Moreover it is often a relatively trivial and superficial record, capturing only the external appearance of its subjects and offering few insights into the processes and relationships, causes and motives which are the historian's concern. It may simply illustrate without helping to explain. This thraldom to externals may seem, too, to make it a difficult medium to employ for historical instruction and interpretation. All these misgivings about the value of film rest on substantial grounds. None constitutes a sufficient reason for excluding it from the field of historical scholarship.

Film, after all, is a fact, which historians can ignore no more than other facts. They labour under Clio's curse, the omnipresence of meaning, which dictates that there can be no area or product of human activity without relevance to their concerns, unamenable to their curiosity. It is not for them so to circumscribe the boundaries of their subject as arbitrarily to exclude any of the available means of furthering it. Whatever exists has to be examined for whatever it can yield, and if the examination suggests new objects or methods of investigation they must be assimilated into the canon, for a conception of history narrower than our means of exploring history is an absurdity. From this standpoint, there is no natural or necessary hierarchy of sources, or, for that matter, of modes of communication, no divine distinction between serious and unserious, trivial and important. There can be only provisional and particular hierarchies related to specific questions and aims. Film will be towards the bottom or the top according to what the individual historian is interested in and wants to know or to do: the bottom if he is studying or expounding, say, conventional diplomatic history; the top if he is studying, say, the development of popular culture, and finds in the mass entertainment aspect of the film not a reason for despising it but an essential source, or if he desires to communicate a body of knowledge to which film is integral. To neglect a source of such multifarious character and vast extent as film is for the twentieth century, to ignore a means of communication which may be peculiarly appropriate to certain tasks of presentation or indispensable in reaching certain types of audience (notably the mass audience now perhaps attainable only through television) deserves the harshest of epithets: it is simply unprofessional. That does not mean that all historians, or even all contemporary historians, are under an obligation to use film; only that none should exclude the possibility of doing so.

Just as there is no immutable hierarchy of sources in terms of their historical significance, so there is none in terms of their intrinsic purity or impurity. All the historian's sources are more or less impure: if they were not, there would be small need for his professional skills. Film sources are not inherently worse than any others. The criticisms outlined earlier of film regarded as record can be levelled at other forms of source material: written and printed documents, for instance, may equally be partial, subjective, tendentious, emotive, and even forged. Nothing has been more curious in discussions of film's role in historical studies than the degree of suspicion directed against it by historians who are prepared to accept verbal material with far less critical apprehension. The pitfalls of film may in some cases be of a slightly different character, and it may require a somewhat different training to detect them, but it is hard to see that they are necessarily deeper or more numerous. It is largely the comparative unfamiliarity of film, decreasing with each new generation of historians, which has earned it such suspicion, and perhaps, too, the insistence of so many of its pioneers on exploiting it as an illusionist device.

Even the criticism that film evidence is often trivial and superficial, which tends again to place film low in a qualitative source hierarchy, has its force only in a limited context. It rests partly on an excessive preoccupation with film viewed as a record of fact and event narrowly defined, especially in relation to conventional political history, and on disillusionment at what may be called the broken promise of reality, a promise held out not by film to its users but by the

6

more naïve of its users to themselves. Since the birth of the cinema, it has seemed at first sight reasonable to suppose that the major advantage of the cine-camera for history would be to permit an exact recording of reality, to enable us to 'see it as it happened'. But what we get from film is only rarely an untainted and unmanipulated reproduction of the external reality at which the camera was originally pointed, and it is always a very partial reproduction of that reality, both because of the circumstances of shooting and editing and because reality does not consist solely of the external physical appearances which may be all that the camera can capture. If film is regarded as a record of facts, of events, processes and people, external to its making, then it is necessary to recognise that it has important limitations, just as it is necessary to assert that it sometimes has considerable merits.

These limitations, however, reduce to their proper proportions when we take an enlarged conception of 'facts' and 'events' and concentrate on the reality represented by, rather than that represented through, film. For a piece of film itself and the circumstances of its making, exhibition and reception are facts and events for which the film is prime evidence. Reality inheres even in a fake: it is a real fake, the result of real events, mental as well as physical, composed of elements individually genuine, and can usefully be analysed in that sense. The film records the outlook, intentions and capacities of those who made it; it illustrates in some way the character of the society in which it was produced and for which it was designed; it is the most perfect record of one factor operating within and upon that society — itself. It is in these aspects, rather than as evidence of external facts seen through the camera lens, that film can offer the richest reward for our interest.

The present book reflects this broad view of the evidential value of film, both in the general discussion of film resources and the evaluation of film evidence conducted by Lisa Pontecorvo and William Hughes and in the contributions on the analysis of fiction film and the historical development of the newsreel by Marc Ferro and Nicholas Pronay. The role that film can play in the factual recording of events, processes, personalities and things is not depreciated, nor is it forgotten that the external appearances which form so large a part of the camera's haul of information are for certain purposes of first-rate importance to the historian, even to the political historian if we think of, say, the theatrical dimension of politics as represented by oratorical style or by the visual self-projection of a mass movement.

But to a large extent attention is concentrated less upon what film overtly records and says than upon what Arthur Marwick has described as its 'unwitting testimony', upon the information that can be derived from it about the mental and social world of its makers and audiences. All categories of film can be examined from this point of view, from the 'factual' to the fantastic. The newsreel may be of value less for the study of its ostensible subjects than for the examination of the assumptions and intentions behind the way it presents them and of the influence which that presentation exerts upon its audience. The documentary film (a misleading title, which has cast a specious mantle of objectivity over some highly tendentious productions) may well turn out to be a document less of what it purports to record than of the values and purposes of its makers and of the manipulations of reality to which these drove them, often, paradoxically, in the interest of the true reality as they saw it.[5] But perhaps it is the fiction film which comes most into its own under this type of analysis. Often neglected by historians whose primary concern is with film in relation to propaganda and mass communication, the fiction film is in fact relevant in both spheres. It is central to the study of mass entertainment and popular taste. Most important, it is arguably (or, perhaps, was until the rise of television) the most 'social' product of the film industry, by virtue of the variety of people employed in its manufacture, its explicit relation to an audience (usually a mass audience), and its influence on that audience. Hence it may well be the richest source of information about the society in which it has its birth and its impact. The exploration of that information by historians is still in its infancy. The best-known attempt to probe the deeper evidential content of the fiction film, Siegfried Kracauer's search for 'the inner dispositions of the German people' as reflected through the medium of the German screen between the wars, in *From Caligari to Hitler*, has not furnished us with a satisfactory analytical model, and it is hard to say that more recent essays in the same direction have been more convincing. Marc Ferro is a leading present-day exponent of the quest for the 'non-visible' beneath the surface of the fiction film, and gives us in this volume a practical example of what it can yield.[6]

Evidently, to say that film reflects and affects aspects of the society which creates it is one thing; to define the nature and analyse the content of its relations with society is another. There are methodological problems of great complexity here, which no one pretends yet to have solved, problems which, of course, have to do not simply with the analysis of film but with the analysis of society. What does a film mean, what does it contain, either for its creators or for any particular audience? These are not simple questions. The difficulty of answering them is intensified by the fact that it clearly does not suffice to look at the film alone. There is a context of production and reception to be examined. Thus we need, for example, what at the moment we scarcely possess, good studies of the motion picture industry as an economic and social mechanism, in order to determine how far and in what ways film has been conditioned by the nature and purposes of the organisation required to produce it. Too often films have been discussed as though generated in a vacuum by the spontaneous power of individual genius: we have much on films as art, too little on films as consumption goods. We need analyses of censorship from within and without, to see how far films have been adapted to conventions and requirements external to the creative impulse. 'When coarse story is being told, Vicar should not be present.' Much history lies in that 1949 comment of the British Board of Film Censors on a scenario submitted to it; still more in its 1932 remarks on the portrayal of strikes and labour movements: 'It is impossible to show such a scene without taking a definite side either with or against the strikers and this would range the film as political propaganda of a type that we have always held to be unsuitable for exhibition in this country.'[7] We need, too, studies of the reception of films. There is frequently no evidence of the effect of particular films on particular audiences, but there is a good deal of the effect of cinema in general. It is important not to neglect the conditions in which reception takes place: we have to study not simply film but the cinema and the nature of the cinematic experience, that extraordinary barrage of sensations falling upon the spectator in an artificial world of darkness and abstraction, relieved sometimes by the diversions to which darkness lends aid and even enchantment. Perhaps there is a special television experience, too, different at least in being fully lit, which we ought to analyse. In all these areas of the investigation of film's relation to society we are simply groping.

How far historians have the necessary skills to grope effectively is a moot point. In order to deal adequately with film, it is probably essential for them to acquire some specialised knowledge of its nature and of the range of possible approaches to its understanding, including such modern fashions as semiology. They must become what Thorold Dickinson has dubbed 'cinemate', as distinct from literate. William Hughes, who outlines below the techniques available for 'decoding the message structure of film', has elsewhere suggested a course for historians wishing to use film, including practical experience in making films, which some would regard as a prerequisite of full comprehension of the medium.[8] Certainly historians engaged with film on a broad front will need sometimes to call in aid practitioners of other disciplines. A practical lead in such collaborative effort has been given by the work of the Göttingen-based Studienkreis Geschichte und Publizistik, devoted primarily to the investigation of film's role as an instrument of mass communication, and combining the talents of historians, sociologists, communications specialists, etc. So far, co-operation with those who would regard themselves as specialists in film or the cinema has been very limited. Film historians tend too often to treat their subject simply as the history of a self-contained art form, ignoring its wider connotations and connections, providing catalogues of technical and aesthetic developments, synopses of plots and roll-calls of directors and their stars, which provide little help in the task of situating film in its social context. From film theorists, analysts and aestheticians there may be more to learn. Historians may well have something to gain from contact with the film studies departments already widespread in North American universities and gradually being introduced, rather tentatively, in Britain, where their survival in a chill economic climate may depend on their ability to strike up working relationships with established subjects and to set their concerns in the widest context.

The need for the historian to extend his skills applies equally if we transfer

9

the emphasis from the use of film as source material to its use as teaching material and as a medium of instruction and interpretation. Even for the simplest presentation of film material to students, some understanding of the medium is desirable in order to guide their appreciation of its content and significance, and in order to gauge the likely character of its effect on them (student response to film as opposed to other forms of communication in history is something which has yet been very little investigated). The students, too, are being required to extend their skills, for critical analysis of film is still seldom taught in schools, and in helping them to do so the aid of film studies departments may again be valuable. The case for the acquisition of specialist knowledge is obviously stronger still when the historian's aim is not merely to show films but to make them. Technical expertise he may not need: the handling of film, television, videotape, etc. by historians as by other academics has been rendered very much easier in recent years by the establishment in most higher education institutions, at least in Britain and North America, of audio-visual units capable of providing almost any service from operating a projector to producing a complete film. But unless he has some grasp of the nature of film and the basic procedure involved in using it as a medium of expression, he is going to find difficulty in ensuring that the media specialists produce the kind of result he wants. It has indeed been argued that the academic should know enough to be his own producer.

The use of film in teaching is surveyed in general terms in this volume by Arthur Marwick, with the advantage of the unique experience of the Open University in incorporating television teaching programmes into its courses, and by Bryan Haworth from the point of view of the schools, while Rolf Schuursma and John Grenville bring to the discussion of the problems and opportunities facing the historian as film-maker their background as pioneers in this field. It is perhaps the making of films that has aroused most controversy in the area of film and history. The initiative in Britain has been taken by the British Inter-University History Film Consortium with a series of productions which, though intended for use in a context of lectures, tutorials and guided reading, set out to provide a rounded exposition and interpretation of their subjects on film. Critics have argued that this impulse to produce a 'freestanding' object involves spending a good deal of time and money in trying to do on film things that film does not do easily or well — providing background information, explaining complicated political and diplomatic manoeuvres, and so on — and that a film of its nature tends towards too dogmatic and un-nuanced a style of exposition to lend itself readily to the needs of historical interpretation. They have therefore preferred to the historiographical exercise in film the alternative approach of producing either editions of film documents or compilations of film source material. The production of editions of film documents, accompanied by printed critical commentaries, has been a speciality for some twenty years of the Institut für den Wissenschaftlichen Film, with its series, 'Filmdokumente zur Zeitgeschichte', on contemporary German history.[9] Compilations of sources have ranged from Rolf Schuursma's *Mussert*, presenting its material almost neutrally, to the Open University's 'War and Society' series, setting the film documents in an evaluative and interpretative frame. It is interesting to note that the Consortium has now begun production of a documents series, without, however, abandoning its commitment to the expository film. The debate between the two approaches, both sides of which are represented here, will no doubt continue. There is one further approach not discussed in this volume but tried out in a few instances, the filming of contemporary events, persons, etc. by or under the direction of historians, for the express purpose of historical record.[10] The problems of selection, method and finance involved will be obvious.

The historian may make films for his students; in the interpretation of history to the general public through film, whether in the cinema or on television, his role will at most be that of an adviser. It is not easy for him to stand aloof from the business of 'popular' history on film, if he cares about the version of history which is absorbed into the consciousness of society. For millions, the television documentary is their only contact with history presented as such. The responsibility which rests on those involved in its production is very heavy, for what they put out does not constitute a part of a continuing debate to which all their viewers are privy. Most of those viewers are not well equipped to evaluate it and are unlikely to be reached by any criticism or refutation of it from professional historians; for many of them it will be not an interpretation but a final statement of the truth about its subject, driven home with all the force of visual demonstration. The historian, then, is under some compulsion to do what he can, when invited, to see that the principles of his trade are observed in the making of the programme to the extent that the exigencies of production allow. The questions which his involvement raises are examined from different, though not opposed, standpoints by Donald Watt and Jerry Kuehl, with the polemical freedom that seems appropriate to the transition from the academic sphere to that of mass communication. Perhaps in the future it may be possible sometimes to present historical topics on television in terms of problems and interpretations to be examined rather than of assumed truths to be conveyed in a pseudo-authoritative commentary, and to provide facilities for the critical discussion of historical programmes at times when there would be some prospect of its reaching the original audience.

In the last analysis, what we can do with film in history depends on what film, and ancillary documentation, we can get. It is with that fact in mind that we have opened this book with a section devoted to film resources and the archives. There are three problems here which are basic to all discussion of the use of film by historians: preservation, information and availability. The enormous task faced by the archives and film collections in preserving film is outlined by Clive Coultass. Much of the early production of the cinema has already been lost. Much has been mutilated: it is not always realised how difficult it may now be to see a film in the form in which it was originally shown.[11] Large amounts of pre-1950 nitrate film are deteriorating towards unusability at this moment. The problem of coping with the huge output of television is not being met. Historians should support their local archive, friendly or otherwise, in attempting to secure the money, staff and equipment which it needs. Perhaps here we should couple with the film archives the sound archives, whose holdings can often usefully be employed in conjunction with film. The provision of detailed information about film holdings (dependent, of course, largely on the capacity of the collections' cataloguing systems) is an urgent need. Historians can turn to no comprehensive inventories of film collections. Those in Britain are better placed than most, since the Slade Film History Register now provides an index to material for history and the social sciences in British collections (excluding television), but the continuation of the Register's work is threatened by lack of funding. There is a need, too, to preserve, list and utilise not merely the films but the associated documents which are vital to their study, from cameramen's 'dope sheets' to the records of the production companies and the censorship. Availability is a question of fundamental importance, and historians have an interest in pressing for film collections to be given and to make use of the means to provide enlarged viewing facilities, as some of them are now eager to do, as well as in backing ventures like the Higher Education Film Library maintained by the British Universities Film Council, which aims *inter alia* to provide hire copies of archive material in requisition by scholars but unlikely to repay commercial distribution.

The use of film in history is still a subject defining its concepts and refining its techniques, assessing its aims and its means. It is important that it should be pursued with appropriate rigour. The entertainment associations of film tend to shed a false glamour on its employment in historical studies and to offer a false promise of escape from the laborious discipline associated with the use of other forms of source and media of expression. In the U.S.A., where it has reportedly been used on occasion to boost student enrolment and to provide a crutch for historians lacking confidence in the future of their subject as traditionally understood, film has been described as a 'sexy' subject. But this is not always the kind of subject that attracts the most virile minds; rather it may attract those in search of quick returns from small endeavour. It needs to be stressed that because of the complexity both of its own nature and of its relation to the world about it film demands just as much critical acumen and effort for its use as any other material with which the historian works.

NOTES

1. 'The Film as Source Material for History', *Aslib Proceedings*, 7 (1955), 230.
2. For the Göttingen work, see K.F. Reimers, 'Audio-visuelle Dokumente in der Forschung und Hochschule: die "Filmdokumente zur Zeitgeschichte" des Instituts für den Wissenschaftlichen Film (I.W.F.), Göttingen', in G. Moltmann and K.F. Reimers (eds.), *Zeitgeschichte im Film- und Tondokument* (Göttingen, 1970), pp. 109–42.

# Introduction

3. D.J. Leab, 'From "Sambo" to "Superspade": some problems in the use of film in historical research', *University Vision*, 10 (1973), 42—3.
4. Quoted in M. Ferro, 'Le film, une contre-analyse de la société?', *Annales*, 28 (1973), 111.
5. 'During the filming of *Borinage* we sometimes had to destroy a certain unwelcome superficial beauty that would occur when we did not want it. When the clean-cut shadow of a barracks window fell on the dirty rags and dishes of a table the pleasant effect of the shadow actually destroyed the effect of dirtiness that we wanted to photograph truthfully, so we broke the edges of the shadow. Our aim was to prevent the audience from being distracted by an agreeable photographic effect from the unpleasant truths that we were showing.' This passage from Joris Ivens' revealing account of the making of *Misère au Borinage*, a film on conditions in the Belgian coalfield after the miners' strike of 1932, should be in the mind of every historian using documentary film. Joris Ivens, 'Borinage — a Documentary Experience', *Film Culture*, 2 (1956), 9.
6. See also his article cited in n.4 above, and for an important essay in the analysis of the fiction film on a historical subject, P. Sorlin, 'Clio à l'écran, ou l'historien dans le noir', *Revue d'Histoire Moderne et Contemporaine*, 21 (1974), 252—78.
7. *B.F.I. News*, 16 (1975), 1, quoting from scenario reports of the British Board of Film Censors for 1930—9, 1941—7 and early 1949, recently acquired by the Information and Documentation Department of the British Film Institute.
8. 'Proposal for a Course on Films and History', *University Vision*, 8 (1972), 9—18.
9. The printed commentaries are re-published in the Institut's serial publication, *Publikationen zu Wissenschaftlichen Filmen* (Sektion Geschichte, Pädagogik, Publizistik).
10. For an example, the work of the Landesbildstelle Berlin, see F. Terveen, 'Historische Filmdokumentation auf stadt- und landesgeschichtlicher Ebene: das Landesfilmarchiv Berlin', in Moltmann and Reimers, *Zeitgeschichte*, pp. 183—9.
11. See G. Sadoul, 'Témoignages photographiques et cinématographiques', in C. Samaran (ed.), *L'Histoire et ses Méthodes* (Paris, 1961), pp. 1404—10: T. Dickinson, 'Some Practical Problems of Film Study', *University Vision*, 12 (1974), 7—8; Lisa Pontecorvo, below, pp. 23—4.

# Part I
# The raw material

---

# 1. Film resources

LISA PONTECORVO

'Film' is as general a term as 'the printed word'. It implies a variety of presentation in what is both an art form and a major technology of the twentieth century. The historian is at home with the forms of the printed word because he uses them all the time, in his daily life. With 'film' he is at a disadvantage, but one that he is well equipped to overcome, if he keeps an academically open mind, and adapts his professional skills to the non-verbal characteristics of the film medium.

What film is used to communicate, and to whom, classifies the type of film. But a fiction film may use documentary techniques and even newsreel material, while so-called actuality film may contain cartoons and acted sequences. So there is a good practical case for approaching film material from two angles: by sponsorship and purpose as well as by aesthetic form and length. I shall deal with both approaches, as the former is more useful for locating a film print and the second is more helpful in assessing its use for historical research and teaching.

Because film and television are expensive to produce, they are always made with a specific audience in mind. This initial target audience will decide the scale of fees paid to contributors and artists, and the charges for copyright material. It is the product's identity tag. Later distribution may extend into other areas than those originally envisaged. Broadly speaking, feature-length fiction films are destined for showing in publicly licensed cinemas. There is usually an embargo on their being transmitted on television for several years if they are of Anglo–U.S. origin, although occasionally a film like *Akenfield* (Peter Hall, 1975) will be released simultaneously on television and in cinemas. The cinema newsreel was produced regularly once or twice weekly for a definite slot in public cinema programmes. The non-theatrical distribution circuit covers the showing of factual and experimental films on a non-profit-making basis to universities, schools, factories, clubs, interest groups, etc., for educational, training,

15

advertising and propaganda purposes. Television transmission is a separate distribution category. To establish the legal identity and distribution circuit of a film or television programme has the incidental advantage for the historian that he has some clue where to begin looking for an old film that is no longer in circulation. If the film has survived, the original purpose of its production will probably determine where it is now kept: a commercial film production library, a state-subsidised archive, a television or a newsreel company library.

Film repositories, like the film industry, tend to be located in capital cities or commercial centres, which makes the historian's task a little easier than it may be with other types of document. In Britain the archive centre is London, with two state-subsidised archives, the Imperial War Museum and the National Film Archive, and three newsreel company film libraries, Pathé, Movietone and Visnews, as well as television companies' and film producers' own libraries, not to mention the vaults of the hundreds of film distributors. In France there are three archives in the Paris area: the Cinémathèque Française; the Centre Nationale de la Cinématographie, Service des Archives du Film (Bois D'Arcy); and the Etablissement Cinématographique et Photographique des Armées at Fort D'Ivry. Three newsreel companies have their film libraries in Paris: Pathé, Gaumont and Actualités Françaises (the last was acquired by O.R.T.F.). Two other film collections are held in the Cinémathèque de Toulouse, and the Musée du Cinéma in Lyons. In Italy there are two main state-subsidised archives in Rome, Istituto Luce and the Cineteca Nazionale; private ones are the Cineteca Italiana in Milan and the Museo Nazionale del Cinema in Turin. In West Germany the documentaries are kept in Koblenz in the Bundesarchiv, the feature films in the Deutsches Institut für Filmkunde, Wiesbaden, or the Deutsche Kinemathek, Berlin. The Germans' richest collection of both feature and documentary film is in East Berlin in the Staatliches Filmarchiv der D.D.R. In Holland, the centre is Amsterdam for the Dutch Film Museum and the Hague for the government film collections, the Rijksvoorlichtingsdienst. In the United States the National Archives in Washington and the Library of Congress have valuable collections along with the Museum of Modern Art in New York, while some of the big feature companies keep their own collections, as does Eastman Kodak in Rochester (N.Y.). There are newsreel libraries in New York.

There may be many film repositories but there are few proper film archives. A film archive is technically like a reference library. Its prime purpose is to collect and preserve a film collection, whereas a film library holds film in order to distribute it or sell it, without necessarily ensuring its long-term survival by copying it to guard against physical deterioration. Film has to be stored in special physical conditions, e.g. colour film has to be refrigerated. Videotapes are susceptible to print-off and magnetic influences and for their long-term preservation have to be copied on to film stock. This brings problems with the preservation of TV programmes. Until 1950 most film was made on a nitrocellulose base, chemically akin to dynamite, and a substance which becomes increasingly volatile with age, and liable to spontaneous combustion. Its chemical life is reckoned to be fifty years, after which the film stock deteriorates to a point where the image is in danger of being lost. It first becomes wet and sticky, and if the picture separates from the base it is lost forever. A planned programme of copying old film on to acetate-based 'safety' stock is ultimately the only way of preserving a film for posterity. A film archive undertakes this sort of programme, and always tries to have two copies of a film for safety: one for duplicating from, usually a master fine-grain print, another for viewing, stored in another part of the archive.

In Britain there is no statutory requirement to deposit film in a national archive, nor are sufficient public funds available to pay film producers to strike an extra print voluntarily for deposit. If the original film producer is still in business, he is likely to have kept the negatives of a feature film or deposited them with a processing laboratory. He may have deposited an old cinema print with the national film archive of the country of production, but he may also have destroyed all cinema copies of the film and even lost or deliberately destroyed the negative because there has been a commercial remake of the film. This barbaric habit flourished for a period, and one of its many victims was Thorold Dickinson's early version of *Gaslight*, which was suppressed for the remake. That story had a happy ending, because a forgotten fine-grain print was rediscovered in recent years and the film is now safely kept in the British National Film Archive. So the historian looking for feature films should go first to the national film archive of the production country, if the film is not readily available on film society booking circuits. If this fails, the original producer should be approached, although the searcher may be unable to see a print because the producer has retained only the negative. If he is lucky, one of the television networks may hold a copy and allow him to see it, privately, since the advent of television has created a new category of film screening rights. Such rights are the basis of film distribution categories. A fiction film can now have television screening rights which are separate from those applying to the public cinema showings. The film distributor may have allowed his lease on the cinema rights of a foreign film to expire, and the television company may be the only holders of a film print. They may transmit it, but not screen it in a cinema.

Documentary film may be available for hire from a sponsor or his agent if it has not become obsolete. If it has outlived its purpose it will have been withdrawn, which means either thrown out and lost forever or deposited in a national, subsidised archive as being of historical value. Survival is undoubtedly haphazard in the grey period before a film becomes old enough to be considered historic, rather than just outdated. Film documentary, as opposed to television productions, tends to be a 'one-off' event, and the myriad documentary producers come and go much more than the large feature-film producers or television companies. So documentary film is particularly vulnerable to loss, as even government-sponsored films are likely to disappear once they have served

17

their informational purpose. Even more so is the television documentary which has been made expressly for broadcasting. It will often not be available for showing on the non-theatrical cinema distribution circuit, because the copyrighted material and artists' fees have not been cleared for that sort of showing, so its physical survival depends on the programming needs and preservation policies of television organisations.

Newsreel libraries are likely to be kept together even if the original producer retires from business, e.g. Gaumont or Paramount, which were bought up by Visnews in London when newsreel production ceased in the mid-fifties. A newsreel library is a business asset built up over the years. It includes not only the accumulated material issued regularly in the weekly newsreel but also probably the film sent in by cameramen that was not used. The library is a constant standby to the newsreel company as a source for obituary films and special reports on crisis areas around the world. Few state archives can afford the enormous cost of acquiring such a commercial newsreel collection *in toto*, far less of cataloguing and preserving it, should it come on the market. Defunct newsreel company libraries tend to be bought up by other film production libraries or by television companies.

Newsreel however is not a monolithic film form, although commercial newsreel like Pathé was a supranational affair from the start, with offices in many countries. Even an internationally produced newsreel reflects the internal politics of individual countries — even more so the state-produced newsreel of Soviet Russia, Fascist Italy and Nazi Germany, or the official British and French wartime newsreels. Such official products remain the copyright of the national government that sponsored them and so tend to be handed over to an appropriate national film archive as a complete collection. This will include newsreels exchanged between wartime allies or captured war booty. There is therefore quite a range of newsreel material held in public archives rather than commercial or private libraries, and so more easily accessible to historians.

A few examples will show the possibilities of these public collections. In London the Imperial War Museum, as a crown agent, holds the official *War Office Topical Budget* newsreel from World War I, the World War II newsreel produced by Paramount for factory workers on behalf of the British government *War Work News*, and *War Pictorial News* produced for allied troops and indigenous middle eastern audiences. It holds the R.A.F. newsreel *The Gen* and the newsreels produced for post-war occupied Germany. Any historian interested in imperial history might like to browse through its collection of *Indian News Parade*. To a fluent Russian speaker, its complete collection of Russian newsreels from 1942, sent over by our erstwhile wartime allies, might be of interest. A representative selection of captured Nazi newsreels of the war period might repay study, particularly if one could compare them with the captured collections in Paris, Washington, East Berlin and Koblenz. A virtually complete collection of the Anglo-French *Journal de la Guerre*, produced from September

*Film resources*

1939 to June 1940, has been assembled by the National Film Archive in London from scattered collections in Europe.

The historian who wishes to travel can spend several weeks immersed in *Les Annales de la Guerre*, the French government-produced newsreel for the army in World War I. This exists complete in Paris in the archives of the Service Cinématographique de l'Armée. The Istituto Luce in Rome has a complete collection of the *Cinegiornale Luce* produced by Mussolini from 1927 to the end of the war. This is of enormous interest, in the history of state newsreel manipulation, as is the post-war Italian newsreel *Settimana Incom*. All these newsreel treasures are in state-run archives where access is free, or at a nominal service charge.

Access to commercial newsreel libraries is based on the assumption that you are in the film-making business, and charges are higher than an individual could reasonably afford. For approximately two weeks' film viewing in Paris during a three-month research trip in 1974, I could have had to pay about £100 (1974 figures) to newsreel archives, from my own funds. Fortunately the film librarians decided my work might ultimately bring them trade and so let me view free. But this is not an assumption that anyone researching in film collections should make. A working estimate of research costs is around £10—15 per day in European film repositories; slightly less in Britain. My own research experience suggests that somewhere between one-fifth and one-third of one's time is spent actually film viewing; the rest of the time is spent on paperwork. These are the sort of costs faced by a historian embarking on film research to integrate film documents with other sources which he studies, if he is communicating in a book rather than on film.

As a practical footnote for the historian who intends to publish his findings in written form, I should mention the dearth of photographic sources to illustrate books and articles. There are no useful photographic print collections taken from frame enlargements of original actuality film. These have to be made specially from archive film prints. Books on the fiction film are often illustrated from production stills taken by a photographer during the shooting of a film. This is not of course done with documentary filming.

What sort of guides are there to help the historian find his way round all the film collections? There is a distinction between the documentation kept by archives and film libraries as an index to their own collections and the kinds of general centralised guide and selective filmography that have been started in a number of countries on the model of the *British National Film Catalogue*. The latter list mainly documentaries and sponsored training and advertising films produced, with full production credits and brief synopsis, but apply only to films in current distribution from the 1960s and include the small amount of television material that is available for hire. They are not likely to be of much use to the historian interested in archive film and particularly in old newsreel. In Britain the most useful and under-used guide available to the historian is the project initiated in 1969 with S.S.R.C. support at University College, London: the Slade Film History Register. This is a centralised register of factual and newsreel film held in Britain, and includes a certain amount of information on foreign collections. The original newsreel issue sheets have been xeroxed, so the historian can either browse through these, chronological and unselected, at his leisure, or use the subject index that is being made on the Universal Decimal Classification system to find selected items.

In Holland the Stichting Film en Wetenschap, in Utrecht, has developed a somewhat similar index to factual film not under its control. No such centralised aid exists in France, Germany or Italy. The American Film Institute is gradually surveying American film archives to safeguard their film heritage but the emphasis has been on fiction rather than factual film, although a recent project has undertaken a survey of television company vaults.

Without the general archive aids a historian may be accustomed to work with in other fields, what sort of paper documentation can he expect to find for film? Catalogues vary from repository to repository. There are two sorts – original documentation made at the time of the film, and subsequent catalogues with some kind of subject classification. This last is usually still in the process of being done and so does not always contain a guide to the whole collection. Sometimes the ancillary paper documentation which would help to make sense of the film document is separated from the actual film can, as I learnt to my cost in Italy. After weeks of reading the original newsreel issue sheets on the *Cinegiornale Luce* at the Istituto Luce I wanted to trace the production background of the Fascist L.U.C.E. organisation. Everybody told me that the company records had disappeared in the confusion of war and occupation. The total disappearance of the business papers of the only Italian film production company operating from 1927 to 1945 seemed to be rather unlikely. After much telephoning I established that something did survive in the papers of the Ministero della Cultura Populare held in the state archives, but that special permission to consult these files had to be obtained. One of the hazards of pioneering is that the film people may not know about the paper records and the state paper librarians do not know about the film collections.

The sort of paper documentation the historian will find with film collections will be related to the contents of the film rather than to the production background: dated original newsreel issue sheets and, if you are lucky, transcripts of the commentary; production credits and cast lists, with synopsis, of feature films and documentaries, in the state archives. The cameramen's 'dope sheets', which are sent in with the unedited film rushes are used to help make up the newsreel or documentary, identifying the location and people in the film. They are unfortunately junked once the final product is made. There are some rare remainders, such as the cameramen's 'dope sheets' surviving with the army record film kept at the Imperial War Museum, but these are exceptional. This sort of documentation is considered as working notes – of no great interest once the film is made. The nearest one can get to it usually is the newsreel company acquisition books, which note when a particular film was received from a cameraman or agency source and whether it was used in a newsreel issue. The Gaumont and Paramount acquisition books at Visnews in London are particularly interesting. For other companies they often do not survive. It is a useful way of checking the authenticity of, say, combat footage in a newsreel: the acquisition book will say if the newsreel company acquired the film from military sources; if the item on Vietnam came from U.S. or North Vietnamese material; if the film of Algerian rebels came from French military sources or the F.L.N.

Production files of documentary and fiction film survive in a haphazard way. It is often hard for a big feature film company to produce a complete script of one of its own films. Documentary producers' files are the first thing to disappear when a company winds up. Television production is a more regularised affair and usually the organisations have some form of central registry where programme files containing versions of early scripts, correspondence, costs, etc., are kept. These files are, of course, private business papers and are not normally available for outsiders to consult. Television organisations also maintain some form of classified register of their productions over the years, although this does not usually indicate whether the programme has been kept. Again it is not usually open to outsiders, who will have to be content with perusing back numbers of the *Radio Times* and *T. V. Times*. There are a certain number of 'mass observation' surveys of audience reaction to films, and of course, television organisations carry out this sort of study all the time. Film journals will contain one critic's view and possibly a synopsis of the content of a film, but for documentation of actuality material I find them unhelpful. They usually add little to what one can find out from seeing a film.

There is a lot to be said for trained historians becoming film historians and applying their methods to the documents of film production, which are just another form of business archive. Unfortunately many of the documents are either un-consultable or destroyed, and film production has the disadvantage that many of the key decisions are taken verbally in the cutting room, rather than recorded in memoranda. Think of a newsreel editor working at speed to make up his edition, selecting his stories from several being screened to him. He will decide on the spot. The surviving film producers, film editors and cameramen, as well as the film censors, need to be systematically questioned about their work, in a multinational oral history project. It is not easy even to find out how many copies of a weekly newsreel edition were struck, far less which cameramen were where, and how they happened to be there; what proportion of a newsreel was made up from agency material and how many of the cameramen's stories were accepted. Even the numerous published interviews with famous feature film directors do not always answer the kind of question a historian would ask.

## Lisa Pontecorvo

Some of the answers to questions about sponsorship and censorship are to be found spread over various kinds of national and local government record: the Gas Council and the Post Office sponsored many films in Britain — as did Bermondsey Borough Council Health Propaganda Department. The British dislike of a government-directed information service, except in wartime, means that there is no convenient batch of ministry papers which consistently covers film matters over the years. The Ministry of Information papers of the Film Division cover only the end of World War I and World War II. Censorship records have not always survived. They are more useful for the study of feature films than for documentary and newsreel. A bomb destroyed many of the British Board of Film Censors' records, and what are left are mainly private committee and other papers. Except in wartime, they do not deal with newsreel. The situation with censorship records will vary from country to country: e.g. in the U.S.A. the records of the Hays Office are accessible. The historian will have to use his traditional methods of ferreting out the right papers, with the disadvantage that the references may be spread over various ministry activities.

So far I have discussed film, its location and documentation from a rather practical point of view. But this is not very helpful without some kind of intellectual orientation towards the opportunities for use of the fiction, factual and newsreel forms in historical research and teaching. If a type of film can be classified by its purpose it also has artistic form. This second approach to the finding and use of film is what I shall now discuss.

Everything on film is a reflection of its own time. When and why certain kinds of film were made and what were the technical and economic bases for their production at that moment of the twentieth century in a particular country is a fruitful study for historians. A Nazi period costume drama about the life of Paul Kruger tells us about Germany at war in 1941 — not about the Boers in 1900. Ideally, the historian's chosen period of study should coincide with an interesting period of film-making: e.g. Weimar and Nazi Germany; Mussolini's Italy; Russia 1917–39; New Deal America; inter-war Britain; the era of Japan's Greater Asia Co-prosperity Sphere; 'Popular Front' France; or France during the occupation, to give a random selection. The historian's approach to such subjects through film can be as varied as his approach to any other historical period, depending on whether he is interested in film content, the history of censorship, the economics of film production, aesthetics, propaganda and information media, or military, social or political history.

Fiction films are of course a very rich source for all manner of historical studies: to mention but a few, class images, racial attitudes, political attitudes and national prejudices, the history of fashion and theatre design, relations between the sexes. It is important to think of a fiction film as a product of its time, whatever the ostensible subject matter, and period setting. Even the Soviet science fiction film *Aelita* (1925) has been analysed by historians as a reflection of Stalinist policy: the revolution to be built in Russia rather than exported

22

abroad. The contrast between the 'realistic' and the 'staged' convention in French and German fiction films tells the historian something about the societies that produced them. Some of Jean Renoir's realistic films of the 1930s were tremendously ill received in certain quarters by a public more accustomed to the studio-staged conventions of a Marcel Carné film like *Le Quai des Brumes* or to the comedies of René Clair. Under Mussolini the films produced were disparagingly referred to as 'white telephone' pieces with no basis in the real life of the mass of the population. The very national film school that Mussolini set up at the Centro Sperimentale in Rome was quietly nurturing young rebels who celebrated the fall of Fascism by producing the post-war masterpieces of neorealism like *Rome Open City*, in marked contrast to the decline of the post-war German cinema once its most skilful practitioners had been discredited by their total absorption in the Nazi film-making style. The production of realistic contemporary 'slice of life' films in Imperial Japan was a quiet protest against the mobilisation of Japanese film production to make patriotic films, in World War II. At the other end of the feature film spectrum, the German censor in occupied France did not realise the hidden message to Frenchmen in such apparently mythical stories as *Les Visiteurs du Soir*.

The fiction film might not on the face of it have much to offer a military historian. But a close study of the feature films made with a military setting would soon show him the source of much footage that passes for authentic military action. There are certain conventions of lighting and placing the camera that would never appear in military record footage, which is usually badly lit and rather shaky as the combat cameraman keeps his head down under fire and certainly never turns his back to the enemy's guns! Those well-known shots of pilots close-up in the middle of bomber raids could not possibly have been taken in the cramped confines of a real bomber cabin.

The study of the feature film by the historian has rich possibilities, as only he has the factual basis in the general history of the period to be able to put such productions into context. In Britain, to date, less attention and sophistication have been lavished on this kind of historical study than on the use of actuality material. It is perhaps more easily dealt with by the historian of ideas, as Marc Ferro's pioneering work might suggest.

There is also the problem, unless fiction films are available for study in a public archive, of how the historian is to set about it. It does take one-and-a-half hours at least to see a whole feature film as opposed to fifteen minutes for a whole newsreel or a short documentary. Film catalogue descriptions may summarise the story but cannot give the historian or anyone else the 'feel' in visual, behavioural terms of a fiction film. It may be a tiny incident that is not even catalogued that gives away the whole atmosphere of a feature film to the historian able to see it.

It is surprisingly difficult to see old film in anything approaching its pristine state. Photographic quality, on which so much of a film's atmosphere depends, is lost in the process of 'reduping' copies further and further from an original negative. I am told that one of the pleasures of visiting Eastman Kodak House in Rochester (N.Y.) is that you can see mint new prints of old American silent films. A professional cinema print has a projection life of a hundred screenings, by which time it will have been scratched and considerably shortened, because every time it breaks during projection as sprocket holes shrink with age, a frame of film is lost splicing it together again. Many famous film classics have had to be reconstructed later from several such 'beat-up' cinema prints, and a new negative struck from this patchwork master print.

Television has done an immense amount as a sort of 'paperback' reissuer of old films of many nationalities. Many of the prints shown by the B.B.C. in seasons such as that of early Chaplins put on a few years ago by 'World Cinema' have been devotedly reconstructed from several different prints to make the longest and most authentic possible version, based on extant scripts. This sort of backroom work often goes unacknowledged, and yet is responsible for a wider dissemination of film appreciation. But the viewer cannot go back and consult these prints once screened. Moreover, those responsible for showing features on television would be the first to admit the limitations of the small screen as a medium for showing 35mm wide cinema films. Television addicts may have noticed that often film titles appear in the middle of their screen, and that much of the picture seems to be cut off at the top, bottom and sides. This is due to the different aspect ratios of the television screen, which is square, and the film screen, which is rectangular. The B.B.C. goes to enormous lengths to 're-shoot' on to videotape the 'pans' and 'angles' of whole sections of feature films before showing them, to try to maintain some of the original framings on the square television screen. Despite these efforts, the pictorial quality is bound to be changed on television, and sometimes this is the most important part of the film in conveying period atmosphere. So it is usually only at the level of plot and characterisation that the historian can use the television feature film screening.

What of the actuality strand of film production? With what mental reservations should a historian approach documentary film? Is the documentary film really 'actuality'? Although the film distribution element is often separate from that of the fiction film the techniques of documentary are less so. Some British documentaries produced in both wars for the Ministry of Information used well-known actors. Even early ethnographic films were given a story line with episodes and identifiable members of the tribe, as in Robert Flaherty's *Nanook of the North*. In a curious way the very interest of a documentary depends on dramatic elements — a strange location in foreign parts, an unknown machine or technical process, a simple development at the 'what happens next' level, watching other people react in a situation. These criteria could be applied to any kind of information film or political documentary. You would identify with the girl making munitions in a British wartime cinema audience; you would cheer Hitler along with the crowds at Nuremberg, in *Triumph of the Will*; you would

24

hope that Nanook could catch the seal and be able to feed his family; you would be willing the closure of the Zuider Zee when the dam was built in Joris Ivens' dramatic film *New Earth*; you would share the despair of the families leaving their farms in the dust bowl as shown in Pare Lorentz's famous film made for the Roosevelt Farm Administration, *The Plow that Broke the Plains*. In an art documentary you would be sharing the artist's preoccupations as the film-maker exposes them through his paintings or as Henri Clouzot allows us to see Picasso's creative processes in live action in *The Picasso Mystery*.

In making a documentary film, the director is not only conveying factual information of a verbal nature. If he is any good at his job, he is conveying the subject's atmosphere in visual terms. What Arthur Marwick calls the 'unwitting testimony' of film evidence comes from the story-telling element in a factual documentary, encapsulating the unwritten values of the times. Story tellers, after all, have to retain their audience's attention, and to do so they use certain conventions which pander to the assumptions of the audience.

The television documentary has taken over some of the functions of the film documentary as an information medium, and covers a wide range of subjects interesting to the historian, because television has to find material to fill up many programme hours. The television documentary is a particularly rich source of archival material of personalities, of places, of customs. The historian who thinks film may be relevant to some specific topic in which he is interested could do worse than mentally categorise the sort of information television documentaries give him well, to get inspiration on how to tackle the material, just as I have suggested he use the television feature film shows to brief himself before venturing into the film vaults.

The great virtue of the television documentary is that normally it is specially created for a specific audience. The subject matter is decided on first, as with the film documentary, and then its presentation is shaped with an audience in mind whose characteristics are known by audience rating techniques. Because the television documentary film fills a particular slot every week or month, certain formats are developed. A degree of audience anticipation grows up with a regular B.B.C. documentary slot like *Horizon*, a popularising science programme, or *Omnibus*, its arts features equivalent, or *Panorama*, a current affairs regular, or for that matter an Open University or schools programme. The only cinema equivalent to this situation would be the political documentary made for the already converted: the British wartime homefront documentary or the Nazi or Fascist documentary that would be shown compulsorily in a feature film programme.

It has to be recognised that, apart from the limited number of programmes any broadcasting organisation makes available for hire and sale, television material is not yet readily accessible for historical studies. I have briefly mentioned the kind of internal documentation that exists in such organisations. One main problem with television is that to preserve it for any length of time it has to be transferred from videotape to film stock. This is an expensive business and not always desirable from an aesthetic point of view, as the electronic magnetic medium does not always translate favourably on to film stock, which basically involves an optical process. Furthermore, editing rhythms are different, and television sound is recorded in such a way that it may not sound the same on an optical film sound track. The aspect ratios of the visuals are square, instead of rectangular, and just as film suffers from being screened on a small screen, so television visuals may not stand being blown up on to a cinema screen after they have been copied from videotape. It is worth noting, however, that a major television series is filmed first and then transferred electronically on television transmission, so that a negative is available from which to make film copies for preservation and sale.

What of the newsreel? Is that, too, like the documentary, fabricated reality? Again my answer would be yes. Newsreels after all can appear twice weekly. The editor will have selected certain events as worthy of attention. The order of prominence in the newsreel issue will vary from country to country. There will always be a sporting event — an obvious case of empathising with the competitors — and there will always be political events. Here there is the satisfaction of seeing those famous politicians performing publicly, or of witnessing the signing of some important treaty, of being addressed by a politician, of being present in the crowd by proxy. There is usually some kind of frivolous or social non-event — a baby competition, a fashion parade, a ship launch or some national achievement. There is always a report on foreign parts usually showing some disagreeable turmoil that makes one glad to live at home, whatever the newsreel country of origin. There is usually a scoop or sensational event of a visual kind — a strike, a disaster, a riot: there is surely a voyeur in all of us. The placing of these items and their length is crucial. Some national newsreels give a dozen items as short snippets, others build up the main item at the beginning or end of the reel.

The newsreel is also fabricated in the sense that it compiles many of its stories from old visual material: the retrospective report or obituary item. If the newsreel was shortsighted and did not collect film of people and events that later proved of moment it will use film library 'wallpaper' visuals.

The personality cult in newsreel is worthy of the fiction film: in the Fascist Italian newsreel Mussolini turns his attention to every small hamlet, but there is also a mass of film of his party hierarchy at routine rallies, acting as his proxies. In the joint Pathé—Gaumont newsreel in unoccupied France from autumn 1940 to 1942 every issue is permeated by Pétain. Nazi newsreels self-evidently star Hitler. Early Soviet newsreels of the 1920s started by starring the common man, using little personified items, to illustrate national recovery after 1917. The Stalin personality cult replaced this, but it is very interesting to see in the World War II newsreels that stories about military victory, or better industrial output for the war effort, or Soviet air strength, or Soviet suffering, are always personified by some obscure officer, or local factory foreman, or suffering refugee, more in the tradition of the Kino Eye newsreels of Dziga Vertov in the 1920s. Some public personalities appear continually in newsreels; others, who may objectively be just as important, are rarely shown.

One of the most fascinating aspects of the newsreel is a comparison of the different kinds of manipulation it is subject to in every country at different times in its history. There are various ways of studying this. One is to check the emphasis in the commentary over a period of time in one newsreel reporting a long-drawn-out civil war or colonial struggle for independence. Another fruitful study is to see how a number of different national newsreels treat the same event or theme, e.g. the slump and unemployment, rearmament, international crises, Fascism, war. One occasionally finds the same visuals shown with completely different commentaries, because the newsreels depend heavily on being supplied by other agencies, and do not film everything themselves. So one finds the British company, Gaumont Graphic, being regularly supplied with Italian film from the Fascist L.U.C.E. productions, which they never appeared to issue. The same material can be seen used by L.U.C.E. in its own nationally produced newsreel *Cinegiornale Luce*. This Italian newsreel in turn received film material from Japan, which was regularly issued. A historian interested in the Manchurian crisis could first study it in British newsreels, and then in Italian newsreels see film sent by the puppet Manchukuo regime. A military historian looking for authentic combat footage in the newsreels would have to know under what conditions an army supplies this sort of film for release as a newsreel. He would find film that was originally shot for release in Gaumont British in 1938, showing the impregnable Maginot line, appearing in Nazi newsreels a few years later, with a rather different commentary.

I have dealt with some of the practicalities of film research, which any historian venturing into the film vaults will have to cope with, and I have tried to outline the nature of the film material he will find there. But if a historian wishes to communicate his findings on film, or simply share his experiences with students by showing them some of the raw material to be found, there is a whole set of new problems for him and considerable expense. His historical training and common sense will see him through the lone research in paper and film documents. The problems there are essentially those he faces with any project, except that film is more cumbersome and depends on technical resources for viewing.

The new range of problems arises when one wants to make old film accessible to other people. There are very few institutions which have a local council licence to project nitrate-based films. Old cinemas built before 1950, and specialist viewing theatres, such as those at the National Film Theatre or the Imperial War Museum, are the only places which can comply with the fire regulations necessary for the projection of nitrate films. Since the changeover to 'safety' film stock there is no need to build cinemas with the requisites for 'nitrate' projection. Because of the expense incurred by archives in copying their

## Lisa Pontecorvo

collections in duplicate, there is little money left over to make viewing copies that can be loaned off the premises, and copyright prevents the National Film Archive lending film. The Imperial War Museum is freer as it owns the copyright on most of its films. If there happened to be a borrowable copy of a 35mm nitrate film available at the Imperial War Museum, it could be shown to students only in a specially-licensed projection theatre. In the case of newsreel material, only a negative and master viewing copy will be held by the newsreel company, and a new film copy would have to be struck at the viewer's expense to show it elsewhere. Feature films are more easily available on 16mm stock because of the film society movement. Most universities have projection theatres that cannot show 35mm gauge even on safety film, and most do not have the kind of 16mm projector able to cope with the separate magnetic track which is standard for the majority of television productions.

What sort of costs is an archive film show going to involve? If you take three to four people to an archive and see original material on an editing table or screened there, relatively little. If you have to print up film, a great deal. An archive hire charge is likely to be less than for the film society hire of a normal feature film (which is around £15). You may be able to negotiate a system whereby your hire charges are aggregated to 'print up' a new film every so often, which remains the property of the archive but is there for you whenever you wish to borrow it or bring students to see it.

With a newsreel company you would have to pay the full cost of printing-up film material, and strictly speaking you should also pay copyright to them. Printing costs for an hour's worth of film would be under approximately £100 on 16mm without a negative. Individual newsreel items can be spliced together on the projector for the film show, if you have a helpful projectionist, or they can simply be run on two separate projectors continuously. It may become possible in the not too distant future, with improved compatibility and cheaper video systems, to make cheap wipeable video recordings from preservation film held by libraries, to avoid abusing their master material by constant screening on a viewing table.

What of the historian who wants to communicate his findings in an edited film? It depends whether he has institutional audio-visual facilities at his disposal. In my opinion a compilation film cannot be produced in less than three months' full-time work even in a highly organised system such as the B.B.C., to the standards of academic and aesthetic authenticity required, from first research to final print, ready for screening with copyright cleared. A month is needed for staggered research and shaping of film ideas; one month for laboratory processing; and one month for film editing and scripting commentary. There are economies of scale in a series. The inexperienced film-maker suffering from lack of funds is likely to take longer. £5–6000 is a realistic estimate for a fifty-minute film if you have no institutional resources to absorb editors' salaries and overheads. In an Open University context where overheads are included in the resource allocation, the price is around £1500 (1972–3 figures), which approximates to the costs of the Inter-University History Film Consortium productions, where again institutional resources already in existence are used. Of these costs about a third will be copyright payments; a reasonable working ratio for film wastage (duping of extra film material to play around with in the cutting room) is about 4 : 1. There are educational copyright rates, and if the film is produced for a limited educational use these will be less than if the film is a commercial venture.

There are two kinds of copyright involved when dealing with film. There is screening copyright, which means that the permission of the producer or his copyright heirs has to be obtained before a film can be released for a public or private screening. If you borrow your print from the original producer you automatically have his permission and if you obtain it through a recognised film distributor he has obtained the permission before you get the film. But if you use a film from the National Film Archive you have to obtain written permission from the copyright owner before they can allow you to have the film off their premises for your use. The second kind of copyright is one more familiar to any writer: copyright involved in reproducing a film to include it in your own production. This copyright, however, sometimes includes performers' rights or music copyright, if you wish to use original sound tracks with music on them, and preserve the original form of the film document.

You should identify the music and composer and trace the music publisher through the records of the Mechanical Copyright Protection Society, and clear the performance with the musical equivalent of the Performing Rights Society. Given the dearth of production records, it is not easy to identify nondescript music on a film sound track, which in the case of newsreel may even consist of stock sounds and not of specific tunes. Common sense prevails once you have contacted the two societies who look after the publishers' and performers' interests. If their records are incomplete no one is likely to sue you. For documentary film, as opposed to fiction film, it is quite likely to be impossible to trace the necessary information, but one must go through the motions of trying. The copyright in the film commentary usually resides with the production company. Should the commentator be a person of eminence who does not normally work for the film company, it is a courtesy practice to ask his or her permission, or that of the heirs, which is normally forthcoming. Copyright clearance is not always a question of money.

One copyright problem for the historian is that he may copy from a film that he has conveniently to hand in a film library and then discover that the original sponsor, the copyright owner, has a negative and better copy and would have preferred that the film be duped from his original. With due apology and explanation this sort of situation can be smoothed over.

The general attitude to 'fair dealing' in film copyright is that every reasonable effort should be made to trace copyright owners and to clear material, but after that: 'publish and be damned'. The onus is then on the wronged copyright owner to prove his obscure claim. There is the slight inconvenience that if you have not cleared copyright the owner could jeopardise your whole film by demanding an outrageous sum for the use of a tiny bit of library film, or with-hold his permission altogether. But no sensible person is likely to do this, since he would not have made any money at all had you not unearthed his film and used it.

A personal reminiscence from a compilation film made at the Open University may show some of the problems and commonsense solutions in copyright clearance. We wished to use a small section from a well-known British wartime documentary *The Five Hundred*, about an airlift of trapped Yugoslav partisans. The film was produced by the Ministry of Information in Britain, and included footage shot by cameramen of the Mediterranean Allied Air Forces, now dis-banded. The film print we used was held in the National Film Archive, London, the copyright being apparently vested in the Central Office of Information as copyright heirs to the wartime Ministry of Information. But they had no pro-duction files to help identify the material. The scenes we wished to use included ground shots of Yugoslav partisans and a British liaison officer, and some air shots from a U.S. plane whose pilot appeared to wear Russian uniform. The Central Office of Information asked us to clear the footage with the U.S. forces, care of the Pentagon, who were most helpful but had no copy of the film or production files. The National Film Archive could not release the film to us without written permission from the copyright owner, and the problem was that no one really knew who that was, as M.A.A.F. no longer existed and had been made up of polyglot allied forces. The Central Office of Information, the spon-sors' heir, felt it could not decently take the cash or the risk of letting us use the film. Finally the Imperial War Museum, who also had a copy, agreed that they would assume responsibility for the film, as they could act as crown copyright agents for the military footage that involved British troops, and was therefore probably filmed by British army cameramen. The only other likely claimant, the Pentagon, seemed to have no interest in the film. To date no one has sued the Open University for using the film.

Often with documentary films of relatively recent date the original sponsor has forgotten the film was made and no production files exist to prove it, even in government departments. On several occasions I have had to go to great trouble to persuade the rightful copyright owners that the film was indeed theirs and to get their permission to screen or reproduce it. When the film is older than fifty years it should be outside copyright. But not much of film history is that old, and those who have preserved such valuable film may reasonably claim a facility fee for letting you use it.

A particular warning should be given to historians about using copies of foreign films, to hand in Britain, that are here because of wartime alliance or victory: e.g. Soviet newsreels at the Imperial War Museum, or captured 'war

## Film resources

booty', particularly German fiction films and newsreels. At the time of writing the question of 'war booty' is *sub judice* and has been rumbling for years. The Americans have returned the copyright to Germany, the British and French have not. If you are making a film in Britain or France you can use the captured film only for showing in these countries and not for screening anywhere else. The whole question is a legal morass, of which the historian should be aware. Less controversial but equally hard to trace is the copyright holder for French wartime material held in Britain from Free French sources. The copyright obscurity surrounding some resistance films made by exiled Poles, Czechs and Yugoslavs in London during World War II defies common sense.

Unless you enjoy playing 'spot the actor' you will probably find it hard to identify individual players from inadequate wartime cast lists, should you also have to obtain their courtesy permission before using scenes from a government-produced propaganda film. That nightmare does not happen too often.

To end on a cheerful note, recognised British educational institutions are allowed to record educational radio and television programmes 'off-air' as long as they destroy the recording within a certain time and use it only in a teaching context in that institution.

As this account should show, the historian who wishes to use film resources for historical research and teaching has to be versatile. He has to use quite a lot of initiative before he can be in a position to do so seriously and to draw conclusions about film's value as evidence. Far from ousting the teacher, film makes him much more indispensable. The more film is used, as film, the more it needs to be circumscribed with written explanation and additional research to put the film artefact into a historical context.

# 2. Film preservation: the archives

CLIVE COULTASS

The film archive is the repository of visual media which the historian who wants to investigate these sources will have to use in the same way as he finds his more traditional forms of evidence in a library of written or printed materials. The basic research principle is similar but the various complex factors involved in the collection and safe keeping of historical film have a bearing on what kind of facilities may be open to the historian and on the methods he is able to employ.

Film of some potential historical value may be found in many different kinds of collection. Before considering the archives themselves, which are essentially institutions for the keeping of public records, one should take into account all other sources. These begin at the smallest level with personal and private films taken by amateurs on 16mm or 8mm, often kept by their owners as souvenirs of the events photographed by them in the past. Some of them, or copies of them, may eventually pass into the larger archives. They can be important supplements to the normal visual records because the private individual may catch incidents and personalities which the official or commercial cameraman had no brief to film at the time.

A few examples of these may make the point. The Eva Braun home movies now held by the National Archives at Washington D.C. have become relatively well known through their re-use in various compilations. One documentary film even saw fit to do a synchronised voice track, but the unusual value of the originals, showing Hitler and his friends in relaxed mood at Berchtesgaden, will no doubt allow them to survive such treatment. Another colour film, shot by a Hamburg fireman after the R.A.F. fire storm raids, revealed devastation and death on a scale which was censored out of the official newsreels. Thames Television in making their *World at War* series also discovered an amateur film of V.E. Day celebrations in London where colour again gave an extra dimension to the reality of these events. The Imperial War Museum has in its collection a private film made by a Royal Naval Officer on the China Station in the 1930s, and apart from happening to give the only first-hand coverage of the incident in the Sino-Japanese war when H.M.S. *Capetown* was cut off in the Yangtze it also illuminates details of both routine and informal naval activities never photographed in such a way by professionals, thus preserving almost accidentally a visual record of a part of Britain's imperial life which now belongs to history.

## Film preservation: the archives

There is always the chance that the amateur film enthusiast may inadvertently be in possession of something of such unique value.

Amongst the more familiar and larger collections are news libraries of different kinds, both those founded originally to keep film made for newsreels in the cinema and those which belong to television companies. These differ from the public archives in one important respect, and the distinction between a library on the one hand and an archive on the other needs to be made clear. Indeed the term 'archive' is frequently misused. The definition of a film archive which is acceptable to the International Federation of Film Archives (F.I.A.F.) is that of a collection of film stored with the specific object of preservation for posterity. This, strictly, rules out the news libraries whose aims are more immediately commercial. They do have master material but their main purpose in keeping it is to facilitate the use of their film as visual journalism, either within their own organisation or by sale to other companies.

The cinema newsreel of the inter-war period perhaps represented the most distinctive form of this kind of communication before television made it an anachronism. It was terse, factual and on the whole uncritical in an age of social and political change. In Britain the only company still producing these items is Movietone. The famous Pathé collection exists now almost solely as a source for re-exploitation as stock shot material. Stock shots, it should be explained, are the film researcher's basic tool. A shot taken, for instance, of a national event in the 1930s and edited into the framework of a newsreel reportage of that time may now be selected again, purely as a shot and without the sound track dubbed on to it in the older issue. It can then be used once more, perhaps in a new television documentary about the period. All libraries which sell film in this way are accustomed to indexing easily retrievable stock shots of particular value, either for their historical content or for their visual quality. If the intelligent television viewer complains that the same old shots keep turning up time and again in documentary programmes, the likely reason is that pressures of schedules and economy leave the researcher with little choice.

The original Gaumont British and Paramount libraries are now incorporated in Visnews, an international news organisation active in the television field. This is a particularly rich collection and the company has shown in recent years some awareness of the needs of historians. The Inter-University Consortium's historical films have been largely built up on stock shot material supplied by Visnews from the original newsreels. Whereas a public archive may be inhibited by lack of funds from making its holdings widely available, a newsreel library usually suffers no such constraints. It is in the business primarily to sell film. In the past it might have been easier for a group like the Consortium to view and purchase its film from Visnews than from the National Film Archive, but this can be partly explained by differences in ultimate aims and in financing.

Visnews recently have taken the momentous step of ridding themselves

entirely of their 35mm film and transferring all their holdings to videotape. This
has certain obvious advantages. 35mm film is a cumbersome medium. It is stored
in large cans which are heavy to transport from the vaults to the viewing area. It
needs a special type of viewing machine, reliable enough when handled by a
professional but unlikely to be left to the mercies of the casual student. Videotape on the other hand requires less storage space, it is easily transportable and it
can be seen on a small machine which an untrained person may operate safely.
Visnews have elected to use half-inch tapes for viewing and as soon as these are
worn out they can be renewed from one-inch masters. The costs of this reproduction are substantially less than those for the duplication of film prints.

Nevertheless, the use of videotape in this way may have its pitfalls. Even as a
viewing facility there would seem to be some drawbacks. A researcher is accustomed to running film backwards and forwards, fast and slow, on a machine
which retains vision in all these circumstances. A videotape viewer does not have
this versatility and so locating, identifying and selecting a shot may actually take
longer. However, more serious queries are really concerned both with the dura-
bility of videotape itself in a physical sense and with its likely continuance as a
viable medium in the future. Some recent technological developments in the
field have foundered very quickly and there can be no real guarantee that videotape will not be obsolete within a decade or two. It is difficult also to transfer
back from videotape to film without an appreciable loss of quality.

Visnews, then, have taken something of a calculated risk, but not in fact by
losing all contact with their original film masters. Many of these have been transferred to the National Film Archive and a small number to the Imperial War
Museum. It is conceivable that if the medium changes again Visnews might have
to come back to the archives at some time in the future to effect another change.
In the meantime the archives have been left with the critical problems of storage
and preservation of more 35mm film, most of it nitrate based. An understanding
of these questions, which may well absorb most of the time, funds and energies
of an archive, is crucial to an appreciation of how such an institution functions
and what it may or may not do now and in years to come.

Film is a fragile agent and even before the archival idea had gained any kind
of acceptance the film industry had a policy for ensuring the preservation of its
products as long as they were commercially exploitable. This drew a distinction
between the show prints made available for projection, which would have a
limited life through the wear and tear of cinema use, and the master material
whose existence could guarantee the continued production of more copies for
further distribution. Prints were taken from negatives and the more a negative
was used in this way the more it too was likely to suffer damage. As an added
safeguard the film company would also keep a special quality fine-grain print,
known as an insurance print, which would be used for no other purpose than the
production of new negatives. Archives adopted the same principles, so that their
ultimate ideal would be to hold a fine-grain print, at least one negative and a

viewing print which would be available for researchers or students. Unlike film companies, who might let their master material fall into neglect when a particular film seemed to have ceased to have value for them, archives keep film in perpetuity.

Unfortunately the reality of the matter is not so simple. It often happens that the film deposited with an archive is a show print, perhaps already worn, and for the time being this alone has to be kept as a master and not used in any way until either a second generation negative can be made from it or — more fortunately — the original negatives and insurance print are passed over. Occasionally an archive may get a negative and nothing else. The whole process of acquiring film can be such a muddle that at some stage a formidable and expensive policy of duplication has to be undertaken in order to gain the necessary full archival coverage.

The question is further complicated by the fact that all 35mm film produced before 1952 was based on nitro-cellulose stock. The potential inflammability of this was early recognised but a more disturbing aspect was its capacity for deterioration over an uncertain period of time. Such a change could occur very rapidly without much early warning until the image itself was actually fading. The factors hastening this change are so variable and inconsistent that it has never been possible to predict on grounds of age alone when a particular film would begin to crumble away. High temperatures can be fatal and there have been instances since World War II of valuable nitrate collections in Canada, Czechoslovakia and Austria being destroyed through spontaneous combustion. The only solution is transference of all nitrate film, master material and viewing print alike, either to the safe acetate based stock which became common from 1952 or to another medium altogether.

The nitrate problem has been highlighted at this point because the great bulk of the collections held by the cinema newsreel libraries has been in this form. As the years advance the threat of deterioration or destruction of these millions of feet of history on film, even if kept in air-conditioned vaults, has gone on increasing. The Visnews solution has already been noted. But it was recognition of the short-lived nature of 35mm film in its original form which produced the film archive movement as a means of coping with a conservation situation different in character from that of other categories of record. Quite simply, nothing costs so much as film to preserve or to reproduce.

The first group of historically interesting films to be permanently preserved in Britain was the official records of World War I, including 'campaign' compilations like *The Battle of the Somme*, *The Battle of Arras* and *The Battle of the Ancre* which had been produced for propagandistic and informational purposes. At the end of the war they were seen initially to be valuable for their commemorative interest and were put in the care of the Imperial War Museum, an institution set up in 1917 partly as a national memorial to those who had lost their lives in the war. The Army for its part wanted the films kept so that they could

35

be re-used for training purposes. These motives may have had little to do with long-term historical considerations but the important consequence was that a collection of cine-film, totalling some two million feet, had been placed in the same bracket as more traditional forms of record or exhibit with a guarantee of government funds for its maintenance. The jingoistic epic *The World's Greatest Story*, made for release in weekly parts immediately after the war, was soon added to the list.

E. Foxen Cooper, an official cinematography adviser who had worked for Customs and Excise and the Foreign Office, was the person responsible for providing the films with safe storage conditions. There were the beginnings of an archival policy of re-printing, at that time of course on to further nitrate stock. Foxen Cooper clearly wanted the government to make provision for other films which reflected significant events in Britain's national life but in the politically and economically crisis-conscious climate of the 1920s nothing was done. Public opinion still thought of cinema as little more than an entertainment medium.

Nevertheless, the end of the decade may be seen as a watershed, a time when new attitudes began to make their mark. Foxen Cooper himself contributed a pioneering article in *The Times* (19 March 1929) on the value to the national heritage of keeping historical film records. If this may be interpreted as accurately representing the state of advanced opinion at that time, it appears that only the actuality film was even being considered as a likely candidate for permanent preservation.

Of feature films, which of course were the very backbone of the cinema industry, Foxen Cooper wrote:

> In contrast one notes that there has been, as yet, no general desire to preserve for posterity any one of the masterpieces of cinematography, such as *Quo Vadis?* and *Intolerance*, probably the earliest and most stupendous spectacles ever shown on the screen, or the *Four Horsemen of the Apocalypse*, possibly the finest dramatic war film ever produced. In these unique productions the critic can detect artificiality and excesses which have been employed by the producer to convey his story. Perhaps one day some international society with sufficient means at its disposal will form a library of the great films belonging to the various periods since cinematography came into being. Possibly then these and other earlier productions will be included in such a collection if the negatives are still in existence.[1]

In the same year a Commission of Enquiry was founded to consider means of furthering the use of what were described as 'educational and cultural films'. One of its first stated aims became the creation of a permanent central organisation to handle these activities and to find ways to 'select, acquire, store and otherwise conserve and utilise documentary film, both positive and negative'. It is worth noting also that the Empire Marketing Board Film Unit, now famous historically as the basis of the British factual film tradition, had been set up in

## Film preservation: the archives

1928. Following publication in 1932 of the Commission's recommendations (a booklet called *The Film in National Life*) the British Film Institute was established in the following year as the government grant-aided body designated for the task of promoting the cultural role of the film in this country.

The National Film Archive as we know it today is a division of the B.F.I. It dates from the appointment in May 1935 of a young man named Ernest Lindgren to be responsible for the collection of a library of films of national importance and for taking what measures he could towards their conservation. With no other staff, no funds and no facilities he had at first a nearly impossible task, but the Archive's development in the subsequent forty years derived mainly from Lindgren's single-minded dedication. To the time of his death in 1973, having relinquished his Curatorship of the Archive only in the final months of a protracted illness, he remained faithful to his own intensely personal idealism in marking out the course which he saw as in the best interests of the film and its future.

Over the years the reputation of the B.F.I. has been most associated with efforts to gain recognition in Britain for the feature film as an art comparable to older forms like literature, music or painting. It is right therefore that a prime task of the National Film Archive has been to preserve copies of such films, whatever their country of origin, provided they have been shown and distributed in this country and their artistic merit has been accepted by a consensus of informed opinion. However, leaving aside the question of the interest which the future historian may have in feature films of a period, as expressions in some way or other of the ethos of that age, it is true to say also that the Archive's avowed object has been to treat fiction and non-fiction films on equal terms. Lindgren himself is on record as emphasising that any distinction between film as art and film as document must be purely an artificial one. It was his aim from the beginning to create as comprehensive a collection as possible.

But the nitrate problem had to be resolved. Already vast numbers of earlier films had been lost for ever, either wilfully destroyed or neglected to the point where deterioration set in. The government could only gradually be persuaded to put up the money for re-printing, and in the pre-World War II days there was still no permanently durable form of 35mm stock, so that re-printing on to more nitrate based film would merely postpone the possibility of eventual loss. Lindgren decided that saving what he already had been able to collect must be his first priority. If a show print was acquired it must stay as a master until that time in the future when full preservation coverage had been made possible. He was not blind to the argument that access is as desirable an end as conservation but in the circumstances of the time his hands were tied. Preservation must be guaranteed before all else.

The decomposition of nitrate based film can be slowed up by storing in cool conditions, a sensible precaution also against the kind of combustion which can destroy complete collections. In 1940 work was begun on the construction of air-conditioned vaults at Aston Clinton, not far from London. These have facilities for controlling the temperature at around 14°C. A nitrate fire is extremely difficult to extinguish (water is no use at all) and as a safeguard against the possible spread of such a conflagration the vaults incorporate safety vents leading to the roof. In general, archival policy is to keep fine-grain prints, negatives and viewing prints of the same film in separate vaults as a further insurance against disaster. Not only the Archive's collection but also that of the Imperial War Museum was stored here during the war years at a seemingly safe distance from the hazards being suffered in London.

To combat the possibility, already referred to, of a nitrate film 'going off' before anyone became aware of its condition, a stability test was worked out by the Government Chemist's department. Tiny round pieces are punched out of a film and placed in a heated test tube. Gases from decomposition then react on a filter paper which has been soaked in alizarin red dye and the speed of this process indicates the extent of deterioration. This is the standard test now internationally accepted by film archives. A policy of re-printing can be geared to its findings. It is perhaps not totally infallible because punch-holes are usually made only at the ends of reels of film and it has also the obvious drawback of inevitably damaging one or two frames. The only alternative might be some form of chemical analysis by spectrometry, a method which has been explored more recently by the Imperial War Museum.

From 1952 it has been possible to re-print on to acetate stock which does not decompose, and so a policy of genuinely permanent preservation becomes feasible. However, the rate at which the transfer can be done is regulated annually by the amount of money granted for the purpose by the government and by the number of staff available to prepare prints for sending out to the processing laboratories and for examining and checking the new material on its return. Even if unlimited funds were suddenly released neither archives nor laboratories could cope with the volume of work at a much quicker rate than is common practice at present. The National Film Archive and the Imperial War Museum together still have sufficient quantities of unduped nitrate film to keep them re-printing for most of the remaining years of this century. The laboratories for their part, giving now most of their attention to colour processing for television, have become more reluctant to work with old nitrate black and white stock. Not only is it a fire risk for them but the film has also probably suffered shrinkage with age. Modern printing machines are ill suited to dealing with shrunken film.

An archive must think of the likelihood that within the decade no laboratory will be willing any longer to handle nitrate film. In anticipating this the National Film Archive has developed some facilities for printing but not on a large enough scale to deal with anything like the whole problem. Ideally an archive would like its own self-sufficient laboratory and some in other countries have achieved this, notably Gosfilmofond in the U.S.S.R., the Bundesarchiv in West Germany and the State Film Archive of East Germany. In the meantime the 'Stone Age' era of

38

the visual medium, its nitrate period, goes on throwing its shadow over the work of most film archives.

The problem of course does not end with nitrate film. Colour too is a special case because the dyes can fade in a relatively short time and this deterioration can only be retarded by storage at temperatures around freezing point. The retrieval of colour film from refrigerated vaults must be done by passing it through an intermediary chamber to allow for a gradual process of acclimatisation. For permanency the solution − an expensive one − is to print black and white separation masters of each of the three basic colour groups and when these are satisfactorily matched again a new colour negative may be made. Now that almost all new films are in colour this should be the ideal, but in practice most world archives have not so far been able to deal with their holdings in this way and some indeed are lucky if they can meet the cost of refrigeration on the desired scale.

It will have been seen that most of the positive steps towards setting up a technically fully equipped film archival plant in Britain took place either during World War II or shortly after it. The National Film Archive could never be self-financing and to pay for its film preservation it had to continue arguing the parallel between itself and the British Museum, in much the same way as the National Film Theatre nowadays may justify its need for public funds by comparing its national status with that of our subsidised theatre companies and orchestras. Even if acknowledgement of the standing of film as an art form was still not generally forthcoming, the government was able to consider favourably the case for permanently preserving the best of its own films and in 1958 the Grigg Committee on Departmental Records recommended that they should be deposited with the British Film Institute. The only exceptions were official films 'covering every aspect of the two World Wars and other operations in which Commonwealth forces have been engaged since August 1914', which were to go to the Imperial War Museum. In the aftermath of the war the Museum had extended its terms of reference and its objectives, so that the memorial aspect gradually receded, and as the importance of its now vastly augmented film collection became better understood it was more directly administered by the Museum's Trustees. A substantial annual grant was secured on the Museum's Vote for a staged programme of printing nitrate film, while air-conditioned vaults to house the films were opened in 1969 on the Public Record Office site at Hayes, Middlesex.

To Ernest Lindgren it seemed with some justification that the B.F.I. was being left behind, at least in the allocation of funds. The Governors published in 1969 a report on the Archive under the title of *The Rescue of Living History* and Lindgren grasped the chance of slipping in a footnote which contrasted his annual grant of £5000 with the £17,000 which the Museum 'with a collection considerably smaller' was receiving from the Department of Education and Science for film printing. It is true that the total holdings of the Museum at that time were about a third of the Archive's but the point not mentioned was that almost all of them were of government origin, a situation drastically different from that of the B.F.I. Nevertheless, the imbalance was soon substantially reduced and the National Film Archive was able to have earmarked for itself a yearly fund which could not be used for any purpose other than film preservation. Lindgren had gained a small measure of budgetary security. Given the crucial nature of the nitrate film question, this was a major move, and no archive can feel fully happy unless the integrity of its film preservation funds can be similarly guaranteed.

The process by which government films are passed to the respective archives can still be complicated, not least because the onus of handing over master material rests on the individual department. The most important nowadays is the Central Office of Information which operates its own film production unit. It too has air-conditioned vaults on the Public Record Office site at Hayes, Middlesex, probably the most advanced of their kind in the country. Although the C.O.I. cannot be said to have any commercial interests it, like other government departments, has some responsibility for creating income and so long as a film has revenue-making value or some other official purpose the date of transfer of its negatives is likely to be deferred. The archives must wait until films are virtually redundant to departmental needs and although the system is fairly administered by the Public Record Office, who act as an arbitrating body, there must be some grounds for uncertainty. Some departments may overlook films, even neglect them, or the wrong historical decisions may be made about suitability for permanent preservation. They can also withdraw the films from the archives on demand. However, in spite of these reservations there is at least an existing system and the archives are on the whole assured of a constant flow of material from this source.

For other categories of film the process of acquisition by the National Film Archive is a selective one. This is true also to some extent of the Imperial War Museum, but because its field is more limited it can usually afford to negotiate without much difficulty for most of the non-fiction films that it needs. Decisions are made within the Film Department alone and to avoid overlapping with the interests of the National Film Archive regular contact is kept up between the staff of the two institutions. The Archive, with a very much broader area to take account of, has a more elaborate system and uses a series of committees made up of experts in their particular disciplines, meeting periodically to arrange film viewings and to advise the acquisitions officers. The History Committee discusses both film and television and as a guide it refers to the invaluable *British National Film Catalogue* which lists most films brought out for non-theatrical distribution in Britain. Assessing what is likely to be of interest and enlightenment to future generations is a task which can have few predetermined rules and all archivists know about the wrong decisions of the past when films which would seem now to be of value were ignored or junked. For this reason the

## Film preservation: the archives

Archive's method is as flexible as possible, the acquisition officers themselves having a burden of responsibility in the matter. A good instance of this is the fact that the one questionable selection precept, that film will not normally be taken if the event it portrays has been adequately recorded in some other form, is in practice subject to a wide degree of interpretation. When a film has been recommended for preservation it goes into the records as a selection until such time as it has been acquired, normally by free donation or in rarer cases by purchase with the aid of a limited budget. Unfortunately circumstances may stretch the waiting period indefinitely. The system is not without its flaws but its very existence puts the National Film Archive in a unique place amongst its counterparts in other countries.

Some film producers (including television companies) are reluctant to deposit film with archives for fear of losing their rights over the material. Copyright is indeed a very sensitive issue in the film world but nothing in the National Film Archive's record over the last forty years would seem to justify such suspicions. The situation could be revolutionised by a system of statutory deposit, similar to the right of the British Library to take copies of all printed materials published in this country. Parliamentary action to secure such a measure has so far failed although the last time it was discussed (in 1970) there seemed to be general agreement about the principle. The root of the problem has been the appreciation that printing costs of the deposited copies would have to be paid by the B.F.I. out of its government funds. It would be unreasonable to expect small-scale producers or distributors to find the money themselves, but the Treasury might have to grant a relatively large sum to make the scheme work. It was this realisation more than anything else that relegated the proposals to the never-never land of a 'more favourable economic climate'. Even so, the difficulties do not end there. Foreign films are a special case because only the distributor in Britain could be compelled to deposit copies with the National Film Archive and the British industry has foreseen a reciprocal situation internationally where they would have to supply copies for a number of national archives in other countries, some of whom might not scrupulously respect copyright laws. At some time in the future, perhaps in the general context of all audio-visual records, the matter will have to be re-opened. In the first instance it might be easier to secure statutory deposit for British films only.

The film deposited with an archive has at some time to be made available for viewing since the ultimate purpose of keeping material at all is to allow it to be seen in controlled conditions by researchers and students. It is worth reiterating that the too familiar situation where archives tend to receive worn show prints is totally unsatisfactory because a decision to pay for a duplicate negative, thereby safeguarding the film, partly depends on whether there is a likelihood of obtaining at some future time the original negative from which better quality prints may be made. Considerations like these inhibited Ernest Lindgren from granting the desired amount of access to some films, copies of which were

41

known from the catalogues to be held by the National Film Archive. It was a view which invited much criticism, his attitude being contrasted with that of Henri Langlois, a great personality and impresario in his own way, who has shown willingness to screen practically everything in his important collection at the Cinémathèque Française; but from the strictly archival standpoint Lindgren was undoubtedly right.

Using the methods employed by the National Film Archive films can be catalogued alphabetically by title. Production of a definitive index, however, usually requires a viewing of the film, at least to establish items like cast, credits, length and other relevant information, and perhaps also to include a short synopsis on the title card. Newsreel film, on the other hand, needs to be analysed further to enable registration to be made of places and personalities and all other items which would be of value to the historical researcher. Subjects can then be put on another comprehensive index so that, to take specific examples, all films which show Churchill or deal with the United Nations may be located. Unfortunately it can be a wearisomely slow process. Some items one might want to index may not be explicitly indicated on the sound track and the cataloguer has to be prepared to undertake some research in order to identify them. With a limited staff and with further acquisitions coming in all the time a cataloguing activity of this kind may seem to many archives to be like walking the wrong way along a moving escalator. They become accustomed to having in their vaults hundreds of cans, the contents of which are only vaguely known and which might not even be retrievable if no one has been able to spare the time to enter them on to index cards. It is to the credit of the cataloguing department of the National Film Archive that in spite of its problems it does enter some kind of information for each film received, no matter how small the film or how simple the entry. More detailed cataloguing can follow in course of time, even if there is little hope of keeping up, but it is extremely important to register some kind of 'instant' indexing so that the film can be located. Moreover, it is important too that printed catalogues should list what an archive holds and in this respect also the National Film Archive has a better record than anyone else.

There is one category of film which is especially difficult to index. That is the kind of original raw material in a mute form, the rushes of a film production or the left-over unused film of a television programme, which sometimes may be passed on to an archive. An edited film is a final fashioned product. The historian may attach as much value to the pre-edited sources, in themselves perhaps more authentic than the film which is seen after it has been made up into a compilation. This is not the place to go into the question of the degrees of honesty which particular film directors or television producers bring to their use of historical film but it is obvious that the researcher will have more chance of verifying a shot if he can go back to it as it was actually taken by the cameraman. As soon as one compilation film misuses a shot the error is likely to be repeated indefinitely. An instance of this is the well-known newsreel shot of a battleship capsizing in World War I with its crew desperately scrambling over the hull, used on more than one occasion as being the German battle-cruiser *Blücher* during the Dogger Bank engagement. In reality the original film was taken of the Austrian battleship *Szent Istvan* sinking in the Adriatic after being struck by Italian torpedoes.

The Imperial War Museum, where the major part of the film collection is composed of mute records, probably has more experience of coping with this kind of material than any other archive in the world. After World War II millions of feet of unedited nitrate based film shot by the various military services were deposited with the Museum. Ideally the preservation programme, to span a period of forty or fifty years from the original date of acquisition, should be phased to take account of two factors, the physical condition of the film in the first place and also the relative value of the subject content in different reels. It is a demanding task for a small staff. Their earliest clues in documented form to the content of individual reels are the cameraman's 'dope' sheets, some of them surprisingly informative and improving as the war progressed. Film taken, for example, by the Army Film Unit in South-East Asia was very well listed and the cameraman usually added an explanatory paragraph to justify his selection of photo and use of film stock. Not only events concerned with actual fighting were photographed. One reel (of about five hundred feet) shows distribution of food and provision of medical aid by the British to villages in Burma and here the cameraman has written at length about the effects of war and occupation on these people. Immediately after the war these activities by the Army might have seemed mundane, hardly worth preserving a record of, but the continuance in recent years of conflict in South-East Asia has given a new perspective to this film.

Certainly much of this mute material is repetitive and dull, frequently showing only the most routine activities behind the battle lines, but comparable footage say of Wellington's Army in the Peninsula campaign would now be very fascinating indeed. When the Museum held in 1974 an international conference on 'Film and the Second World War' the audience was riveted by a reel which had been shot in the north German town of Uelzen as British troops were capturing it in 1945. No one is seen to be killed or injured, the Germans appear only as prisoners or as frightened civilians and the soldiers seem to spend much of their time battering down the heavily bolted, obstinately resistant doors of German houses. But taken as a whole the reel is a striking reminder of the visual reality of the time, a small German town, drably dressed civilians, British soldiers wearing campaign-worn uniforms (not costumed as in a feature film), soldiers hunting for snipers and some of them casually smoking cigarettes, a touch which the average feature-film director might veto as unlikely or unbelievable. Naturally there are occasions when a man seems to pose for the camera or the cameraman will shoot some fairly obvious cut-aways but the record is as close to actuality as one can get.

*Clive Coultass*

The Imperial War Museum's Film Department has been a fruitful source for television programmes and in this respect it functions as a stock shot library. In some cases active co-operation has gone further, with for instance the Thames *World at War* series where a close relationship was set up. Revenue is made for the Treasury because the films are the property of the Crown. By contrast the National Film Archive owns copyright on none of its films, but does supply extract material to television companies and film producers, while ensuring that this activity does not compromise preservation and research priorities. Nevertheless, one ignores this outlet at one's peril because the exhibition of historical film to a mass audience on television, provided that it is used scrupulously, is as valuable and legitimate an objective as storing it away for future use by academic historians.

The Museum's experiences in supplying stock shots no doubt mirror those of the newsreel libraries. It is impossible for any one person to view all of the Museum's footage and detailed information necessarily has to be provided by the subject index cards, shot sheets or other documentation, which can only go so far and might not adequately give an impression of the visual composition of a shot, or it can be obtained from one or other individual who has personally seen different parts of the collection. The danger for a stock shot library is that one senior film librarian may accumulate a great deal of knowledge himself and even though he may transfer the basic details to the cards he can be so harassed by pressure of demand and shortage of staff that his own intimate acquaintance with the collection is only sporadically passed on to his subordinates, themselves busy with day-to-day administration and with scarcely any time to look at film. The sudden death in 1971 of the film librarian at the Imperial War Museum, the energetic and much liked John Sutters, left his colleagues groping in the dark for a time. It is essential that a library or archive both records its information fully and encourages its staff actually to view film. An ideal balance might be a combination of the cataloguing methods used by the respective British archives. While the National Film Archive tends to employ people with some librarianship qualifications and classification is based on the Universal Decimal System, the Imperial War Museum has attempted a more detailed scheme devised by history graduates. As a step towards greater speed and accuracy the Museum has also introduced a programme of computerisation, beginning with the recording of technical information which relates to the testing of nitrate film.

The International Federation of Film Archives dates from 1938 when the National Film Archive was one of its founders. It has grown now to a position where most of the major film archives of the world have membership and representatives normally meet annually at a congress which is held in different countries. Luckily international politics have rarely interfered in the work of F.I.A.F. and for many years its distinguished president, Jerzy Toeplitz from Warsaw, was able to keep the Federation away from partisan issues. Its greatest value is to provide a forum for people working with common archival problems.

## Film preservation: the archives

A series of committees tackles specific questions, like preservation, documentation and cataloguing, and the published products of their work can act as guides for newer archives in developing countries.

Full membership is granted only to those archives whose main concern is with the art of film, while a specialist organisation like the Imperial War Museum is admitted as an associate. The distinction has given rise to much argument within F.I.A.F. Many members are 'cinémathèques' who keep and preserve film, mostly feature films, but who have an exhibition function by running programmes in their own cinemas. The National Film Archive is in a rather different situation because, apart anyway from having a much broader collection, it does not possess its own integrated viewing theatre where it can show archive films continuously, although active use is made of the National Film Theatre as a public outlet. The invidious line of demarcation which F.I.A.F. appears to draw between film as an art form and film as a record might actually discourage a few archives from joining and from the historian's point of view it is unfortunate that these include some, like the U.S. National Archives and the Soviet Documentary Film Archive, which have major collections of non-fiction film. Looking at F.I.A.F.'s work in the past thirty years it is difficult to avoid the conclusion that however much it has done for exchange of information about feature films it has scarcely taken the historical film seriously.

Much the same might be remarked about its attitude to television. Indeed a few F.I.A.F. members have gone so far as to reject collections of television material altogether. The ultimate absurdity of this view hardly deserves comment. Television libraries are not encouraged to join F.I.A.F. because their main commitment is not to preservation for posterity and in this respect the principle is justified. But television does incorporate some of the most advanced technology in the film world and in a field like subject indexing the experience of television libraries (and stock shot libraries generally) is unrivalled. If F.I.A.F. disregards this it must again be because its members are unwilling to concern themselves with actuality film. In spite of its limitations F.I.A.F. sometimes seems to behave like an exclusive club with a unique right to determine international standards. The ideal of keeping together a close-knit group of people who know each other makes some sense and experience of a more diffuse organisation like the International Film and Television Council has not been too encouraging, but there must be room for a widening of interests.

The main barrier no doubt is the fact that whereas discussion between archivists of different countries about classic films can start with some common assumptions there is unlikely to be the same amount of general agreement on historical matters, especially when all the history in question is of the twentieth century. Few film archives employ history specialists on their staffs. With almost all of the major national archives putting the art of film concept first it is inevitable that leadership in the historical area should pass to those institutions more specifically concerned with film as a documentary record. Assessing and cataloguing the film and making it available to researchers and users remain the principal activities. However, one can go further by exhibiting the film in some programmed way. In the U.S.A., for instance, this is done by the National Archives with their regular series of public film performances. In Britain the Imperial War Museum has developed a somewhat similar function and has tried also to stimulate a broader interest in film by putting on a number of historical film seminars and conferences, some in association with other bodies, and incidentally not confined to the war theme. This is an outward looking function which an archive ought to be prepared to undertake if it has the resources. The National Film Archive for its part has mounted at the National Film Theatre at least one successful season with the collaboration of historians.

The reluctance of some film archives to take account of television springs to some extent from the very nature of the medium itself as an agent of communication. Selecting from an endless output of information and news material is a formidable if not impossible task. Much of it in any case is ephemeral, being recorded on videotape which can be wiped immediately afterwards. The National Archives have permission from C.B.S. to make video cassettes of their news transmissions and this experiment might be a model for the future, but a comparable policy in Britain would need a considerable amount of government support. It is still too early to make definitive comment on the conservation prospects for videotape or on other developments, like the video-disc, which might gain more ground in the next few years. Completed programmes from the companies still tend to be acquired in the form of 16mm film. An annual grant from the Independent Television Companies' Association helps the National Film Archive to purchase some of these and there are occasional donations, like an important *This Week* series formerly belonging to Rediffusion. The Imperial War Museum, by reason of its copyright ownership of stock shots, can sometimes negotiate for material and in the case of *The World at War* it has received not only the programmes but also much that was untransmitted. The B.B.C. in general has been more cautious about releasing its holdings to archives and its library would probably claim that it has its own long term preservation policy. Even if that argument can be accepted, it does not help the public to gain access to the B.B.C.'s collection.

This chapter has concentrated on the film archival situation in Britain but the various questions discussed are common throughout the world. The trend on the whole has been for each country to build up a single national archive, a pattern usually broken only by some of the larger and richer states. As one would expect of the most advanced capitalist country, the U.S.A. has more variety than anyone else with at least four large institutions (Library of Congress, American Film Institute, National Archives and Museum of Modern Art) concerned with film preservation. F.I.A.F. has tried to encourage the national archive concept and the East European countries have rigidly followed the idea by their representation within the Federation, even the U.S.S.R. where the film archive structure is in fact not so clear-cut. West European countries like France, West Germany, Italy and Austria each have more than one film archive, catering for different aims and different interests and not all members of F.I.A.F.

As the technology of audio-visual media advances the need for newer and more diverse kinds of archives and collections may be predicted. Even in Britain there could grow up some form of regionalisation and already the Scottish Film Council, with its own local sources of revenue, has come forward with a strong interest in selecting and keeping film about Scotland. This has to be balanced by the case for a centralisation of resources, especially where such an expensive process as film printing makes up a major part of an archive's budget. Lord Eccles, when he was Minister for the Arts, suggested that in the course of time visual and sound records could come under the wing of the British Library. In theory this kind of rationalisation has much to be said for it. It cuts out duplication both of costs and of effort. Against it one might argue that individual historical interests, whether those of a region or of a particular specialised subject, are better served by being under the control of separate bodies. Whatever the future, a national film collection should retain a degree of budgetary and policy making control, even inside a larger organisation with wider aims.

In favour of Lord Eccles' idea is the implied recognition of the national status of audio-visual records including, one would expect, some form of statutory deposit provision. The outcome of a recent decision to transfer the film archive of the Canadian Film Institute to the Public Archives of Canada will be watched with interest. The way ahead for Britain certainly should contain some plan for systematising the many confused processes by which film of historical value is first identified and then put into a permanent national repository.[2]

NOTES
1. Reproduced by permission of *The Times*.
2. The writer wishes to thank David Francis, Clyde Jeavons, Roger Holman and Victoria Wegg-Prosser of the National Film Archive, London, for their help in preparing this chapter.

# Part II
# Film as historical evidence

# 3. The evaluation of film as evidence

WILLIAM HUGHES

## Introduction

Although historians' connection with film has been only a brief encounter, a 'conventional wisdom' already pervades professional discussions of film as a source of information about the past. I am referring to the notion that, except for a few minor technical differences, film is just like other historical documents, and may be understood and criticised in the same manner. This insistence on preserving old and familiar orthodoxies is perfectly understandable, for historians — like other academicians — are extremely conservative on matters involving the fundamentals of their discipline. By tradition, we have preferred written documents over other sources, and it is reassuring for us to believe that a few simple refinements of our familiar research strategies will enable us to master the accumulated motion picture record. Acceptability, as J.K. Galbraith observes, is the hallmark of conventional wisdom.

Admittedly, there is some merit in even the most conventional of our professional wisdom. With film, as with other sources, we must be concerned with the familiar problems of dating, authorship, point of view, authentication, and verification. To resolve these problems we may adapt and apply to film sources the established techniques of internal and external criticism.

The projected film will often provide useful data in the form of slating, credits, and date of copyright. Certain stylistic elements of a film (editing or lighting styles, for example) may indicate the source of a film, or its approximate date. In addition, the visual content of a film may provide important clues. Architectural styles, landmarks, the level of technological development, modes of transportation, fashions, furniture and other decorative items, placards,

49

symbols, uniforms, even patterns of language and behaviour, are useful indicators for the historian who is trying to place his footage chronologically or geographically.

A film also reflects the state of film technology at the time of production, so that such factors as the size and shape of the picture may enable us to determine that our film was made before or after the introduction of 'cinemascope' (*c.* 1953). Was the film shot in colour and, if so, which process? Does the film have a synchronous sound track? Did the cameraman use a zoom lens? In answering even such rudimentary questions, anyone familiar with the evolution of film technology should be able to formulate relatively accurate estimates of the date and authenticity of the footage in question.

The researcher may extract other useful information from the film stock itself. Film manufacturers often mark and number their products directly on the stock. These punch-marks and latent images may enable the historian to determine whether his print is an original or a duplicate of much later vintage. If he is working with an original print, these markings may lead him to the source or approximate date of his footage.

Certain supporting documents provide much useful information. Back issues of distributors' catalogues describe the contents of individual films as well as their running times. Such information is helpful in establishing whether the footage available to the historian has been altered from the original version. The historian working with film sources also may have access to cameramen's reports in archives or company files. In addition to supplying dates and locations, these reports may reveal the existence of valuable historical footage not used in the final version of a film. The researcher may be able to locate 'trimmings' and 'out-takes' which enable him to piece together a more complete visual record. If the additional film has been lost or destroyed these reports provide at least a brief account of the missing material. Whatever they may reveal about the event in question, such data help the researcher judge the quality of his source because they provide clues to the film-maker's pattern of selectivity in constructing his finished film.

In using film sources historians will have numerous opportunities to apply various techniques of internal and external criticism, because such methods constitute a most effective means for resolving problems of authenticity and verification of evidence. But we should not limit ourselves to these measures, for if we treat film as just another document — more like than unlike our traditional sources — we ignore some important problems of evidence, and we limit unnecessarily the range of information we might extract from film sources. If we rely exclusively on such a narrow research mode, adding only our common-sense interpretation of what we see on the screen, then we presume, without justification, a high level of visual literacy on the part of the researcher; we ignore the substantive differences between various film forms; we deny ourselves, unnecessarily, the relevant analytical techniques developed by the new disciplines of communications research; we tend to concentrate on record film, to the exclusion of fiction film; we assume, incorrectly, that the camera makes an objective record of actuality. If we are interested in the informational content and message structure of film, or its possible effects on audiences, we must broaden our methodological concerns.

Certainly we are obliged to maintain the same high standards of accuracy for all our sources, including film. But in order to comprehend fully this new source we must take into account those qualities of film that set it apart from more traditional forms of documentation. Film, whatever its similarity to other written or pictorial records, has its own distinctive forms and 'language'. We must recognise, also, that economic, technological, and sociological factors peculiar to the medium may influence the structure and content of the film message. The emphasis of this chapter is on these aspects of film as history. It begins with a brief examination of the language of film, especially its capacity for recording and distorting actuality, followed by a survey of various categories of film, and the range and reliability of information associated with each type. The chapter concludes with a review of techniques for determining and interpreting the message structure of film.

## Film as language: reality and illusion

Film is a unique 'language', but the historian's professional training provides no guarantee of his cinematic literacy. As Joan and Louis Forsdale have argued, 'the higher reaches of literacy in the new media are all but barren slopes' – even in America and Europe where motion pictures and television have been for decades a part of everyday life. According to the Forsdales we rarely explore the content of visual images beyond the level of mere recognition.

For historians, the great value of film is its capacity for recording actuality. But the medium has equal potential for distorting reality, and for disguising discontinuities in its recording of events. Historians who would work with film sources need to know how films are structured and how structure shapes meaning. Each component of the cinematic language may be used in numerous ways and in various combinations to produce a visual message. Just as they must often learn a foreign language in order to utilise essential written documents, historians must know how focus, camera placement, framing, lens selection, lighting, film emulsion, editing techniques and other factors combine to determine the form, content and meaning of a given length of film.

It is not practicable within the scope of this chapter to survey all the elements of film as language. For a more complete introduction to the subject, readers should consult the many fine texts on film-making and film theory. Here the case for cinematic literacy must rest on a brief exploration of the language of film as it conveys and distorts actuality.

*William Hughes*

Any suggestion that film might not convey an accurate representation of reality seems an affront to common sense. From the very beginning of the cinema film-makers have used their cameras to explore and record aspects of reality. This impulse, as critic Roy Armes has noted, is fundamental to the cinema: 'The camera is a unique instrument for capturing the surface details of life. It can show faces, streets, landscapes, human groups and activities as well as tiny quirks of behavior, all with great power. Life itself is so engrossing on this level that the material can never be exhausted.'

Another commentator, Siegfried Kracauer, has based his elaborate theory of film upon the medium's capacity for recording and revealing physical reality. Kracauer argues that film, as an extension of photography, shares with its predecessor 'a marked affinity for the visual world around us'. Films may claim 'aesthetic validity' only when they reflect this affinity for reality. Kracauer's argument is often arbitrary, convoluted, wrong-headed. In certain particulars, however, he has articulated with great precision the 'recording' function of film.

According to Kracauer, film and science stand in the same relation to their subject matter. 'Like science', he writes, film 'breaks down material phenomena into tiny particles, thereby sensitizing us to the tremendous energies accumulated in the microscopic configurations of matter.' Film has other revealing functions. It captures and records the least permanent components of our environment. Through slow and fast motion (i.e., the manipulation of time), or through special lenses, it makes visible movements so transitory or items so small they would be otherwise imperceptible. It forces us to explore 'the blind spots of the mind', areas of perception that habit and prejudice cause us to overlook, things that we 'know by heart' but not with the eye. Film forces us to notice these things, and perhaps see them in new ways, in new relations. Film is a celluloid memory, preserving events, customs and fashions from our past. And as a witness to the catastrophic events of our epoch, it retains a level of objectivity that is often beyond the capacity of the agitated human participant. Kracauer admits that 'films cling to the surface of things', that they do not penetrate the inward life, or effectively treat matters of spirit and intellect. But, in sum, 'films evoke a reality more inclusive than the one they actually picture ... they suggest a reality which may fittingly be called "life" '.

There is much to be said for Kracauer's observations. Film reality is so powerful as to be almost self-authenticating, to the point that we sometimes judge the authenticity of a moment or place by relating it to a visual memory from a film. The journalist A.J. Liebling, for example, once reported in a dispatch from the German front that a battle never seemed more 'real' than when it evoked the memory of scenes from Hollywood war movies.

Film records time as well as space and motion. Historians, of course, are concerned with events in time, with problems of chronology. Knowledge of the technology of film-making, particularly its timing mechanism, is not irrelevant to these concerns, for, as Mark Slade has noted, 'In nearly every respect a film projector is a clockwork mechanism; it ticks, not in seconds, but in twenty-fourths of a second. Each frame (or event) is separated by a twenty-fourth of a second.' The Warren Commission staff exploited this aspect of film mechanics in its use of the Zapruder film to reconstruct certain events of President Kennedy's assassination. The film did not simply picture essential details of the event, it 'clocked' the action as well.

And if film captures only surface realities, as Kracauer admits, these externals are not without their value for historians. As Mario Praz has written: 'The inner history of a period is liable to misconceptions because the essence of ideas is subtle and deceptive . . . All things considered, one is led to wonder whether we should not be on safer ground in studying the temper of a period from its externals . . . ' By 'externals' Praz means more than the monuments of the past (palaces, cathedrals, and the like); he means, in addition, the simple utensils and fashionable knick-knacks that are so much a part of everyday life. Though it may be a secondary, even unintentional, aspect of the film-making process, film is unsurpassed in its ability to capture these items that seem so commonplace in their time. This is because film shows them in their functional contexts, in everyday use, not as mere curios or museum pieces.

Against these views of film as reality may be set certain other traditions and characteristics of the medium. From the start cinema has displayed a dualistic nature, encompassing both realism and fantasy. For every Lumière using the camera to record actuality there is a Méliès inventing new cinematic techniques to create fantasy images. This duality carries through the history of film, even to the contemporary documentaries of Frederick Wiseman and the kinetic, structural and computerised visual experiments of today's *avant-garde* film-makers.

Beyond this manipulative impulse, film has certain intrinsic limitations as a recorder of reality. As Roy Huss and Norman Silverstein note in *The Film Experience*, the motion picture camera is 'bedeviled by many hazards and ambiguities which clearly demonstrate that it does not see precisely the way the eye sees'. For a start, the camera reduces three dimensions to two. Colour is lost to black and white film, and even colour film does not reproduce the colours of the visible spectrum with complete accuracy. Motion pictures do not even provide an entirely accurate picture of motion. The spoked wheels of a moving wagon, for example, may appear to be moving backward — an effect which occurs whenever the speed of the wheels is out of synchronisation with the rate at which the film passes through the camera.

There is, in addition, the plasticity of films, which enables them to be shaped and reshaped to produce a variety of meanings. This quality of film may work for or against realistic representation. The editing process, therefore, is one of the most crucial functions of film-making. The great Soviet director V.I. Pudovkin, who (with Lev Kuleshov) conducted important early experiments in montage, has written of the place of editing in structuring our impressions of cinematic reality:

> it appears that the active raw material is no other than the *pieces of celluloid* on which, from various viewpoints, the separate movements of the action have been shot. From nothing but these pieces is created those appearances upon the screen that form the filmic representation of the action shot. And thus the material of the film director consists not of real processes happening in real space and real time, but of those pieces of celluloid on which these processes have been recorded. This celluloid is entirely subject to the will of the director who edits it.

A good example of Pudovkin's point is the case of an enterprising film promoter who arranged non-related bits of footage into a film that could be used to exploit public interest in the Dreyfus case. From a scene of a French army parade led by a captain, a Paris street scene showing a large public building, pictures of a Finnish tugboat approaching a barge, and some travelogue material picturing the Nile Delta, Francis Doublier compiled a film which purported to depict Dreyfus in the days before his arrest, the scene of the Dreyfus court-martial, Dreyfus transported to the ship that would take him to Devil's Island, and the scene of his imprisonment.

The sequential arrangement of individual shots can create new meanings not inherent in the separate shots that make up the sequence. To put it another way, the same shots can be arranged and rearranged to produce a variety of meanings. This aspect of film language suggests that a simple shot-by-shot analysis, though useful, misses an important dimension of the cinematic message. Montage creates an additional level of meaning, so it is necessary that any system of film analysis take into account the effects produced by the sequential arrangement of shots, as well as the contents of each separate shot. The plasticity of film, and its capacity for representing time and motion, also cast some doubt on those critical approaches based on analogies between film and static pictorials, such as paintings or tapestries.

Despite some apparent contradictions or tensions between the recording and formative aspects of film, the cinematic language is capable of resolving this duality. It is precisely through its manipulative or plastic qualities that film manages to depict reality. As Huss and Silverstein contend, 'Objective or photographic reality has a way of eluding the simple and direct gaze of a camera lens and can be approached only through a carefully calculated series of oblique maneuvers.' This process necessarily involves utilisation of all the elements of the cinematic vocabulary. Visual information is selectively recorded and structured to create a pictorial message — whether the film is realistic or fantastic. Film editor Robert Vas is on the mark when he says 'Cinema is reality sifted, pointed and intensified.'

### Film as artefact: varieties of film form and function

Film, like other artefacts, is an article produced or shaped by human workmanship. In its form and function it reflects the economic and technological impulses of the culture that brought it forth, and it reveals something of the values of that culture. As form is related to function, it is useful to identify and describe the range of film formats with reference to the variety and reliability of information associated with each type. As the archaeologist K.C. Chang has noted, in the analysis of cultures types and modes are better suited for historical study than are individual artefacts. By this emphasis on typology I do not mean to suggest that some forms are necessarily more 'historical' than others, but that different formats may provide different kinds of historical information.

This section of the chapter surveys various types of 'factual' or record film, as well as fictional feature films (including historical re-enactments.) It is not possible, for reasons of space, to treat non-linear or experimental films here — though they too have their historical value. Although any of these formats may depict virtually any topic, each format organises and presents its images in a distinctive way. They differ in structure and purpose, and these differences must be taken into account by historians who wish to draw reliable inferences from this kind of evidence.

### The film of record

In its various forms the film of record constitutes a vast visual record of all kinds of human activities during the eight decades following the invention of motion pictures. This broad category includes actuality footage (edited and unedited), newsfilm, newsreels, magazine films, documentaries, and compilations.[1] Two other variations, newsfilm and documentaries made for television, will not be treated here.

Actuality footage consists of a single motion picture sequence showing ordinary people and unstaged events which are not in themselves newsworthy. Many of the first motion pictures were actuality films. (These films made news, of course, but for their technological novelty rather than for their specific visual content.) These simple films, which generally lasted only a few seconds, conveyed scenes of contemporary life much in the manner of today's 'home movies'. Such footage may be unedited (retaining all technical flaws as well as irrelevant or excess footage shot on the same reel), semi-edited (irrelevant and technically inadequate material removed), or edited (restructured to better convey the intentions of the film-maker). The trims and out-takes which are the by-products of the editing process also may contain visual information of some specific interest.

Newsfilm consists of motion picture footage of a single newsworthy event or personality. Such film might have been shot continuously by one camera and screened in unedited version, but even abbreviated coverage of a single event ordinarily involves considerable editing of material shot discontinuously from a variety of perspectives. Such films, as distinguished from newsreels, were not released in series on a regular schedule.

55

*William Hughes*

Newsreels are a potpourri of news footage edited into a conventional format and released in series on a fixed schedule (often semi-weekly). They generally conform to a standard length (one reel, or about ten minutes), and include several newsworthy topics, usually unrelated. Throughout the history of newsreel its content was just as conventional as its format. Humorist Oscar Levant's description of the newsreel as 'A series of catastrophes, ended by a fashion show' is only a slight exaggeration. If anything, the emphasis was more on pageantry than on politics — and not without reason. As an editor for Paramount News explained in 1937, newsreels had to be treated as entertainment: 'The theatre managers who have to show our newsreels do not think their function is to educate. They go to great effort in their theatres to set up the desired atmosphere of romance, happiness, music and soft light, and along comes a newsreel with the latest race riot or something else that makes the audience hot.' Hence the concentration on the ceremonial aspect of public affairs, the emphasis on sports, fads and fashions, parades, bathing beauties, ship launchings, and mere curiosities.

Newsreels were standard fare in motion picture programming even before World War I, and they lasted until the maturation of television news. The term 'newsreel', however, was not limited to the standard commercial product released through the major theatre chains. During the Great Depression some American labour groups, perhaps in reaction to the unfavourable treatment they received in the conservative commercial newsreels, organised their own 'Workers Newsreels'. And recently a group of radical film-makers in America revived the label for their films, which are not newsreels in the conventional sense but separate documentaries.

Magazine films, like newsreels, were released in series on a regular basis, though magazine films were usually longer, covered fewer stories, and appeared less frequently. These slight changes in format, pioneered by Louis de Rochemont for *The March of Time* series, extended the potentialities of visual news by allowing the producers to probe their topics in greater depth than newsreels had ever done. Freed from the semi-weekly deadlines of the newsreel, editors had greater opportunity to manipulate their footage for dramatic effect. Out of this new format emerged a distinctive journalistic style, one in which the drama of the event was heightened by the drama of the presentation. *The March of Time*, which typically treated from two to four stories in the course of an eighteen to twenty-two minute programme, completed its evolutionary departure from the newsreel in 1938 when de Rochemont offered the controversial single-story issue 'Inside Nazi Germany'. Other magazine films (such as *This is America* in the United States, *World in Action* in Canada, and *This Modern Age* in Great Britain) followed much the same format developed by *The March of Time*.

The documentary label has been applied to a wide variety of films. It is a term that for some is synonymous with realism and objectivity, while for others it is avowedly propagandistic. Even in the early years of documentary that term embraced films as dissimilar as the lyrical personal visions of Robert Flaherty and the programmatic social documents of John Grierson. More recently new forms have evolved under similar banners, including *cinéma vérité*, which purports to depict real people in undirected situations (the so-called uncontrolled documentaries of D.A. Pennebaker and Richard Leacock, for example); the 'fictional documentary' (the use of nonscripted, unstaged material in creating fiction film, as in Allan King's *A Married Couple*); and the 'semi-documentary' (a fictional film set within an actual event, utilising much actuality footage – as in Haskell Wexler's *Medium Cool*, which is set against the violence of the 1968 Democratic National Convention).

Obviously so diverse a means of expression is difficult to define, though many have tried. John Grierson once described documentary as 'the creative treatment of actuality'. While this may not be a satisfactory definition, it should serve to put historians on guard concerning the difficulties inherent in using documentaries as visual records. Grierson's remark reminds us that the documentary film-maker feels free, indeed obliged, to reshape his materials to fit his personal vision of contemporary realities, or even his dream of an alternative future. Clearly this kind of film-making does not preclude the staging of scenes or the re-enactment of events. As Richard D. MacCann, a student of the documentary tradition, has noted, 'The important thing is not the authenticity of the materials but the authenticity of the result.'

Unlike documentaries, which generally are shot from a single point of view, compilation films are constructed out of extant archival footage. They are films made in the editing room. The editor's challenge is to overcome a certain 'schizophrenia' in his materials by shaping into his own point of view footage that originally was shot from many perspectives and for unrelated purposes. Often the compiler uses footage in ways that are quite the opposite of what the original film-maker intended, as when Frank Capra used excerpts from the Nazi propaganda film *The Triumph of the Will* to make an anti-Nazi film for his *Why We Fight* series. All films, as we have seen, are subject to a certain amount of manipulation – even distortion – but the compilation format has been abused repeatedly by film-makers willing to join authentic footage with stock shots and staged sequences, without informing audiences of these practices. For the historian, problems of attribution and documentation are more troublesome with compilations than with films originating from a single source.

Notwithstanding its capacity for recording events, personalities, and material culture, the film of record – from the simplest actuality footage to the most subtly edited compilation – has serious limitations which historians must take into account if they are to use such material as a source for history. Of course, there is always the problem of the personal biases and intentions of those concerned with creating a film. This is a factor in dealing with any historical document. But with film sources the limitations also include a tradition of deliberate deception; the influence of sponsorship, censorship, and other organisational factors upon the standards of selectivity used in the creation of these films; and the inherent superficiality of so much of the extant visual record.

The histories of several forms of record film reveal deeply ingrained patterns of falsification and misrepresentation. As early as Méliès, film-makers peddled re-creations of news events to an eager and curious public, but most of these films were understood to be staged versions of the events in question. On occasion, however, the combination of plasticity and publicity proved too tempting to film promoters, and they pieced together bogus or unrelated materials and offered their creations as authentic visual records of current events. Doublier's *L'Affaire Dreyfus*, mentioned previously, is an early example of this practice.

Such activities were widespread among early newsfilm producers. As Raymond Fielding reports in his account of the American newsreel industry, 'Apparently there was not a single major producer in the period 1894 to 1900 that did not fake newsfilm as a matter of common practice'. These fakes gener-ally consisted of re-creations of news events (sometimes using actors, at other times using the original participants), or outright manufacture of unverifiable activities (for example, shots of off-duty soldiers pretending to be in battle were sold to the public as scenes of actual Boer War combat). According to Fielding, these early news fakes succeeded because they were very brief and of poor optical quality so that it was difficult to observe enough detail to judge their authenticity. In addition, audiences had little or no standard for comparison because extensive photographic coverage of newsworthy events was not yet commonplace.

Fortunately, we have much more film experience than those audiences that viewed the earliest newsfilms. Modern researchers are less likely to be fooled by fake footage — particularly as viewing devices in the archives enable us to slow the action or run it again for careful analysis. Although Fielding maintains that some fakes were 'virtually impossible to detect without evidence and testimony from the participants in the production', my own experience in viewing early newsfilm in the Paper Print Collection of the Library of Congress is that fake footage is relatively obvious. It is usually characterised by amateurish, excess-ively animated 'acting', obvious miniatures, and painted cardboard backdrops. Even the more realistic fakes often give themselves away by the poorly ex-ecuted action and the location of the camera. In *Advance of Kansas Volunteers at Caloocan* (Edison, 1899), for example, the camera is in the centre of the action. In the opening shot the enemy is firing directly at the camera from close range with no apparent effect. This action is followed by the appearance of U.S. troops, from a different angle, and the retreat of the enemy. It is improbable that the news cameraman with his bulky equipment would have advanced ahead of the troops, and even more unlikely that the enemy would misdirect their efforts toward the camera if U.S. troops were only a few feet off to the side.

The tradition of deception in early newsfilm carried over into the newsreel

and the magazine film. The repertoire of misrepresentation was much the same
– mislabelled stock shots, staged scenes, re-enactments. Louis de Rochemont,
who made the transition from newsreels to *The March of Time*, transformed the
re-enactment from an expedient into a credo. The practice took hold in *The
March of Time* because it was not always possible to have sufficient film and
sound recordings to construct a continuous narrative of the event in question.
Often the only solution was to re-enact or reconstruct dramatically the elements
necessary for story continuity. Unlike many of its predecessors, however, *The
March of Time* did not try to disguise this practice. Instead, it actively promoted
the notion that even authentic news footage was only symbolic of reality. 'What
mattered', as A. William Bluem has written in *Documentary in American Television*, 'was not whether pictorial journalism displayed the facts, but whether,
within the conscience of the reporter, it faithfully reflected the facts.'

Because so many creators of compilation films rely on old news footage,
often without verifying and authenticating their materials, compilations can
perpetuate the kinds of misrepresentation that characterise other forms of
record film. Documentary film-maker Joris Ivens takes a more positive view,
however, contending that the 'resurrection of the newsreel' in later compilations
gives the original footage 'historical perspective' by juxtaposing it with other
visual materials and adding new information to the narrative. But this 'historical
dimension' is only as valid as the footage on which it is based. On occasion the
impulse to impose historical perspective has produced a treatment of both the
film and the facts that fundamentally violates the methods and purposes of
history – whether perceived as art or science. A case in point is Emile de
Antonio's powerfully engrossing compilation from the kinescopes of the Army–
McCarthy hearings, *Point of Order*, in which the film-maker quite deliberately
distorted the time sequence to impose his meaning on the events depicted.

Beyond this tradition of misrepresentation there is the web of social, economic and political relations which influence the content and credibility of the
various forms of record film. These contextual factors take the form of sponsorship and various forms of information control (censorship, selectivity and ac-
cessibility of materials).

The major newsreels, for example, were subsidiaries of the same companies
that produced and distributed most of the feature films. In Great Britain,
as Nicholas Pronay reports, newsreels were operated by the leading film companies as 'a break-even advertising unit to keep their names before the cinema-
goers and to keep off others who would undoubtedly have filled their time on
the screen'. As a consequence there was a great deal of commercial pressure on
the producers to follow popular tastes in their newsreels just as they did in
their features. In America the pattern was quite similar. The newsreel was part
of the programming service provided by the major production companies in
the days of block booking. Designed for presentation as part of an entertainment package (along with cartoons, travelogues and features), its contents

59

generally were not permitted to be controversial or upsetting — as we noted earlier.

Nicholas Pronay's studies have established that the British newsreel industry also attempted to minimise controversy (and, therefore, censorship) by creating structural safeguards. Editors of the five major newsreels met regularly to discuss their handling of potentially sensitive topics. 'The commonest outcome of the meetings which the Editors held over "touchy" subjects was the decision not to cover them at all, so concerned were they with the repercussions of a misjudgement.' This kind of arrangement accounts for much of the banality of so much newsreel footage, for the very structure of the newsreel industry committed that medium to emphasise consensus rather than conflict, to stress 'the points of similarity, identity of outlook and interest between the world of government and that of their working-class regulars'.

This timidity seems unjustified in view of the success of *The March of Time* series, which was willing to undertake controversial subjects and explore them in some depth. Perhaps because of its connection with Time Inc., with all its financial and journalistic resources, this film magazine was able to maintain consistently higher standards of effective reporting than had its forerunner, the newsreel. Launched in 1935, within a year the series was being distributed to more than five thousand theatres in the United States, and its monthly international audience was estimated to be fifteen million. Eventually distribution was extended to reach twenty million people monthly in nine thousand theatres around the world. Still the series did encounter some restrictive action. Warner Brothers refused to show the controversial 'Inside Nazi Germany' episode in its chain of theatres. The same episode faced censorship in Great Britain and elsewhere. In any event, the experience of *The March of Time*, which lasted until 1951, clearly reflects its unique corporate origins, as well as the broader social, political and economic pressures of the industry and the period.

Sponsorship is a central issue of documentary and compilation film production. Neither form has ever enjoyed commercial success, so sponsorship usually has been essential to their very existence. Inevitably this has meant that both forms have been marked by compromise, whether the sponsor was government (Grierson's G.P.O. film unit in Britain and Pare Lorentz's United States Film Service, for example), or private industry (Flaherty's *Louisiana Story*, done for Standard Oil). As Richard Griffith stated at a crucial point in the history of the documentary movement, 'documentary can survive in the modern world, or any conceivable permutation of it, only so long as it knows how to confront the sponsor with the necessary identification of his own interest with the public interest'.

This condition often determines which documentary projects are produced and how they are distributed, as well as influencing their treatment of the topics depicted. A given project may please its director, but the sponsor, as owner of the completed film, may destroy it or withhold it if he is displeased. Thus Pare

## The evaluation of film as evidence

Lorentz's impressive films (*The River*, *The Plow That Broke The Plains* and *The Fight for Life*) languished in government archives for years after their original distribution simply because some influential Congressmen and Senators believed the films to be government-sponsored propaganda for New Deal social programmes, and because the film industry lobbied against competition from government films.

In addition to the influence of sponsorship upon the film of record, the credibility of these visual sources partially hinges upon the principles of selectivity used by film-makers in assembling their footage. In gauging these standards of selectivity, out-takes (all the shots that were not included in the finished film) are very valuable. These unused shots and sequences are essential for any reconstruction of events depicted on film, simply because they provide additional visual information. But, beyond that, out-takes provide some basis for assessing the veracity of the finished film. And by checking the finished film against the out-takes we can determine whether the film-makers' pattern of selectivity significantly altered our perception of the events depicted. In weighing the significance of such material historians would do well to consider the claim of radical film-maker Emile de Antonio that 'the real history of the United States in the Cold War is written in out-takes'. Several of de Antonio's films are compilations of unused network news material. In de Antonio's view 'The networks shoot but don't televise the raw spots which reveal'.

As we have noted, traditional patterns of misrepresentation and organisational restraints on visual reporting are major liabilities of the film of record considered as a source for history. In addition, we must recognise that film provides a special, limited knowledge of events. Film critic Penelope Houston has written shrewdly of this aspect of the visual record:

> It's the record made by and for the man in the street. In peace, the cameraman has been kept on the doorstep, or allowed in for a few carefully posed, unrevealing shots. In war he has been with the troops rather than the generals. He hasn't seen the process of secret diplomacy, the forming of strategy, the details of economic policy.

Regarding Miss Houston's comments, it may be useful to compare film with other records of political history. G.R. Elton has classified these records according to particular stages of political action: discussion, decision, consequences and reaction. In general, the film record best fits within the latter two categories. That is to say, it tells us more about the results of political developments than about their causes. Motion picture archives will reveal little or nothing of the discussions behind the American and South Vietnamese decision to invade Cambodia, but the cameras vividly recorded some of the major consequences of and reactions to that decision, both on the streets and campuses of the United States and in the jungles of South-East Asia. And even though the cameraman may be kept at the doorstep of much political history, he has made an engrossing record of such elements of political experience as the physical appearance and

61

oratorical styles of public figures, the external trappings of power and the symbols of mass movements (the appurtenances of Fascism, for example), as well as the dynamics of crowd behaviour. Certainly such a record, though limited, is not without value to historians.

Sometimes it has been possible for some film-makers to go beyond the limitations noted by Miss Houston, as in the case of the film *Crisis: Behind a Presidential Commitment*. This *cinéma vérité* film enables us to witness political history at the discussion and decision stages (although, as Stephen Mamber has written, the fundamental decision in this episode already had been made). Prepared by Drew Associates for A.B.C. Television, *Crisis* was shot in the offices of the President and the Attorney-General, and on the scene at the University of Alabama, during the integration crisis at the University (though by mutual agreement the sound in certain scenes in the President's office has been omitted and replaced by voice-over narration).

But in its penetration of the corridors of power this film raised an important issue for students of the film of record: to what extent was the camera an 'affecting presence' in these events? That is, did the presence of cameras influence the behaviour of the participants in the events? Did the subjects behave as they would have in the absence of the cameras? These are questions which get at a basic premise of *cinéma vérité* — that filming can be handled in such a way that the subjects retain their integrity and spontaneity. In the case of *Crisis: Behind a Presidential Commitment*, the film-makers insist that their presence did not affect the behaviour of their subjects, though many commentators doubt their claim.

In view of our knowledge of the categories and general characteristics of the film of record, we may elaborate several means by which such material may be utilised as a source for history.

First, certain film may be used as a partial record of events and personalities. Actuality footage, as defined earlier, is best for this purpose because it has undergone a minimum of editing and restructuring. But if out-takes and trims survive, along with other supporting documentation, it may be possible to disassemble film that has been heavily edited into newsfilm, newsreels, documentaries, even compilations, and to reconstruct it in its original form. Here the principles of internal and external criticism will determine the validity of any such reconstruction. It is legitimate to question whether the anticipated results of such reconstructions would be worth the trouble. In particular cases the answer depends, of course, on the significance of the event in question, and on whether other sources may be more revealing or more readily accessible. When we make such an assessment, indeed whenever we consider film as a record of events, we come up against Penelope Houston's remark, cited earlier, that film is nothing more than 'the record made by and for the man in the street'. If so, the film record would serve as a useful corrective to the elitist bias inherent in so many of our traditional sources. A source which records the responses of those millions affected by decisions of the few can make a valuable contribution to our understanding of the dynamics of this age of the masses. It may be noted, however, that the film record has not simply documented the public's responses to official policies but has often played a role in triggering or conditioning those responses.

Second, some categories of the film of record (those made on a regular basis for mass distribution, such as the newsreel and magazine film), may be viewed as a partial record of what the public saw of events and personalities of the day. This approach has the practical merit of allowing the finished film to speak for itself. No search for out-takes or other documentation is necessary; the historian wants to see exactly what earlier audiences saw, not what was left on the cutting-room floor. There are other problems, however, concerning the nature of the audiences who saw these films, and the impact of the films upon their attitudes. Audience research generally has been unsatisfactory, possibly because audiences are so varied and transitory, and attitudes are so ephemeral. Certainly the inferences that historians may draw from audience studies are rather limited.

Nicholas Pronay's account (*History*, 56, November 1971) of the audience for British newsreels during the 1930s demonstrates both the potentialities and limitations of this approach. By carefully analysing census data, the distribution of cinemas, and statistics concerning cinema attendance, Pronay establishes that, on the whole, the British film audience during the 1930s was predominantly working-class. He asserts, also, that producers geared their product for this particular group, though he does not identify or elaborate any mechanism by which film producers ascertained the specific preferences of the working class. Pronay's analysis is very useful, but it does not tell us how particular audiences reacted to particular films. It would be useful to know how many people may have seen particular newsreels, but attendance does not necessarily denote agreement with the newsreels' handling of certain topics − particularly as most members of the audience probably came to see the feature, not the newsreel. Nor do Pronay's figures indicate whether Mayfair audiences, for example, reacted differently from film-goers in mining towns or industrial cities. Along these lines, Pronay maintains that working-class audiences were likely to be uncritical of what they saw on the screen, accepting it as 'real'. He says, also, that 'the intellectual effort involved in grasping the very difficult concept of "montage" . . . was in any case beyond the powers of the great majority'. There is some recent experimental evidence that frequent film attendance correlates with perceived similarity between film life and real life, but it is problematical whether these findings are applicable to British audiences of the 1930s. As for the intellectual challenge of montage, it might be argued from Pronay's own data that working-class audiences were the most experienced cinema-goers and the ones, therefore, who were most likely to be conscious of the devices of film-makers. In any event, the most elaborate montage techniques generally have a 'distancing' effect (i.e., they tend to draw attention to the technique rather than the content) and are not used to achieve greater realism, at least in the conventional sense.

Third, sponsored films, for all their inadequacies as record film, do provide insights into the motives of sponsoring institutions by revealing the views which they wanted the public to hold on the vital issues of the day. (Sometimes film-makers may even shape institutional policies with their films, as Frank Capra claims to have done with his *Why We Fight* series.) Many such films are best viewed as propaganda. As such, these reels of celluloid preserve through time the most carefully calculated contemporary estimates of emotions and issues that would move the public mind in a given situation. They are the organisational message distilled to its emotional essence. In addition, representative films of this type produced over an extended period of time reflect changing styles and techniques of mass persuasion, a matter of some significance for historians interested in the communications revolution which is so much a part of the modern experience.

Fourth, these films may be considered a source of their own history. Each category of record film has a history of its own. These histories intersect with and illumine other aspects of our culture. Documentary film, for example, was a vital part of a widespread documentary movement in America during the 1930s. This form of expression was the guiding impulse of the culture of the period. Certainly a topic of this importance and centrality deserves serious study by historians, and the films themselves are the best source for such efforts.

In this vein, films also are a primary source for studies of individual film-makers. Though many films clearly are the work of collaborative effort and cor-porate enterprise, personal documentaries, such as those of Robert Flaherty, may provide insights into the views of their makers. Certainly these film-makers deserve study, for their work has reached more people than that of many artists, philosophers, or minor statesmen who have received much more attention from historians. A film-maker's work reflects his background and his attitudes toward the age in which he lives. If the film is a historical compilation it also reflects the film-maker's view of the past, as well as his notion of his function as compiler, and his attitudes toward his materials. The Inter-University Film Consortium's film of the Spanish Civil War provides an interesting example of the interaction of these concerns. Based largely on newsreel archive material, the film wavers somewhat between the position that newsfilm is a record of events and the view that such film is simply a record of what people saw of events. What we get is a carefully researched visual chronicle, heavy with narration, which incorporates some newsreel clips exactly as they were shown at the time. This film, then, records a particular view of the Spanish Civil War. But, in a sense, it is also a reflection of the dichotomous view of visual history held by its compilers. To put it another way, like all films it is partially about its makers.

Sixth, censored footage and even some out-takes that never reached the censors provide a record of those social and political issues that were most likely to disturb significant groups at a given historical moment. Studied over a period of time this material records shifts in these concerns and values.

### Feature films as sources for history

To this point the emphasis has been on 'factual' films, but historians can find something of value in fictional feature films as well. There are several possible approaches. Here we shall consider the views that feature films, though predominantly fictional, capture at least the surfaces of reality; that historical dramas or period pieces serve as a visual 're-creation' or 'history' of some earlier period; that feature films reflect popular attitudes; that feature films serve as indicators of covert culture traits and values; that films are primarily a source of their own history. An additional possibility, that films can be studied as a force in history, is beyond the scope of this essay. Each of these approaches, of course, presents unique possibilities, problems and limitations.

**Feature films and the surfaces of reality.** Because so many Hollywood feature films are done in strikingly realistic style, many observers — critics and theorists, as well as a large part of the audience — see a direct connection between the images on the screen and the real world. Michael Roemer, a film-maker and critic, says we make this connection because film 'must render all meanings in physical terms', and that film's 'affinity for real surfaces, combined with great freedom of movement both in time and space, brings film closer than any other medium to our random experience of life'. So even fiction films may capture the 'surfaces of reality', i.e., the way things look and sound, and there might even be some information of historical value in these surface images. Films shot on location, for example, do convey a partial visual record of a particular place at a particular time. More specifically, Reyner Banham, an architectural historian, has cited early American silent film comedies (shot on location in and around Los Angeles) as 'an archive of urban scenery around 1914—27 such as no other city in the world possesses'.

But some observers seek a more significant connection between Hollywood films and the real life of the period from which they spring. Critic Robert Garis, for one, feels that amidst the surface reality, hidden away in all the formulas of plot and style, it sometimes is possible to locate 'a passage that showed that somebody had looked closely and well at American behavior'. What is expressed in this view, I think, is that feature films reveal some occasional 'truth' about American life. But this is the cinematic equivalent of the novelist's truth, not the historian's. As a matter of fact, those feature films that deliberately try to expose certain conditions of American life most often take the form of melo-dramas, and do not usually convey factual information that is not more completely available elsewhere. When we view a typical 'problem film' of the 1940s for example, we are left with a relatively accurate impression of the way things looked in the forties — the clothes, the buildings, the cars, the furniture. The film may even make us conscious of contemporary slang and the changes that have developed in everyday speech patterns. But such a film is not likely to provide much, if any, useful information about the problem it purports to depict. Indeed, Hollywood did not usually undertake a problem theme until well after the problem had ceased to be an explosive one, and even then film-makers tended to avoid the hard issues raised by these problems. Such films stand in much the same relation to history as did the social novels of the nineteenth century. As William O. Aydelotte has written, 'The historical value of fiction, often misconceived, . . . is not for the history of facts but for the history of opinions'. Just as Mrs Gaskell's *North and South* is not the best source of information concerning labour—management problems in mid-nineteenth-century England, so John Ford's film of *The Grapes of Wrath* does not provide a very complete account of the American depression and the plight of migratory workers. Each, however, provides us with a set of important contemporary opinions on these problems. (The matter of film as a reflection of popular attitudes will be taken up later in this section.)

**Historical re-creations.** At least as far back as the meetings of the International Iconographic Commission in the late 1920s and early 1930s, historians were expressing their disapproval of the elaborate costume dramas or period pieces which were passed off on the public as 'historical re-creations'. The Commission rejected such films as history because film could not serve as a record of events that took place before the invention of motion pictures. Re-creations were, by definition, fictions. These glossy epics generally have been full of howling historical errors, reflecting the industry's indifference to the facts of history and its disregard for the discipline of history. Even when preparations for such a film include the most thorough-going research (as in the case of De Mille's second version of *The Ten Commandments*), accuracy is readily sacrificed for drama once the cameras start to roll. We now have it on good authority that even the costumes, which we once took to be the one element of the past that was accurately reproduced for our historical epics, reflect modern conventions of costuming more than they do the fashions of the past. Anne Hollander, a costume designer and student of costume in art, theatre and film, has written:

> In the movies the public has always accepted historical characters wearing the faces of their favorite stars, providing the clothes gave the right idea in at least a few scenes, or perhaps only in a few particulars. Queen Elizabeth is always recognizable because of the familiar image; but for many others less easily schematized, specific costume conventions have long been established . . . that now serve to signal the person or period in question without resembling anything actually worn at that date.

Notwithstanding criticism by scholars, the film studios of Europe and America continued to produce these profitable staples. Surprisingly, the

## The evaluation of film as evidence

American Historical Association's Feature Films Project is based upon just such films. The Project provides excerpts from feature films, such as *Juarez* and *Martin Luther*, which treat historical characters and events. Intended for classroom use, these excerpts are packaged in cassettes and are augmented by relevant documents and interpretations. The films themselves were selected presumably for their quality as historical re-creations. It is regrettable that the prestige and good intentions of the major organisation of professional historians in America could have been committed so uncritically to a concept of such dubious validity. Still, the episode does show how deeply entrenched is the popular notion that 'history' is simply a matter of 're-creating' the past.

This is not to say, however, that historical re-creations have no value as evidence, for these epics, like most films, reflect popular attitudes. It is the peculiar value of these films that they reflect popular attitudes concerning particular historical periods, and toward history itself. Garth Jowett has established this point with his extensive analysis of historical films made in America between 1950 and 1960. His studies indicate that American films reflect certain attitudes toward historical themes. First, some historical topics are used so frequently they have become paradigms for the public's concept of these topics. These are generally 'safe' topics which do not require much interpretation and which are least subject to divisive emotional responses. Second, American historical films seldom, if ever, provide accurate historical renderings (except, perhaps, for their presentation of the material culture of the period in question). Third, films made for the commercial market seldom deviate very far from those social values which are basic to American society. In this sense, historical re-creations reflect general attitudes of the period in which they were made. To cite just a few examples, Alexander Korda's *Lady Hamilton* and Carol Reed's *Young Mr Pitt*, both purportedly about England in the Napoleonic era, very much reflect the concerns of an England at war with Hitler. Similarly, Griffith's *The Birth of a Nation* is not simply an account of the Civil War and Reconstruction. As Everett Carter has explained, Griffith's film is also a vivid and dramatic reflection of 'the ways in which a whole people have reacted to their history'. But beyond that, it embodies the anti-Negro attitudes held by Griffith and a great many of his contemporaries.

**Feature films and popular attitudes.** We have considered two approaches to the feature film and both have pointed toward the notion that feature films reflect popular attitudes. This is a rather large and imprecise claim, and we need to scrutinise it carefully before we set out to base historical generalisations upon feature films.

For a start, we need to determine whose attitudes are expressed in particular films. We know that the attitudes which come through to us from a novel are the novelist's, but a film is not quite the same. A film is not the work of one person, it is a collaborative effort. Sometimes it is possible to determine whether a particular point of view expressed in a film originated with the writers, or the director, or the producer. But, unless we are doing a study of a particular film or a particular artist, that kind of specific attribution is beside the point. For no matter who first articulated the point of view, it must receive broader endorsement within the production company to survive several script revisions, the shooting and re-shooting of scenes, and editing.and re-editing. Films, in short, are group products, and in the narrowest sense they reflect the attitudes of those social groups that make films (the attitudes of Hollywood, to oversimplify somewhat).

To what extent can we assume that the attitudes of the people who work in the film industry correspond to the attitudes of the larger society? If we turn for our answer to gossip columns, fan magazines, and even the films Hollywood makes about itself, we can only conclude that there is little connection between the film capital and the rest of America. But this view of Hollywood as 'tinsel town' is not very good sociology. Leo Rosten, who studied the sociology of the film industry in the late 1930s and early 1940s, found Hollywood to be 'an index of our society and our culture'. He concluded that 'the aberrations of our culture are more vivid, more conspicuous, and more dramatic in Hollywood than in New Bedford or Palo Alto. Our values are extended to the strident and the unmistakeable in Hollywood's way of life . . . A study of Hollywood casts the profile of American society into sharper relief.'

This observation should not be surprising, for Hollywood did not then, and does not now, exist in total isolation from the rest of the nation and its attitudes. Hollywood's technicians, writers, directors, stars and producers are products of the larger society, and they bring their attitudes and values with them when they come to Hollywood. Moreover, the social structure of the film community is not unlike that found elsewhere in the country. There is a large working-class element (observers have catalogued more than 250 occupations in the film industry), in which skilled technicians rank highest. There is a middle class of writers, actors and studio officials, and an upper class of the most successful directors, stars, executives and financiers. Like the larger society, Hollywood has been characterised by considerable mobility, and status there is determined largely by wealth.

In general, film people share the national commitment to the American Dream of success, as well as the nation's basic technological orientation. The great film-maker Frank Capra is a case in point. The child of Sicilian immigrants, Capra was obsessed by his desire to shed all traces of his family's traditional culture and to win social acceptance by achieving success on purely American terms. He did it according to the classic formula: hard work, education and good fortune. He managed to earn a degree as a chemical engineer, but the economic dislocation after World War I left him unemployed and embittered. He bummed around the west for a while, and somehow talked his way into a film job. Clever and brash, he worked his way up from prop man to editor, then to gag writer, finally becoming a director. His personal success re-enforced his childhood enthusiasm for 'the American way', an enthusiasm which comes through such films as *Mr Deeds Goes to Town, Mr Smith Goes to Washington, Meet John Doe,* and *It's a Wonderful Life.* The popular reception of Capra's films has often been taken to be a measure of the director's mastery over the symbols and values of American life. But Capra's recent autobiography, *The Name Above the Title,* suggests by its form and substance that Capra was more the servant than the manipulator of the American Dream, for the symbols and values of that dream first moulded his aspirations, then found expression in his films, and finally determined the structure of his personal narrative, which is cast in the form of the classic American success story.

And it was no mere coincidence that executives in the Louis B. Mayer mould (self-made men, immigrants or sons of immigrants) dominated the studios at a time when audiences were simpler, less well educated, and generally uncritical of the basic tenets of American life. Nor is it surprising that in the post-war period independent producers, such as Stanley Kramer, should emerge to offer a more diverse and critical view of American life to an audience that had become better educated, more sophisticated and less tolerant of the older values and attitudes. There is, in sum, plenty of circumstantial evidence to support the view that throughout its history Hollywood has been more like than unlike the rest of America, both in its social structure and its values.

But there is additional support for the notion that films reflect the attitudes of a wider public. It is a truism that one value strongly held by those who make films is the desire to achieve financial success by attracting and satisfying audiences. To that end, their films will necessarily reflect film-makers' best estimates of those themes, attitudes, values, stars and styles which will best guarantee popular success for their products. According to sociologist Herbert J. Gans, most of those involved in the creation of a film develop an 'audience image', an internalised notion of the anticipated attitudes and preferences of the people who will see the finished film. To some extent this audience image is the product of audience studies conducted by public opinion specialists hired by the film companies. But film audiences are so diverse and transitory that it is very difficult to formulate definitive, or even functional, conclusions about them. As a result, Gans says,

> The audience image is not a unified concept, but a set of numerous impressions, many of which are latent and contradictory. These impressions deal primarily with how people live, and how they look at, and respond to the roles, personalities, relationships, institutions and objects that movies portray. These impressions develop and accumulate in the mind of the creator in his contacts with potential audiences.

The film-makers' audience images must take into account that the audience for any film consists of any number of groups or 'publics'. Although every member of a given audience will have made the same basic choice at the box

69

office, each person will have his own reasons for that choice. Similarly, each individual member of the aggregate will respond to different aspects of a film, depending upon the predispositions each brings into the theatre. For any given theme or attitude his response may overlap with that of other members of the audience, thus creating a 'public' for that particular topic or point of view. As Gans notes, 'The total potential movie audience is thus composed of innumerable publics, and every movie attracts a distinctive combination of them.'

In addition to these subjective audience images and the studio-commissioned audience studies, the film industry receives other cues concerning the acceptability of film themes and attitudes. These cues may come from critics, pressure groups, censors, box-office receipts, even informal audience comments passed back to producers by exhibitors. In sum, it is not unreasonable to assume that the people who make feature films share many of the attitudes of the larger society, and that the industry makes a conscious effort to ascertain and appeal to public attitudes (though it may not always hit the mark, for in a modern pluralistic society public attitudes are diverse and often contradictory). Controversial attitudes, of course, generally are avoided.

One final question comes to mind concerning this notion that films can be a useful source for cultural history because they reflect popular attitudes: whether the element of calculation we have explored affects the validity of this source. Historians generally have maintained that 'a primary source is most valuable when the purpose for which it was compiled is at the furthest remove from the purpose of the historian', as Arthur Marwick puts it in *The Nature of History*. Certainly there is a sense in which the film-makers' interest in American attitudes coincides with the concerns of the cultural historian. Both are consciously concerned with ascertaining popular attitudes at a particular time (though one is interested only in current attitudes, while the other wishes to determine past attitudes). And they differ, of course, in the uses to which they put this information.

The finished film is, in part, a conscious probe of American values based on the film-makers' own intuitions and values, as well as their shrewdest calculations. Though this commercialised self-consciousness deprives films of the innocent or naïve spontaneity of folk culture, it does not render film unacceptable as a source for popular attitudes. Historians usually are concerned that the self-conscious document is somewhat suspect because it is likely to be a self-serving document. But in Hollywood the self-serving document (i.e., film) is the one, whether through calculation or instinct, that best reflects popular thinking and values. The film that entertains while it affirms cherished attitudes has an excellent chance to win wide public acceptance, and in the film industry this means wealth and status for the film-maker. (Ironically, it is in Hollywood's films about itself that we are most likely to find the kind of distortion that historians associate with the self-conscious document.)

What I mean to suggest here is that the element of calculation in feature films

70

does not necessarily corrupt the attitudes they depict. They are not — strictly speaking — personal attitudes, as with a novel or other works of individual art; nor are they spontaneous as are the attitudes expressed in folk culture. The attitudes conveyed by film are, for the most part, collective attitudes, and they should be evaluated accordingly. Because the finished film is, in part, a conscious probe of audience values, it is, in a sense, a complex of hypotheses. Our concern as historians using film sources should be whether these hypotheses about popular attitudes are accurate ones.

One of the virtues of this particular source is that the public's choices at the box-office provide a crude measure of the accuracy of film-makers' hypotheses about popular values. Admittedly, many factors influence the success or failure of individual films. But audience studies suggest that, although people attend films for innumerable reasons, both individually and collectively they tend to reject those films which contradict their basic attitudes. A film which accurately reflects their attitudes can fail (perhaps because of poor advertising and distribution, poor plot, bad casting, even general economic conditions), but a film which does not share some of the audience's fundamental orientations will not often succeed. In using feature films to gauge popular attitudes there is some basis, then, for working with successful films, particularly genre films. In addition, it is best to base our estimates of popular attitudes on a wide sample of films from a given period. As a check on the accuracy of our findings we can compare the results of our film analyses with studies of popular attitudes reflected in other forms of popular culture from the same period, and we can relate our findings to contemporaneous sociological studies of norms and values. For example, the vast literature on the nature and evolution of the American national character provides an extensive and intensive charting of American values over an extended period of time, against which we can compare the values and attitudes we detect in popular American films.

**Feature films as indicators of covert culture values.** We have examined the view that films reveal popular attitudes, often quite consciously. But films, like other forms of cultural expression, can reveal more than they intend. That, at least, is the view of those who see popular forms of expression as indicators of covert culture values, i.e., values seldom acknowledged by those who possess them. To those who adhere to this view, such as Bernard Bowren, Leo Marx and Arnold Rose, popular culture may be studied for 'what it betrays as well as what it depicts'. In their view the covert values that sometimes emerge from popular culture should not be taken as more 'true' or 'real' than the values we consciously acknowledge, but they are equally representative of people's attitudes and behaviour. The utility of this approach is that, where it is applicable, it can suggest some underlying tensions or contradictions in a given culture at a given moment in history. This is in sharp contrast to the more overt and calculated attitudes mentioned earlier, which are likely to reveal only consensus.

*William Hughes*

The depiction of Negroes in American films provides an interesting example of this two-dimensional aspect of popular culture. The films of the 1890s reflected some typical Southern rural stereotypes of Negroes, but, as Thomas Cripps has noted, 'the depiction of urban Negro characters was remarkably like that of all other urban immigrants'. Film exhibitors simply did not want to alienate any group of potential customers, so racial stereotyping had not become a factor. By 1915, however, racist attitudes were not uncommon in films. This new tendency reflected, perhaps, the general notion of accommodationist racism that had taken root in the country. Certainly it reflected the attitudes or biases of a few film-makers, most notably the Southern romantic D.W. Griffith. It was not, however, the systematic policy of an entire industry. As yet the image of the Negro in American films remained unformed.

It was Griffith's massive masterpiece, *The Birth of a Nation*, and the public reaction to it, that brought this issue into the open. In response to the film's vividly hostile portrayal of Negroes, the National Association for the Advancement of Colored People campaigned against the film, hoping to restrict its distribution or to have the most offensive portions deleted from the film. The N.A.A.C.P. and its sympathisers were not successful in blocking the film, but their efforts made film producers and distributors more sensitive to the problems created by such malicious racial stereotypes. The film studios did not want to antagonise the black minority, nor did they want to lose what they perceived to be the predominantly white 'Southern box-office'. Consequently the studios appear to have made a conscious effort to eliminate overtly vicious Negro stereotypes (black 'villains' are very scarce in films produced after 1915), but neither did they wish to portray many assertive, competent, virile black heroes. Indeed, many film-makers must have felt that the best way to avoid such problems was to eliminate Negro characters from their films, a view which minimised the employment of black performers (and probably reflected a certain amount of racism within the film industry). In its conscious efforts to avoid racial controversy the film industry developed what it took to be harmless or neutral images of the Negro, leading to the now familiar stereotypes of the servile, loyal, ineffectual — even shiftless, comic, likeable — Negro. Which is to say that the industry's efforts to minimise overt racism saw the same attitudes emerge in covert form. Even the new black heroes of the 1960s and the super-heroes of the 1970s are essentially false and incomplete images, reflecting the industry's and the society's continuing failure to come to grips with the realities of black existence in contemporary America.[2]

The problem with the overt—covert approach is that it is not so much a systematic method of analysis as it is an angle of vision. As such it depends very much on the researcher's insights, which are not necessarily verifiable. Such method as there is for this approach has been developed for literary rather than cinematic sources, and is based on close scrutiny of recurrent images and metaphors (Leo Marx's *The Machine in the Garden* is a good example). Applied to film analysis this approach would involve merging this particular angle of vision with detailed content analyses of cinematic images, icons and themes.

**Film history.** Feature films form the mainstream of film history. To most academic historians, however, this may seem a trivial subject, particularly in view of that concoction of nostalgia and gossip that so often passes for film history. But if we are to study film as evidence in any of the ways outlined in this chapter we must have accurate information about the films themselves and the circumstances of their production. To date even the best film histories have stressed aesthetic considerations rather than concern for the social, political and economic aspects of film production. Presumably the participation of professional historians in the research and writing of film history would broaden the range of film history while bringing greater depth of analysis and higher standards of accuracy to this field of study. It is an undertaking that is worthy of the attention of trained historians. We have already noted some of the possibilities for using film as a source for social and cultural history. Patterns of film censorship, for example, reveal moral and political impulses that would interest historians. In addition, economic historians will be challenged to make sense of a major industry, yet one whose company records have scarcely been tapped by researchers. There are also great opportunities for the historian of ideas. As Michael T. Isenberg has written:

> there is little doubt that historians, dealing with ideas presented on film are dealing with numbers far greater than those associated with the more traditional concerns of historians of ideas. Further, in an age of mass communication and public opinion polls, it is becoming increasingly clear that the line between 'high thought' and 'low thought', if it ever existed, is becoming increasingly vague with each passing decade.

Regrettably, many of the important sources of film history, i.e., the films themselves, have been lost or destroyed. In this case the culpability of the motion picture industry in neglecting, even destroying, its own products must be shared by historians, who have failed to provide leadership in recovering and preserving this matchless resource. (It is doubtful that historians would have been so complacent about the destruction of written sources, however trivial.) On the positive side, the American Film Institute has mounted a continuing effort to locate, restore and preserve this source in its National Film Collection. In addition, its catalogue of feature films, when completed, will be a significant research tool for historians and other film scholars.

## Film as message: some approaches to film analysis and interpretation

A significant portion of the vast literature on film is devoted to various social, cultural and psychological analyses and interpretations of film. Some of the social and cultural perspectives have been alluded to elsewhere in this chapter.

73

*William Hughes*

The psychological approaches to film often have been crude efforts to read Freudian meanings into films and to use these meanings as the bases for inferences concerning the mass audience. So that, for example, the horse in western films becomes a totem laden with underlying sexual implications for the collective subconscious of the masses. In addition, the literature of the psychology of film includes numerous experimental studies of audience responses to particular films, as for example the studies by U.S. Army psychologists of the reactions of soldiers to a number of orientation films (such as the *Why We Fight* series). Such efforts provide useful information, but audiences seldom are so homogeneous, nor are films usually shown under such controlled conditions.

The emphasis here, however, will be on those approaches to film which offer 'objective' techniques for decoding the message structure of film. The basic concern is to identify and review briefly some modes of analysis which minimise the subjectivism of film viewing, i.e., the tendency for each viewer to see a film in a purely personal way. This commitment to the systematic viewing of films leads us into a consideration of such techniques as quantitative content analysis and various forms of structuralism. It is the underlying assumption of this part of the chapter that the social, psychological, or cultural significance of film material cannot properly be assessed until the message structure of that footage has been articulated.

It is useful, I believe, to begin our consideration of film analysis from the standpoint of communication theory, for film is the central element of an act of communication. Even in its simplest form the communication situation involves the following processes: a source or transmitter encodes some content into a transmittable form (words, signs, or other signals) which is decoded by a receiver. The decoding process results in a representation of the original content. If film is the instrument of communication the situation becomes much more complex, involving — as we have noted earlier — all sorts of variables at the production level; transmission is complicated by the distribution network, and reception is subject to all sorts of audience attitudes. But, in any event, the message itself is a key element in the act of communication. It is, in a sense, the medium of exchange.

Quantitative content analysis is one means for identifying and evaluating the components of message systems. Although there is considerable disparity in content analysis literature, there is common agreement that this method focuses primarily on the manifest content of messages. It is not concerned with intentions, latent meanings, hidden attitudes. Fundamentally, the method consists of identifying and classifying words and signs on the basis of explicitly formulated rules (in order that the findings will be consistent if the material is subjected to the same rules of analysis again, either by different analysts or by the same analysts at a later time). The rules are intended to minimise subjectivity and ambiguity. On a very simple level quantitative content analysis may simply involve counting the number of times a given word or topic occurs in a text or series of texts. As applied to film a great variety of classifications may be developed. Analysts may wish to identify films by type (western, romantic melodrama, historical epic, etc.), locale, period in which the story is set, number of men, women, children (or various ethnic groups, or occupations, etc.) depicted, social relations of characters (married or unmarried, employer or employee), themes, motifs, values, attitudes, and activities – just to mention a few items that have been included in various studies. Leo Handel's analysis of newsreel content between 1939 and 1948 simply identified the items according to topic (political, religious, military, foreign, labour, fashion, disaster, etc.). But even such simple classification revealed significant shifts in newsreel content during that decade, though the method of analysis reveals nothing about the newsreels' treatment of the substance of these stories. It should also be noted that the categories used in content analysis are developed *a priori* by the researchers. The findings are limited therefore, to those categories that have been articulated in advance of the analysis. All other items within the message presumably escape identification and analysis. Nor does such a method reveal anything about the relations between the items identified, i.e., how these separate items function in relation to each other to create a coherent message. This method, then, hardly takes into account such factors as style, the plasticity of the medium, or even the totality of the film message based on a perception of the relation of the parts to the whole.

Structuralism, in its various forms, undertakes to isolate the components of the message without losing sight of their relations. As Marina de Camargo has written, this approach is concerned with the message as a structured whole: 'the interest is not centered in the explicit content of the signs, but rather on the relation they maintain with each other and how they are articulated to form the message with various levels of signification'. In contrast to content analysis, the place of each element within the structural totality is more important than the number of times an item might recur.

There is no single definition of structuralism because there is no single method of approach, but among cine-structuralists, who generally are more eclectic than some of the more rigid schools of structuralism, there is some common ground. The fundamentals of semiology (the theory of signs) form the basis for much of cine-structuralism. In order to convey meaning a message organises a set of signs which are selected and combined according to certain rules. These elements constitute a code. There are numerous codes, and semiology attempts to identify their components and rules (i.e., the structure of relations within each code). Umberto Eco, for example, has identified various codes and subcodes which occur in the definition of a visual message. They include an iconic code which spells out the iconological, aesthetic, erotic and montage aspects of the visual images, and a linguistic code which details the stylistic and conventional aspects of the message. Other cine-structuralists, such as Christian Metz, emphasise the linguistic aspects of film particularly as they apply to cinematic narrative. Peter Wollen, on the other hand, combines semiology with the *auteur* approach to illumine certain aspects of the work of individual film-makers. American cine-structuralists have been concerned with determining audience responses to isolated elements in the cinematic structure. Their work has been directed toward practical application in instructional media.

The structuralism of Roland Barthes touches upon the cinema but ranges into other aspects of cultural expression as well. He suggests, for example, that such forms of cultural expression as clothing, furniture and architecture are analogous to linguistic codes. That is, they can be said to form a system, or code, that consists of constituent elements and the rules that determine the relations between these elements. Together they form a kind of message. It is possible that this conceptualisation can be used in the analysis of certain aspects of cinema, particularly the treatment of 'surfaces of reality' mentioned earlier. Seen from the perspective of Barthes' theories, relations between the objects constituting a system (the system of clothing, for example) may be taken to constitute part of the total message structure of a given film. Barthes' treatment of film itself focuses on the iconographic and mythological aspects of the semiology of film. (See, for example, his treatment of 'The Face of Garbo' and his analysis of the mythological elements in the film *The Lost Continent* in *Mythologies*.)

Barthes' treatment of mythology as a semiological system provides a possible link between cine-structuralism and the structuralist anthropology of Claude Lévi-Strauss. Lévi-Strauss has endeavoured to formulate a science of mythology which would enable the analyst to explore 'certain fundamental structures of the human mind'. Like the semiologists, Lévi-Strauss utilises linguistics as a model for his studies of cultures and their myths. The object of his studies is myth, not cinema. Myths are analysed with a view to isolating basic units of the mythic structure: a term and a relation which constitute one half of an antinomic pair. A given term exists in various dialectical relations to other terms within the system of myth. It is a mode of analysis which emphasises the importance of polarised thought. The logical function of myth is to mediate or reconcile these polarities. Or, as Lévi-Strauss puts it, 'myth works from an awareness of oppositions to their progressive mediation'. Myths, however convoluted and contradictory they may appear on the surface, are structured techniques for clarifying and ordering important aspects of man's intellectual or psychological environment. The meaning of a particular myth is not usually self-evident from surface details. Meaning is exposed only by penetrating mythic structure. As a system of thought myth is dynamic. Though individual myths are subject to permutations, the structural logic of myth is consistent. Because myths are logical attempts to express and resolve cultural dilemmas or contradictions, myths 'die' or become fossilised, when the dilemmas or contradictions to which they give expression have been resolved or made irrelevant by time and events. Lévi-Strauss' structuralism, then, is a systematic technique for identifying cultural polarities, tensions and contradictions, and for analysing the structures of thought by which those matters are reconciled in a given culture.

Lévi-Strauss has not applied his analytical techniques to the cinema but, if it can be established that films are basically analogous to myths, anthropological structuralism may have some utility in the study of film and its relation to the structures of popular thought. Films, like myths, are fabricated narrative structures that are, in a sense, expressions of communal concerns. (Lévi-Strauss' view of myth is broad enough to include any manifestation of the social or intellectual activities of a community.) Genre films may be viewed as repetitions of basic 'mythical' patterns and concerns. Their perpetuation and mutation are suggestive of the continuation or evolution of certain basic culture concerns. Assuming for the moment the validity of the analogy between myth and film, this brand of structuralism would appear to have particular application to American films. American culture, as Michael Kammen notes in *People of Paradox*, is characterised by various deep-seated cultural tensions, uncertainties and 'biformities' — it is a contrapuntal civilisation. One thinks of particular cinematic manifestations of these 'biformities': the transmutation of the frontier myth in *Easy Rider*; the dichotomy of the machine and the garden in Sam Peckinpah's *The Ballad of Cable Hogue*; the emergence of the anti-hero in the western film; Hollywood's treatment of black Americans; the displacement of *film noir*, so characteristic of film melodramas during the 1940s, by the family melodramas of the 1950s (only to see its basic elements resurface in so many adult westerns of the 1950s and 1960s).

Although Lévi-Strauss' approach is fundamentally non-historical, at least one historian foresees possible applications of structural anthropology in historical studies of culture. George L. Mosse, in a review essay on 'History, Anthropology and Mass Movements', has written:

> Lévi-Strauss may not point the way out to historians trying to cope with the phenomena of popular and mass movements, but he does seem to come closer to posing the problem than other anthropologists. He attempts to deal with the role of the human mind in forming and reacting to social systems, and he advocates a specific research strategy. Lévi-Strauss recognizes the necessity of investigating the relationship between the unconscious working of man's mind and the reality of the social system. Language may indeed be a useful bridge between the mind and the system, but the statement that 'myth is language' must be broadened to take in visual means of communication as well.

A balance sheet on structuralism would have to acknowledge its theoretical richness and diversity; its apparent suitability for cinematic analysis; its systematic character, which gives it the aura of scientific objectivity. These attributes are offset somewhat by the scarcity of case studies utilising these theories; by the counter-claims of some critics that film is not analogous to either language or myth; and by the fact that, for all its rules and rigour, structuralism (particularly as practised by Lévi-Strauss), is highly personal and idiosyncratic. Still, as Howard Gardner observes in his study of the structuralist movement, 'the most dramatic property of structural analysis is the possibility it offers for deducing the existence of hitherto-undiscovered phenomena'.

For historians working with film the particular utility of structuralism is that it forces us to concentrate on the message structure of film without losing sight of broader social and cultural concerns, for all these elements are brought together in a single system of analysis. Structuralism, as we have noted, is basically non-historical, but it is not antithetical to history. Indeed, the development of that dimension may prove to be the historian's contribution to this mode of analysis. It is more likely, however, that historians would be most comfortable with structuralism utilised as part of an eclectic approach, typified by the 'reading' of John Ford's *Young Mr Lincoln* done by the Editors of *Cahiers du Cinéma* (reprinted in *Screen*, Autumn 1972). This study combined a structural analysis of various of the film's components with the more traditional social, political and economic concerns of the historian or socially-oriented critic. It provides a useful model for future structural-historical analyses of the cinema.

## Conclusion

Concerning film and history H.J. Hanham recently commented: 'It would scarcely be necessary to mention that the coming of camera, radio, and recording machine made a very big difference to the raw materials available to historians of very modern history, were it not that there is little evidence that historians have been able to discover ways of dealing with them.'

This chapter is not intended to fill the methodological gap to which Hanham alludes. I have not attempted to articulate a single comprehensive methodology, nor even a theory for the treatment of film as evidence. Rather I have attempted to identify and explore aspects of cinematic communication that any such methodology or theory must take into account. I believe we must acknowledge the limitations of our traditional methods as they apply to film. We must recognise the complexities of cinematic communication. For a start, we should be alert to the relation between film form and film content, and we need to be aware of the ways by which organisational factors influence both form and content. In developing our methodology for using film as evidence we must concentrate on the centrality of the film message. We should be flexible enough to draw on the analytical techniques of other disciplines if they might be helpful in defining and analysing the message structure of film. Only if we are prepared to broaden the scope of our professional dialogue on film can we escape Hanham's judgement. This chapter is offered as a contribution to that dialogue.

## The evaluation of film as evidence

NOTES

1. These typologies of actuality footage, newsfilm and newsreel derive from Christopher H. Roads, 'Film as Historical Evidence', *Journal of the Society of Archivists*, 3 (1966), 184, and Raymond Fielding, 'A History of the American Motion Picture Newsreel' (unpublished dissertation, University of Southern California, 1961), 5–6.
2. Although I have relied on Thomas Cripps' copious research in developing this example, Cripps himself does not utilise the overt–covert culture dichotomy in his approach to the subject. *Fade to Black*, Cripps' forthcoming study of the depiction of Negroes in film, will constitute the most scrupulous and comprehensive account of the topic.

# 4. The fiction film and historical analysis

MARC FERRO

## Historical analysis and the different types of film

All films are objects of analysis.

It is true that only newsreels and pieces of reporting are at present regarded as documents; fiction films, the 'cinema', are held to belong to the realm not of knowledge but of the imaginary; they are supposed to convey not reality but its representation. Hence today, through application to the image of the dogmas of the written tradition, only meagre credit is accorded to the scientific evidence of fiction. There is a strong tendency to assimilate it to the novel. Now, it is well known that 'important' men, scientists or politicians, administrators and decision makers put little faith in the imaginary, in the novel. In the East, they trust rather to figures, to statistics; in the West, to calculations of profitability. Like a shadow, historians and economists follow them along that road. But we know the results which that quasi-scientific faith has produced, for example in the East on agricultural production, which according to these people ought not to have stopped rising; in the West on the price of petrol, which according to the 'experts' ought not to have stopped falling.

So, through a kind of assimilation of film to writing, educated people tend to accept if absolutely necessary the evidence of the film document but not that of the film as document. The fiction film is despised, because it dispenses only a dream, as if the dream formed no part of reality, as though the imaginary were not one of the driving forces of human activity.

To come back to the reciprocal role of the documentary (and newsreel) and the fiction film (the 'cinema') for the analysis of societies, it is necessary at least to point out that contrary to what is commonly supposed the fiction film possesses (before any comparison is made of fundamentals) an advantage over the newsreel, over the documentary: thanks to the analysis of critical reactions, to the study of the number of cinema attendances, to a variety of information on the conditions of production, it is possible to get an idea of at least some of the relations of the film to society, whereas one cannot always say as much for the newsreel or the documentary film. True, since the existence of television, it is possible, thanks to that medium, more effectively to compare the relation of those two 'categories' of film to society. But we have insufficient information on the subject; at most, those responsible for television imagine that there is a risk that the content of a documentary film will have *direct* effects on the viewer; hence, at least in France where state television reigns, these films very rarely form the subject of discussion on television. It is not known, however, whether this fear is well founded.

Moreover, if it is certain that the social reality contained in a fiction film is not of the same kind as that which is proffered by a piece of reporting, by newsreels, it needs to be observed that there are nevertheless *areas of overlap* between these two types of film, that the antithesis is not as clear-cut as it is thought to be. It is clear, for example, that in the case of films shot on location a whole body of documentary information is furnished which is of the same nature as reportage even if it does not have the same *function* in the two types of film. We may call it 'film museum', a museum of objects and gestures, of attitudes and social behaviour which often elude the intention of the director. A film, as we shall see, is always overflowed by its contents. Thus, certain films of Jean-Luc Godard, for instance *Deux ou trois choses que je sais d'elle*, are as much documentaries as works of fiction, just like a great many films of the present-day English school.

In any case, every film has a value as a document, whatever its apparent nature. This is true even if it has been made in the studio, even if it is neither narrative nor representational. Through the way in which it acts on the realm of the imagination, through its transposition of the imaginary, every film lays down the relationship which binds together its author, its matter and the spectator. Besides, the unspoken, the imaginary, are as much history as is History, but the cinema, especially the cinema of fiction, opens a royal road towards psychosocio-historical regions never reached by the analysis of 'documents'.

The enthusiasts of the cinema are fully convinced of it. However, for their part, they may likewise tend to arrange 'cinematographic' genres in a hierarchy, to deny for example that a television transmission can be as much cinema as the cinema. This differentiation is related to the habits and defence mechanisms of the profession. The alibi of state censorship or of the assimilation of television to the newspaper industry justifies this critical attitude, which has the paradoxical effect that in cinema yearbooks and catalogues the historical programmes of Frédéric Rossif broadcast on television are ignored, though they are of the same nature as the films of the same Frédéric Rossif, shown in the cinema.

Certainly genres exist, in the cinema as in literature. A documentary, a musical comedy, a compilation film are not the same thing and result from different cinematographic operations. But, for social and cultural analysis, they are *equally* documentary objects: the film work of Elia Kazan, indeed that of Minnelli, imparts and teaches as much about America as a study by Siegfried or Commager. One has only to learn to read it. And documentary is not necessarily more objective, more scientific, more 'real'. Let us put forward this paradoxical

## Marc Ferro

hypothesis: there is no less of the imaginary, of the ideological in the outlook of Antonioni filming *La Chine*, a piece of reporting, than there is of social reality and of analysis in *Le Cri* or *Le Désert Rouge*, imaginative works of the same man.

The paradox is only apparent because it takes up, but in an inverse sense, an old quarrel of the great creative artists of the silent cinema epoch. For Dziga Vertov, there was no reality except in the documentary, and no document except through the medium of external observation: it is the camera eye which grasps the truth; the montage utilises the components, it competes for primacy with the shooting. Eisenstein, on the contrary, believed that one arrived at a more real, a more profound analysis of the functioning of society thanks to the language constituted by montage, a precision instrument permitting every possible reconstruction; the primacy belongs to the act of creation, to the montage. Can we say that there is less *social* reality in Eisenstein's than in Vertov's films? Jean Vigo opened up a third perspective: he put forward something better than a document, better than an analysis, a documented point of view. To that school belongs Joris Ivens, while for the naturalistic films of Flaherty, Rouquier and Dovjenko, at the confluence of these currents, observation is no good without participation, truth being accompanied also by the search for beauty. Would style have no importance in a written work? For its part, the school of Jean Rouch and the Belgian Luc de Heusch has no conception of a document without a point of view. Nevertheless, by contrast with Jean Vigo, its purpose is analysis, hence it presents its work as a document of experimental and scientific research.

Another paradox, it is perhaps historical reconstructions which contain the least historical reality. Look again at *Alexander Nevski* or *Rublev*, those masterpieces; the reproduction of the past is exemplary. Is it yet possible to understand and picture to oneself medieval Russia without driving away the besetting images of Eisenstein or of Tarkovski? In this sense, *Nevski* and *Rublev* are two extraordinary film-objects. But they are nothing more, rather as Michelet's *Histoire* is a book-object: the past that they reconstruct is a mediated past. Via the choice of themes, the styles of the period, the exigencies of production, the capabilities of the script-writers, the slips of the makers, we see the U.S.S.R. of 1938 as its rulers wanted it to be, the U.S.S.R. of 1970 as its opponents experienced it. It is there that the true historical reality of these films lies, and not in the representation of the past, leaving aside the costumes or the scraps of authentic dialogue. In the same way, *Jew Süss* is more important for the vision it offers of Hitlerian ideas and of what Nazism thought it necessary to tell the Germans about the Jews than for the picture it provides of Germany in the eighteenth century.

Thus we see the degree to which the distinction between the different kinds of cinema does not arise from the same categories in the eyes of the historian or the sociologist as it does in the eyes of the historian of the cinema. The contrast between document films and fiction films nevertheless remains partly valid, to the extent that these two types of film frequently call upon processes of

82

filming, similar indeed in one way, but essentially different because of the different nature of the original rushes, which have not been filmed to the same end.

### An example. The study of Stalinist ideology through a film: *Tchapaev* (1934)

The analysis of a fiction film derives from procedures which bear on (1) the transmitting or receiving society, (2) the work itself, (3) the relation between the authors of the film, society and the work. To these may be added a complementary study, (4), when, after its production, the filmic work has a history of its own: for example, the *Bonaparte* which Abel Gance modified several times between 1927 and 1965; or again *La Grande Illusion*, presented after the war in a slightly different version from the original, and above all *received* in quite a different way in 1937 and on the morrow of the war in 1946.

In order to sketch the outlines of a general methodology for the analysis of a fiction film, the example of *Tchapaev* (1934) has been chosen here. Starting with the screen play, we shall examine first of all the reception of the film compared with the intentions of its authors; then, on the basis of some aspects of the production, we shall contrast the explicit content of the film with the latent ideology of the text and images.

*Tchapaev* presents a rare circumstance: on its appearance it was greeted by a front-page editorial in *Pravda*; this film was a model; Soviet film enthusiasts should draw inspiration from it. 'We do not insist on a new *Tchapaev* every day', another leader wrote modestly a few weeks later. For the first time since 1917, *Pravda* was soon devoting an entire page to Soviet cinema. S. and G. Vassilev, authors of *Tchapaev*, had the lion's share of it. The reasons for this enthusiasm were clearly expounded in the editorial of 21 November 1934: the film 'showed the organisational role of the party, how a link was established between the party and the masses, how the party had organised and disciplined spontaneous reactions'.

Abroad, the communist parties joined in the chorus. It is significant that in Madrid the republican government saw to the showing of the film in the midst of civil war. The cinema newsreels provide evidence of the poster publicity given to the work of the Vassilevs. The reasons are understandable. *Tchapaev* depicted the civil war of the years 1918–19, the Reds were put forward as an example, but above all the film showed the necessity of centralisation at a moment when, in Spain, that problem was at the heart of the conflict between communists and anarchists. *Tchapaev* shows that heroes make mistakes, that spontaneity leads to errors, that individuals die, while the party sees straight, does not make mistakes and never dies.

Let us call to mind the synopsis of the film as well as the commentary on it verbatim that a Soviet critic gave in 1934.

*Marc Ferro*

**Synopsis of the film.** The action takes place in 1919, during the civil war. Tchapaev carries on a victorious but somewhat disorganised fight against the Whites. In order to bridle him and educate him politically, the party sends him a political commissar, Furmanov, who shares command of the division with him. The film traces the relations between the two men, as well as the general conditions of the struggle against the Whites.

**Commentary.** The film begins with an episode of Tchapaev's retreat under pressure from the White Guards who, in 1918, are operating on the Volga and in the whole of the eastern Soviet Union. Tchapaev's troops, composed of heterogeneous elements, put up little resistance: it is clearly apparent that we are not yet dealing with the Red Army, but simply with one of those spontaneously formed partisan detachments which later provided it with many recruits. But here is Tchapaev, rising up in the middle of this rout. He halts the fugitives and leads them back to the attack. It is he who organises the battle and aims the machine gun. And immediately the spectator is captivated by the fiery temperament of this legendary leader, sprung from the poor reaches of the peasantry. His soldiers halt at the sight of him, and turn round victoriously upon the enemy, whom they wipe out. Retreat is changed into victory. Tchapaev thanks his comrades for their bravery and energy. But at once he becomes the stern teacher that every true popular leader must be. He insists that all those who have thrown away or lost their rifle in the retreat should find it and present it to him. There they all are looking for their rifles, some even plunging into the river. Meanwhile, Tchapaev's division finds itself reinforced by a workers' detachment from Ivanovo-Voznessensk, led by Furmanov who is henceforth to fulfil the functions of political commissar. From that moment complex relations between the two men are formed.

Furmanov understands the difficulty of the task which falls to him: to re-educate the partisans in order to make self-conscious Red soldiers out of them and to help their extemporary and talented leader to become a commander of the regular Red Army. What bolshevik tenacity, patience, tact and firmness he will have to display to gain that end! The film shows us with astonishing profundity that process of political re-education, which is carried on not on school-room benches but under the whistling of bullets, in the feverish and strained atmosphere of a divisional headquarters. Bit by bit, Furmanov brings about the triumph of bolshevik ideological control, and at the same time his authority grows in the eyes of the combatants.

But does not the most arduous aspect of Furmanov's task consist in the re-education of Tchapaev himself? At their first meeting, Tchapaev is unwilling to put up with the intrusion of the commissar newly posted to his division. He does not want to subordinate himself to anyone. Tchapaev takes the opportunity of the first military conference which brings them together on the eve of a battle to test the knowledge and character of the commissar by asking his opinion on the plan of operations. Perhaps he would have found a malicious pleasure in making fun of the commissar, if the latter had let his ignorance of the military art appear. But Furmanov does not conceal that he asks only to educate himself in that art at Tchapaev's side, and he continues calmly to study the commander, the soldiers and the surrounding environment.

We are soon present at a scene which reveals new aspects of Tchapaev's character. Brigade commander Yelan, wounded in the hand, is met by these gruff words from Tchapaev: 'Wounded! There's a fool for you!' Yelan replies, altogether shaken: 'Bullets don't choose.' 'It's up to you to choose!' roars Tchapaev, 'you need a bit of gumption!' And in front of the commissar, under the ingenious guise of a lesson in practical matters, he shows the brigade commander how the battle should be directed. Tchapaev appears to us here in a somewhat unexpected light. Despite the spontaneity of his military talent, he completely excludes chance from strategy. He insists on a conscious control of the battle: 'You need a bit of gumption!' And it is thus that a second essential trait in Tchapaev's character shows through: the need for reason, organisation, discipline, exact military calculation; a trait which in the end, under Furmanov's impulsion, will definitely get the upper hand.

There is nothing more remarkable than the scene in which Furmanov and Tchapaev talk of Alexander of Macedon. It causes us to take a further step in knowledge of Tchapaev. He thinks himself versed in military history: but it turns out that he has not even heard of the great Macedonian and he feels hurt because of it. It is in vain for Furmanov to try to console him by telling him that Alexander the Great has been dead for a long time and that many people know nothing about him. Tchapaev is not satisfied with that reply. He has in the highest degree the feeling of dignity of the worker who has broken the chains of oppression. 'You know it', he replies, 'so I must know it.' His thirst for knowledge is as impetuous as his military activity. It is enough to look for a moment at his face and to catch his glance to feel all the impetuosity and all the mental élan which are at work behind that broad brow. Thought is for him inseparable from action.

From the time of his first meeting with Furmanov, he is very conscious in his innermost heart that his division and the partisan spirit of his soldiers leave a great deal to be desired. He draws the conclusion that his knowledge is inadequate and expresses the wish to educate himself with Furmanov.

Thus there appear in Tchapaev the characteristics of those men who re-create themselves in the very process of the struggle for socialism.

Alongside these two heroes of the civil war epoch, Tchapaev and Furmanov, depicted in striking relief, we see in addition other characters appearing who have the effect of completing them and making them stand out still more: several officers of Tchapaev's division, simple and austere men, deeply devoted to the revolutionary cause, full of decision, courage and energy. And what an unforgettable figure is that of Tchapaev's orderly, Petka, this petulant, observant young peasant, gifted with deep sensibility, open to all the joys of youth, who falls gloriously as a hero of the revolution!

Several types of peasant also pass before our eyes. Sometimes they belong to the soldiers of Tchapaev's division, sometimes they are peaceable villagers. We find a typical example of the general tendencies of the middling peasantry during the civil war in a peasant living in a village occupied by Tchapaev's troops, whose part is played by the actor Tchirkov. Fearless, but circumspect and unrelentingly suspicious, he observes successively the Whites and the Reds, and finally makes his choice by joining the ranks of the defenders of the proletarian revolution.

The Whites themselves are depicted in an interesting and objective manner. We see setting himself up against Tchapaev a colonel, made wise by experience of life and war, who understands perfectly that the greatest danger for him lies in his rear. That is why he would like to modify the conduct of the officers towards the men. He does not want to be simply a stern commander for them, but also a 'patriarchal' leader. But all his calculations are overthrown by the logic of the class struggle. The 'psychological attack' of the Whites, by the way perfectly authentic, has a striking impact. There they are advancing in close columns, in impeccable order and with affected swagger, smoking cigarettes as they march to the assault of the positions held by Tchapaev's division. Already a section of the Red troops, seized with panic, is retreating. But Furmanov brings the fugitives back to the attack, and Tchapaev delivers the decisive blow to the enemy at the head of his cavalry.

The film ends with the disappearance of Tchapaev, an episode which reproduces with great historical truth the glorious death of this legendary hero of the civil war.'

In fact, this 'commentary', written in 1934, provides only a summary of certain sequences of the film, and those the most spectacular. We may compare it with the screen play, which we have abridged here where it covers the sequences selected by the 'commentary'.

Sequence 1    Tchapaev emerges in the midst of the rout of his men. He restores the situation.

Sequence 2    Tchapaev as teacher, the rifle scene.

Sequence 3    Arrival of commissar Furmanov and the worker volunteers.

Sequence 4    Noisy meeting between the worker volunteers and Tchapaev's soldiers. Petka, Tchapaev's orderly, calls for silence: 'Tchapaev is thinking things over.'

Sequence 5    In front of the map: Tchapaev tests Furmanov: 'what does the commissar think about it?' Furmanov replies that the leader's opinion must be followed, not that of the man who states his disagreement with Tchapaev.

Sequence 6    The tactical lesson given to the wounded man, known as the apple scene.

Sequence 7    Petka teaches Anna, the working girl who has volunteered as a soldier, how to handle the machine gun. He tries in vain to caress her and seduce her.

Sequence 8    In the White camp. Colonel Borozdine explains to a more traditionalist officer that one must understand how to treat subordinates in a more human manner and how to maintain 'patriaarchal' relations with them.

Sequence 9    First clash between Tchapaev and Furmanov. A veterinary surgeon complains to Furmanov that Tchapaev is insisting that he should award someone the title of doctor, which he is not competent to do. Furmanov supports the veterinary surgeon. 'You're defending this rotten intelligentsia', says Tchapaev, 'you don't want a peasant to be able to become a doctor.' 'He can't, he hasn't got the right', explains Furmanov.

Sequence 10   Furmanov educates Tchapaev; he teaches him the history of the past and of the great commanders.

Sequence 11   In the White camp. The colonel's servant begs his mercy; his brother is going to be shot for desertion. The colonel grants it: Potapov's brother will be flogged.

Sequence 12   Second clash between Tchapaev and Furmanov. Tchapaev's men are increasingly pilfering from the peasants. Furmanov puts their lieutenant under arrest. Anger of Tchapaev: 'Bureaucrat, you want to pinch someone else's glory; who's in command of the division?' he asks. 'You and I are', replies Furmanov. Tchapaev's and Furmanov's men nearly come to blows. Furmanov has had given back to the peasants what had been stolen from them. A delegation of them comes to thank Tchapaev. 'It was getting impossible to tell who was White, who was Red.' Modest triumph of Furmanov.

Sequence 13   Petka expresses his admiration for Furmanov to Tchapaev. 'They wouldn't have sent Tchapaev a bad commissar', replies Tchapaev.

Sequence 14   In a meeting, Tchapaev expounds to the peasants and soldiers his conception of fairness and of command.

Sequence 15   The last lesson. Anna knows how to dismantle and reassemble the machine gun. Petka leaves on patrol, with orders to bring back a prisoner. Farewell scene: he does not dare kiss her. She is moved and watches him for a long time disappear into the distance.

Sequence 16   Petka takes prisoner the colonel's servant, who is catching fish for his brother, dying from his flogging. Touched, Petka lets him go and keeps his rifle.

Sequence 17   At Tchapaev's headquarters, Petka gets reprimanded for not having brought the prisoner back.

Sequence 18   In the White camp. The colonel plays the piano while his servant polishes the floor. Close-up of Potapov's face, which expresses anger, hatred, temptation to murder in regard to the colonel. He does not have the strength to do it, and explains to the colonel that his brother has died of his injuries. The colonel expresses his grief.

Sequence 19    Sentries in the Red camp. They are discussing the merits of Tchapaev. Furmanov passes, checks the alertness of the sentries and jokes with them. A White soldier crosses the lines and comes over to the Reds: it is Potapov.

Sequence 20    Potapov informs Tchapaev and Furmanov that the White offensive is scheduled for next day. 'They're preparing a psychological attack.'

Sequence 21    Eve of battle. In their quarters, Tchapaev and Petka gossip and sing 'The Black Crow'.

Sequence 22    The morning of battle. Potapov with the Reds. 'Why are these men going to die?' asks a child. 'So as to live', replies Potapov.

Sequence 23    Before combat. Tchapaev has to leave the field of battle to put down a mutiny. 'The soldiers are saying they want to go home.' He executes one of the mutineers. Order is restored.

Sequence 24    The 'psychological' attack of the Whites; to music, in white gloves, marching in step.
Anna lets them come close in order to decimate them with the machine gun.
Tchapaev's cavalry pursues the Cossacks.

Sequence 25    After victory. At the White headquarters now occupied by the Reds. Tchapaev congratulates Anna.

Sequence 26    The departure of Furmanov, posted to other duties and replaced by another commissar, Sedov. Emotional farewell from Tchapaev.

Sequence 27    Tchapaev's encampment attacked at night by the Whites. Taken by surprise, the Reds have to flee. Tchapaev is wounded.

Sequence 28    The Whites pursue Tchapaev who with Petka's aid tries to reach the river Ural. In fighting on the cliffs which overlook the river, Potapov kills his former colonel.

Sequence 29    Tchapaev tries to swim across the Ural. He is hit by a bullet and dies.

Sequence 30    Arrival of the Red cavalry who ensure the victory of the revolutionaries.

The lesson of this conclusion and the lessons of the whole film are clear. Heroes die, but not the communist party which assures the continuance of victory. This moral supplements the rest of the film's teaching, the calm and thoughtful superiority of party members over even well-intentioned heroes, and finally and above all the justice of the cause which they are defending against the Whites.

*The fiction film and historical analysis*

Contrasted with other historical testimony, compared especially to Furmanov's text on which the film rested, these lessons appear somewhat forced, notably the principal theme. The superiority of organisation over spontaneity, over anarchy, is a theme which constantly crops up; even if the latter word is never spoken, it is nevertheless present, at least for the spectator of 1934, a spectator knowing about Russia's immediate past. In the meeting sequence (sequence 14), a peasant asks Tchapaev if he is 'for the bolsheviks or for the communists?' Tchapaev does not know how to reply; pressed by the rustic, he looks at Furmanov, who smokes his pipe with amusement while waiting with curiosity for Tchapaev's response. After some hesitation, the latter replies that he is 'for Lenin'. The tension of the bystanders is relieved. Now, in 1934, if a member of the party knew very well that it had changed its name in 1917, that the social democratic party (bolshevik) had become the communist party (bolshevik), nevertheless a certain ambiguity remained for those who also remembered that the name communist had been coupled with that of anarchist. In the film, Tchapaev is obviously displaying his ignorance of the subleties of the vocabulary of political life; the sequence nonetheless has the effect of dissociating him from all possible attachment to any tendency other than the leninist, which hence-forth will alone be identified with the revolution. In the same year, another film-maker, Dzigan, similarly blotted out the activity of the anarchists in *The Sailors of Kronstadt*, merely stressing the turbulence, politically anonymous, of these revolutionaries. But the Vassilevs go on to further expurgations. They make Trotsky disappear: he is never referred to as head of the Red Army, although the action of the film takes place precisely at a moment when he is in command of it. His successor, Frunze, who at the time was commanding only a single front, is named instead of him as the sole arbiter of the decisions handed down from above; he is referred to several times, more than is his due, as if to obliterate retroactively all recollection of Trotsky in the audience's memory.

Another wink at Lenin, comprehensible only to old activists: sequence 18, when the colonel plays . . . the 'Moonlight Sonata'. Everyone knows that this was Lenin's favourite piece, and that he said that it was dreadful to think that while one was listening to the height of beauty horrible scenes were happening elsewhere. Now, exactly at the moment when the colonel is playing the sonata, his servant's brother is dying.

There is scarcely any question in the film of a problem which was neverthe-less essential in 1919 and which Furmanov's text grapples with: the relations between the officers of the old army who had come over to the new regime and the new commanders sprung from the ranks or from the party. In *Tchapaev* only a single reference is made to it when, in the sequence of Furmanov's test (sequence 5), the officer who states his disagreement with the tactics planned turns out to be precisely an officer of the old army. It can be seen by his uni-form. Now the shot is done in such a way that he is hardly visible. Thus the problem is spirited away, though Furmanov, by contrast, explains in his book

89

that from the moment of his joining Tchapaev to that of his leaving him the latter was increasingly hostile to any collaboration with these officers; he adds that this problem was an absorbing one. There are reasons for this excision: any explicit allusion would refer back to one of the quarrels between Trotsky and Stalin in which the latter finally adopted the propositions of his rival, making use of a large number of officers of the old regime.

This explicit invocation of history is not artless, since it is systematic and without counterbalance. It extends even to the present, that is to say to the period at which the film was produced: for example, it is characteristic that the *rapprochement* between Furmanov and Tchapaev should take place with regard to the peasant question, a link with the peasantry which is thrown into prominence precisely at the moment when collectivisation requires a reconciliation between the party and the peasant masses.

So the legitimisation of the party as ruler, on the one hand, and the legitimisation of the dictatorship of the proletariat, on the other, definitely form the intended objectives of the film. The production achieved these objectives since, as has been said, the authorities applauded the film and held it up as an example.

From there, it may be useful to proceed to another type of analysis of the film in order to examine what other messages it transmits, which were likewise accepted as being representative of the views of the regime, even if this non-visible content of the film was not directly amenable to the will of the directors or to the analysis of contemporaries.

An examination of the film's construction brings out the division between two types of sequence: those which show groups or masses, in which long shots predominate; those which show two leading characters, in which close-ups predominate. The first are animated essentially by actors' movements; their impulse is lyrical. The second, more analytical, can be grouped in several combinations according to the table on page 91. The numbers indicate the sequences in which the characters are brought together.

Thus, sequences 16, 20 and 25 aside, the most frequent combinations feature four pairs of characters:

| | |
|---|---|
| Tchapaev–Furmanov | six sequences |
| Anna–Petka | three sequences |
| Petka–Tchapaev | four sequences (often short) |
| Borozdine–Potapov | four sequences |

These pairs of characters can be found in other sequences, but they no longer animate them, other characters playing that role. In sequence 25 for example, Furmanov is present but he does not take part directly in the scene, he is simply a witness of it.

These pairs form the basis of four stories which can be isolated for analysis as plots in themselves, independent of the plot of the film and its main thread.

1. Let us examine in this way the development of the relations between

| | Tchapaev | Furmanov | Petka | Anna | Borozdine | Potapov |
|---|---|---|---|---|---|---|
| Tchapaev | | 3,5,9,10, 12,26 | 13,17, 21,28 | 25 | | 20 |
| Furmanov | 3,5,9,10, 12,26 | | | | | |
| Petka | 13,17,21, 28 | | | 7,15, 25 | | 16 |
| Anna | 25 | | 7,15, 25 | | | |
| Borozdine | | | | | | 8,11,18, 28 |
| Potapov | 20 | | 16 | | 8,11,18, 28 | |

Tchapaev and Furmanov, the principal 'pair'. In the film, they have difficult relations from the outset, relations of animosity, whereas in Furmanov's text, written in 1926, he explains that he had been 'thrilled' at the idea of seeing the famous Tchapaev; in the film he is reserved and polite along the lines required by the ideology of the main story. On his side, Tchapaev is aggressive; he hardly turns round when Furmanov introduces himself. It is the start of a real duel, a struggle for power, which to begin with follows certain rules, obeying conventions which are violated when Tchapaev bursts in on Furmanov during the incident of the veterinary surgeon. They are violated still more when the former's lieutenant is arrested and he threatens to come to blows over it, giving an imitation of the display of a gladiator stripping off his insignia. Then comes a sudden turnabout in their relationship when the peasant delegation arrives to thank Tchapaev. Subsequently, the relations between the two men get better and better. They become relations between brothers in arms. Thus the relations of rivalry have turned into fraternal bonds.

2. The relations between Anna and Petka develop similarly from a negative to a positive pole. At the beginning of this encounter between a young working girl and the soldier, which symbolises the relations between town and country, Petka wants to make love to Anna. Now Anna represents the self-conscious revolution. She has got to display her virtue, and refuse that kind of relationship with Petka. She fights him off. Petka keeps his hold on her because he teaches her to handle the machine gun; she is grateful to him for imparting his knowledge to her, but that is his duty. All the same, it is clear that she has a liking for him. The long caresses that she gives the barrel of the machine gun (sequence 15) are obviously caresses for Petka, and it matters little whether they come from the actress or from the instructions of the director, whether their significance is conscious or

91

unconscious. Yet, when Petka leaves to carry out a mission, risking his life and
so performing, in some sense, a ritual test, and wants to embrace her before
setting off but has not the nerve, she controls herself in his presence; hardly has
he gone than she rushes to the window to look after him. The music emphasises
the nature of her feelings. After the victory (sequence 25), Petka and Anna have
both succeeded in the rite of passage: Petka has done better than take a prisoner,
he has made a recruit to the cause out of him; Anna has dispersed the enemy
with the machine gun. When Anna enters the soldiers' quarters for the first time
to receive Tchapaev's congratulations, her liaison with Petka is henceforth legitimate; she lets herself be held by the waist. Tchapaev is present playing the role
of father, and in some sense legitimates their union, looking at Petka in order to
speak of Anna. Petka's first action after this token of recognition is to cut open
the egg which Anna is going to have for her meal. The symbolic significance is
unambiguous. Thus this series of sequences moves from condemnation of illicit
liaisons to the vindication of marriage.

3—4. The other two 'series' of sequences feature father—son relationships,
between Tchapaev and Petka and between the colonel and his servant. In the
first case, these relations work well. The father dies before the eyes of his son,
who has reversed the protective relationship when the wounded father had need
of his youthful vigour. Contrariwise, the relations between Borozdine and
Potapov do not work, although they have been explicitly defined as 'patriarchal'.
In a society 'condemned by History' the protective function of the father cannot
be fulfilled. Despite his efforts, the colonel does not succeed in saving the life of
Potapov's brother. Furthermore, Potapov goes over to the enemy and kills the
father who has failed to protect him.

So, at the implicit level, the systems of relations between individuals are all
situated and develop on the plane of the functioning of the family; and not, for
instance, on that of the class struggle, *which is present only in the general context* of the war against the Whites. Whether because of the situation in 1934,
class relations in the countryside, for example, are never brought out, although
they were in a lively state in 1919.

In this film, 'positive', 'normal' family relations function only in the society
legitimated by History, that of the Soviets. The proposition can be turned
round: the Vassilevs, sanctioned by the regime, judge the nature of a social
system, Good and Evil, from the starting-point of the traditional functioning of
the patriarchal family. The latter constitutes the basis and the criterion of a
regime's legitimacy.

The observation may seem paradoxical; at least it illustrates the defeat of
Alexander Kollontai's notions. But in reality its significance is more substantial
since, in the film, it is corroborated by other features which complete *the model
of values taken up by the regime in the Stalinist period; this model constitutes
at least a partial inversion of the value system of the revolutionary society of*

*1917*. Such is the case, for instance, with the attitude adopted towards the institutions of learning and military discipline.

The problem of the validity of degrees is in fact the ground of the first clash between the state (Furmanov) and society (Tchapaev). The latter supposes that with the success of the revolution access to learning is henceforth open to all with its corollary, the conferring of degrees. For a man of the people like Tchapaev, the veterinary surgeon and the doctor belong to the same world, that of learning. In that sphere the interchangeability of roles and areas of competence operates. For example, it allows Stalin to judge problems of science, art and linguistics. But Furmanov undeceives him; the law is not the same for everyone; a veterinary surgeon cannot award a doctor's degree: 'he doesn't have the right'. The ambiguity of the legitimacy on which the bureaucracy bases its power is thus uncovered: it allows the bureaucrat Furmanov, because he is a member of the party, to be joint commander of the division; it does not allow a veterinary surgeon to play at doctors. The revolution has developed occupational and social mobility to the extent that one adheres to the party. Otherwise, it blocks it. *Such is the new divide*. The new authority reinvests itself with the old learning. It revives its forms: all Furmanov has to say about a graffito that makes Tchapaev laugh is that 'the versification is bad' (sequence 25). The reinvestiture with traditional values is manifest at all levels of the film: for instance, through the music; the stretches of symphonic music are reserved for them; they extol separation, victory, licit love and death.

The falling-off by comparison with revolutionary ideals appears still more in the sequences on military matters. In the Vassilevs' film, Furmanov requests Tchapaev to 'attend to his dress' so that he can be recognised as the leader; he 'commands a division of the Soviet army'. Later, Tchapaev sees to his uniform, the peasants having failed to identify him (sequence 12). There is a comic sequence a little further on: in his turn, Tchapaev advises Petka to take care of his appearance, etc. This concern about appearance has no place in Furmanov's account; on the contrary, he writes: 'it would have taken a very clever man to pick out the leaders'. Moreover, in the meeting sequence, Tchapaev expounds his ideas about discipline: the leader should be shot like anyone else if he disobeys regulations, his table is open to all, etc. But the film's images contradict this profession of faith: there is the officers' mess and the soldiers eat separately. Above all, the attitude of the command in the mutiny scene (sequence 23) seems still more significant. The soldiers who do not want to fight repeat exactly what the Russian soldiers said in 1917, when they were fraternising with the Germans and Lenin was encouraging them at it. Here the inversion of sense accompanied by obliteration is complete: in Vassilev's film the mutineers are executed with the spectator's approval. Tchapaev adds this sentence, which is not in Furmanov's account, and goes to the very depths of traditional morality: 'The blood of the country's finest sons will redeem your faults.'

*Marc Ferro*

We may add that the taking over of the countryside by the town is represented by a remarkable inversion. At the start of the film, the battalion of worker volunteers is nothing, Tchapaev's division is everything. Among the workers, Anna symbolises this lack of competence of the town: she is learning to use a weapon while the leader, Tchapaev, is teaching tactics and strategy. At the end of the film, when Tchapaev's headquarters is surprised in the early morning, there is general confusion; Tchapaev himself is at a loss. By a complete reversal of functions and roles, it is Anna the worker, representing also the party, who was nothing at the beginning of the film, who henceforward gives the orders. The countryside has nothing more to do but obey the orders of the party, which represents the central authority.

Thus, on the implicit level, we observe a fairly coherent identification with the value system of the Whites: redemption through blood and myth of sacrifice, army discipline, exhibition of rank, legitimacy of institutionalised learning, glorification of the patriarchal and legitimate family, obedience to the central power. We may likewise note that the attacks against the 'rotten intelligentsia' and the assimilation of officers to the intelligentsia (sequence 24) convey another feature of society, the plebeianisation of the institutions of government, which is one of the characteristics of the Stalin era.

The latter displays other features, certainly; but the process of reversion which the regime endorses and encourages is systematically hostile to certain kinds of transformation, whereas for a worker or a peasant only the sexual problem is dissociated from the liberating phenomenon of the revolution.

# Part III
# Film as historical factor

# 5. The newsreels:
# the illusion of actuality

NICHOLAS PRONAY

During the sixty years which followed the invention of photography, engineers, chemists and optic scientists gradually solved the problems of the photographic reproduction of movement. The final step, taken around 1894, was the adoption of the projector which allowed the human brain to reconstruct from a series of photographs the movement itself.[1] It was incidental to the purpose of the men who struggled with the task of photographing movement that projection also allowed a large number of people to view the picture simultaneously. But it was this element which turned a scientific invention into a major entertainment industry and, in a few years, also turned it into a medium of mass communications. 'Film' was an invention of considerable scientific utility; the 'cinema' was the new entertainment industry and medium, which resulted from the fortuitous fact that it was the entrepreneurs of the fairground and vaudeville business who were the first to take up film as a commercial proposition. It was a match which lasted and which determined the development of the cinema as fundamentally as the decision to make radio into a public utility came to determine the evolution of broadcasting.

The cinema grew upon the old business of entertainment by optical illusions. Its roots were in that fascination for optical and mechanical 'ingenuities' which had kept ringing the tills of the great nineteenth-century fairgrounds and amusement piers in Britain and the 'English Gardens' of the continent, and on a higher social plane paid handsome fees to a peripatetic order of magic lantern lecturers. 'It won't draw the public for more than a month. They soon get tired of these novelties', Sir Augustus Harris the rumbustious impresario told Robert Paul the magic lantern manufacturer who invented a projector attachment for them. 'Are you however prepared to come in on sharing terms of 50% of the receipts?'[2]

The result was the Theatograph at the Olympia and the beginning in Britain of the 'cinema industry' as we know it.[3] 'Monsieur Trewe the Magician' soon officiated at the first London showing of the Lumière programme and with that the competitive element, so essential in the history of the cinema, had also arrived.

The fact that it was as a novel form of amusement by optical illusions that commercial capital came to be applied to the development of film led to the initial primacy of those two forms of film which most particularly utilise its power to create illusions. The first of these was the 'actuality' film, its final form being the 'newsreel', which created the illusion that the viewer was actually witnessing an event, which in reality took place far away both in terms of *distance* and in terms of *time*. The second of these was the 'trick' film, its final form being the 'cartoon', which created the illusion of witnessing episodes in the life of creatures which in fact could only exist as images on the screen. These two types of film, from the beginning to the present day, represented in the purest form the power of the cinema to create illusion: the illusion of actuality and the illusion of reality, respectively.

Feature films developed later and represented much less the illusion-creating power which was *sui generis* to film, in as much as feature film began as a reproduction of a real performance by real actors (named and known) on a stage and a set. Later of course, in addition to sets, location shooting came, thus adopting something of the illusion of actuality, and many of the techniques of trick films were also adopted. With these the feature film developed into an art-form. The 'youngest art', one of the most vigorous children ever of the ancient art of the theatre, nevertheless relied basically on the age-old spell of the theatre. Whether ultra-realistic or ultra-ritualistic, its essence was the magic of acting, and not of the camera. But it could develop into mass entertainment for the same reason that made the newsfilm into a medium of mass communications. That was the possibility inherent in photography, and therefore film, of reproducing exact copies of an original performance in limitless numbers and at a very cheap price.

The ability to reproduce cheaply theatrical performances and to show them simultaneously almost anywhere where a darkened room and a relatively cheap projection apparatus could be found transformed the economic basis of entertainment. It turned it into an industry. It held out the prospect of building up large, centralised business organisations in which considerable capital investments could be made, offering glittering profit in return. It was this economic aspect of the cinema which, more than any other factor, conditioned the history of newsfilms, because it linked inextricably the development of film as journalism to the development of film as the new entertainment industry. Neither the capital nor the entrepreneurial energy, which fuelled the incredibly rapid spread of the cinema, and within it the newsfilm, would have been available without this link. Without it the newsfilm as a medium of communications would not have remained confined to operating within an entertainment context, the chief cause of its failures — but then without that context it might never have reached a mass audience at all.

The history of the newsfilm falls into three periods. The first began with the birth of the cinema itself, in 1895—6, for the very first programmes already included topical items. It ended around 1910 with the introduction of the first regular weekly newsreels. This period saw the experimental development of most of the basic techniques of news-communication by film, and it coincided with the newspaper revolution associated with the Harmsworth brothers. The second period, between 1910 and 1928, was the age of the silent newsreel, during which the structure of the elaborate international newsreel organisations was fully evolved and the newsreel's potential political significance foreshadowed, though its political impact was in fact severely restricted by the limitations inherent in a purely visual medium. The third period, the golden age of the newsreel, during which it emerged as a fully-fledged journalistic medium and as a potent form of political persuasion, began with the introduction of sound newsreels in 1927 and ended with the supplanting of cinema newsreels by television news in the course of the 1950s.

The first period of newsfilm production can be said to have begun on 10 June 1895, when the Lumière brothers filmed the arrival of the delegates to the Congress of the French Photographic Societies, for exhibition before them the following day. By a remarkable coincidence, Birt Acres of Britain was then already preparing for the filming of the opening of the Kiel Canal by Kaiser Wilhelm II a week later. These two films, in their separate ways, are indeed the archetypes of the newsfilm. They set out to interest a *specific* audience by reporting an event which had *news value* not because of the inherent pictorial interest of the subject, but because the audience was already interested, had already been *conditioned* to be interested in it. Pictures of soberly dressed Frenchmen disembarking from an ordinary riverboat on a very ordinary promenade were not intrinsically fascinating even to the average Frenchman. But if the audience was composed of people already interested in photography and if they were *told* that the pictures showed the arrival of leading French photographers at their annual conference, then these unexciting pictures would be invested with a significance, by the mind of the audience itself. The Lumière brothers in fact translated into a new medium two of the cardinal techniques of local or specialist journalism. A good speciality journalist (whether on a local paper or on a trade journal) should not ask when considering a news item, 'is this interesting?' but 'will this interest the readers of *my* paper?' The second tenet was the rule of Northcliffe, that readers are perennially fascinated by news items about people they can identify with or already know, their neighbours, their colleagues or their vicarious familiars, such as public 'personalities'.

Birt Acres' *Opening of the Kiel Canal* was a classic newsfilm applying the rules of national journalism. It provided a report which was not visually exciting, for canals look pretty dull and very much alike, but covered an event over which there was already public sensitivity and which the mind of the audience would invest with great fascination. British concern over the increasing might of German naval and military power came to be a staple for the other media of popular journalism as well as the newsfilms in this period, as witnessed by Northcliffe's *Daily Mail.*

In the following year Francis Doublier and Felix Mesquich, working for Lumière, became the first of the full-time film reporters, with assignments ranging from the coronation of Czar Nicholas II to the bullfights of Spain. It was however in Britain that the next step in the development of newsfilm was taken. Birt Acres and Robert Paul — it is not clear to which the priority belongs — conceived the idea of filming the Derby on 3 June 1896, *and* arranging with great ingenuity and organisation to project the film the following evening at the Alhambra, that is while the event was still current news. This element of rushing an event of entirely ephemeral but great topical interest to the public had been missing from the work of the Lumière organisation. Newsreelmen themselves always regarded the 'Derby Film' as the first true newsfilm. The success of this venture led to a potentially very important further step. Robert Paul signed a contract with the Alhambra for the presentation of a regular weekly programme. This might well have been the beginning of the regular weekly newsreel. As it happened Paul — an inventor primarily interested in the technical aspects of the cinema — was however not the man to take this step.[4]

The outbreak of the Spanish American War in the spring of 1898 and then the beginning of the Boer War in the autumn of the following year offered an opportunity for the establishment of the newsfilm over the whole of the western world which could hardly have come at a better moment. Manufacturers of cameras, projectors and film stock were now capable of providing at least serviceable equipment. Public and exhibitors' interest in film had been aroused. There was by then a sufficient number of producers experienced in the rudiments of cinematography to take the chance offered by spectacular events far away in which there was intense public interest everywhere. These two events, America's first and Britain's last major colonial war, established the newsfilm in its own right as a new medium of communication and persuasion.

The huge number of newsfilms which were produced as a result of an insatiable public demand explored to the full the possibilities of silent films as a medium of communications. By the end of the Boer War in May 1902 there emerged three basic characteristics.

First, the film coverage had shown beyond any doubt that film was capable of communicating something of the feel and character of events which was different in kind from what had lain within the powers of the news media before. Second, the reception of the films had shown that the cinematic presentation of news could evoke a greater degree of rapport and emotional involvement from the audience than printed words and pictures could, especially so in the case of the semi-literate majority of the ordinary people. The films themselves, third, proved again beyond doubt that despite its photographic technology, film was neither a less 'flexible' nor a less 'imaginative' medium of reportage in the hands of skilful, or unscrupulous, reporters than either the written or the spoken word had been – only it carried more conviction.

The cheers, boos, foot-stamping, the stunned silences and the wild cries of joy and even the tears observed in audiences of these war newsfilms demonstrated their power to affect their audience on a highly emotional level. But the evo-cation of such *crowd* responses evidenced for the first time also that peculiar power of newsfilm which it did not bequeath to its successor, television. News-film could act upon the audience somewhat like a demagogue, it could reduce the individuality of the people in the audience and substitute a mass response for a critical and individual assessment.

The war newsfilms also settled the question, at least as far as producers were concerned, whether film was a visual *recorder* of events, or whether it was a *reporter*, a teller of tales whose truthfulness depended entirely on the veracity of the bearer of the tale. Discounting the admitted 'reconstructions', such as the films produced by Robert Paul in England and Georges Méliès in France amongst many others, and discounting doubtful ones, it is nevertheless certain that at least two-thirds of the films surviving in the archives today were anything but 'visual records'. Faced with the difficulties of filming in the midst of an actual battle, with the imponderable chances of getting cameras into the actual place where the 'event' was to take place, with the unreliability of equipment and their dependance on the vagaries of the weather for good light even if they did happen to be present at the right place at the right time, the great majority of the producers gave up almost at once any attempt at treating the camera as a 'recording machine'. In fact, what emerged as the first lesson of the war was how woefully inadequate the camera was in fact to cope with almost any subject which had not been staged in the first instance. Parades, ceremonies, training exercises and the like were suitable subjects because cameras could be set up at suitable vantage points, the filming could be planned and rehearsed, and such was the keenness to get on to the screens of the nation that often it was possible even to persuade the participants to repeat their performance if something had still gone wrong. For almost everything else connected with war or politics or crime or accidents the camera was heavily handicapped.

By the end of the pre-newsreel era, the newsfilm producers had had to learn, perforce, all the basic techniques of news reportage by films which the great *creative* possibilities of the camera, as opposed to its limitations as a recording device, had made possible. These techniques did not change in any fundamental way to the end of the newsreel period, indeed they are daily used today, nor were any substantially new visual techniques subsequently to be added. It may be convenient to review these techniques at this point.

The newsfilm producers learned that it was almost as effective to use shots taken before and after an action — for example, showing troops preparing equipment and marching off to a battle, followed, after a few indistinct views, by soldiers herding back prisoners, shots of the wounded, etc. — as it was to try to film in the smoke and confusion of actual fighting. They discovered that one burning house or one smoking gun muzzle looked so much like another that it made no difference at all whether it had been filmed at the place or at the time in which the sequence of the finished film made the audience imagine it. It was also learned that a close-up of a general, or of a pretty nurse, or of the unshaven face of a prisoner of war, or of a thumbs-up sign from 'one of ours' was in fact a better stimulant to the imagination of the audience (even if it happened to have been taken months earlier) than long-shots of distant figures on an actual battle-field. Above all they gradually evolved the techniques of juxtaposing such shots with shots of the location of the event and thereby leading the mind of the audience to make up its own sequential story from them. The discovery that people wanted a story instead of scenes, and that this could be done by a sequential juxtaposition, was a fundamental one. In addition, many of the producers also learned the exciting possibilities of intermixing 'real' shots of the exterior of buildings etc. with re-enactments of what might have been happening inside.[5] They also learned the use of models, from battleships in Manila Bay to rubber figures 'leaping' from a burning hotel and from firework volcanoes to panoramic models of earthquake-stricken Los Angeles,[6] which was based on the realisation that both perspective and scale are in any case an artificial product of camera optics. Some of these techniques were later known in the newsreel industry as 'faking', and there had been always a good deal of debate amongst the newsreelmen where the line ought to be drawn. In fact the first published discussion of this question appeared as early as August 1900 under the title 'Sham War Cinematograph Films'.[7] Models and re-enactments were always regarded by some newsfilm producers as unacceptable; by the majority as only to be used in the very last resort; and by some as quite legitimate techniques, because truth, in their view, resided in the truthfulness of the *story* told by the film *as a whole* and not in the photographic credentials of any one shot.[8]

Towards the close of the pre-newsreel period appeared the first exploration of another form of 'faking' which exposed the central problem of news communications by film, the fact that in films *time* as an element of reality is always purely artificial. The order of sequences, hence the apparent order of the events, the inclusion or exclusion of anything which took place between those sequences and the time elapsed between them were entirely in the control of the film-maker. Moreover, since there is only one screen in the cinema irrespective of how many cameras might have been employed, events which occurred simultaneously in real life could not also be shown at the same time. Thus with the purest motives and the best will in the world, the newsfilm maker had to distort the element of time. In fact he had to create an illusion of time and had to create a sequence in the light of his own interpretation of the causal relationship between the shots. Thus the *story* of what happened was just as much a creation of the newsfilm maker's interpretative mind as if he had written it or described the story verbally.

The technical limitations of news cameras, which were not substantially removed until the introduction of 16mm safety film after 1945, clinched this point for the whole of the newsreel period. The cameras were incapable of filming continuously for more than about ten minutes, at the most. In the case of a military or political event stretching over hours, days or even weeks, as most of them had a habit of doing, the complexities of telescoping the time element into the scale of a newsfilm (or news broadcast today) were so self-evident and the scope for distorting the story by the inevitable imposition of an artificial sequence and time-scale so great, that merely photographic 'fakes' paled into insignificance. A complete travesty, even a fantasy, could easily be woven out of perfectly genuine shots, taken at the proper time and at the real location, if the man who created the sequence and created the time factor chose to do so, or was simply ill-informed or had misjudged the story. The emergence of the 'editor', the man whose job this became, over the cameraman was just beginning at the end of the pre-newsreel period. He became, of course, the key figure in the newsreels, and the supersession of the camera-recorder by the editor as the journalist represents the transition from the 'actuality' or 'topical' stage to news-reel journalism.

The realisation of *all* the basic principles and techniques of sequencing and time manipulation by the juxtaposition of shots (montage) for the purpose of telling a news story can already be observed in the film made about the coron-ation of King Peter of Serbia, in 1905:[9]

> *Le Couronnement du Roi Pierre de Serbie, Belgrade*
> Long shot of the Danube outside Belgrade; group of men paying off a boatman; group of women standing waiting, having arrived presumably for the coronation; busy street-scene, decorations, a contingent of soldiers, close-ups of people hurrying on foot to the procession; procession itself, with heralds, cavalry and infantry; a group of women in national costume watching; open carriages with representatives from foreign countries and army officers; more shots of streets and sightseers; King Peter returning from coronation, medium close shot; followed by carriage bearing the orb and sceptre, the rest of the procession including a group of men in ermine robes and a mounted gun carriage; medium close shot of two women unidentified; out in the open fields where a cavalry exercise is held; King Peter on horseback takes the salute at a march past which ends with a charge of the cavalry. (A total of 790 feet, approx. 8 minutes running time.)

Perhaps for the first time, we have here a classic demonstration of the tech-nique of news communication by film. This film would be accepted as a 'good story' not only by the editors of both the silent and sound newsreel periods, but by the news editor of any television station today.

## Nicholas Pronay

The techniques of communicating a news story by film were fully developed within a decade of the invention of the motion picture. What remained to be done was to evolve organisations which were capable of producing a *regular* film coverage of the world's news events. This involved the creation of a parallel industry to the elaborate structure, developed over a century, which supplied the newspapers. Considering the capital investment and organisational problems involved, it is an amazing testimonial to the impact of cinema that this step was taken before the cinema was fifteen years old. Such a step could only become feasible after a large and *habitual* cinema audience had already come into being.

The first cinema in Britain, as opposed to music halls, theatres and fairground operators who showed films as a part of their programme, was probably established in 1904, and the first purpose-built cinema was opened in 1907 at Balham. By 1914 however there were 1375 cinemas in towns of a population of 100,000 or more, and between 4000 and 4500 in Britain as a whole. In the United States there were already around 9000 cinemas in 1908 and approaching 14,000 by 1914. These figures show that a very large number of people had already acquired the habit of cinema going — thus the time was ripe for converting the occasional, if numerous, newsfilms into a regular weekly news magazine. The credit for taking this step belongs to the French Pathé Company, headed by Charles Pathé. Early in 1909 his company committed itself to the production of a weekly news magazine; by the end of the same year the Gaumont Company, also French, followed suit. In the summer of 1910 both the Pathé and the Gaumont 'newsreels' were introduced into Britain as a separate British 'edition' and in 1911, at the latest, Pathé opened its United States newsreel branch. By that time Pathé had already reached most of the continent of Europe, including Russia. By 1914 Pathé (and at least some of its main competitors) could effectively cover news events taking place in the whole of what was regarded as the civilised world, and the Pathé newsreels were regularly exhibited in the greater part of the continent of Europe and over the vast territory of the United States of America.

Pathé's crowing cockerel became a common symbol of 'news' for New Yorkers and Parisians, for Magyars and Swedes, for Englishmen and Germans. Thus the might and tradition of the British Empire, as displayed at the Coronation Durbar at Delhi in 1911, became a new, common, shared experience for the ordinary townspeople of France and Austria, the United States and Germany as well as, and almost as much as, for the majority of the common townspeople of Britain itself. The annual Potsdam manoeuvres of the Kaiser's army, relayed by newsreels from 1910 onwards, created for the first time that peculiarly mechanistic German military image which too came to be a lasting shared experience for the ordinary people of the world. Altogether, there came into being a community experience, a common view of the world shared by the lower-class townspeople, who were the cinema-goers. They were becoming more familiar with the far-distant events of the newsreel world than with those outside their own towns. A reviewer of the first American edition of the *Pathé Journal* wrote on 29 July 1911:[10]

> The *Pathé Journal* makes its debut with a mixed program of foreign and domestic events. The foreign events consist of happenings in England, France, Russia and Germany. We see the scenes and display of military splendour at the unveiling of the monument to Queen Victoria in London; the presentation of the colors to a regiment of French Zouaves at the Hotel des Invalides in Paris; the visit of the German crown prince and his wife in St Petersburg; the highly interesting water jousts at Nizza, France and the big military review of the German troops at Potsdam. Of all the foreign features the last named is easily the most impressive. No amount of printed or spoken description could give us as clear and convincing a picture of Germany in arms as this film. For the first time we understand what is meant by the military prowess of Germany and the splendid physique and perfect drill and discipline of its soldiers.

The impact and significance of the world *coverage* combined with world *distribution* can hardly be exaggerated. Nothing like it had been achieved by the press, the printed news medium. No newspaper had breached the frontiers of language to reach an international readership of ordinary people (unless the personnel of the foreign offices were to be so regarded). Very few newspapers in the world, outside Britain, had even a genuinely national circulation. The United States, for example, had, and still has, none. Even in Britain, whose press was far in advance of the rest of the world, it is questionable if the newspapers could really be said to have breached the inner frontiers of education and class: the total circulation of the whole of the national daily press in 1914 was just over four million, out of a population of over forty million. Just how many of the 'compulsorily educated ones', in Bernard Shaw's phrase, amongst the working class were in fact up to reading a report of the German army by Wickham Steed, let alone digesting any of it, after their long working day?

There was no lack of consciousness of the significance of what they had started, amongst the newsreel men or amongst the cinema exhibitors. They had no doubt at all that by moving from occasional to regular newsfilm they had crossed into journalism. F.A. Talbot's *Moving Pictures*, first published in 1911, devotes a chapter to 'The Animated Newspapers'. He describes how 'the topical film which presented in a tabloid form an assortment of news was given a newspaper title. The animated "Graphic", "Gazette", "Chronicle" appeared, while to render the newspaper idea more pronounced the exteriors of the picture palaces were emblazoned with placards drawn up in the most approved newspaper style.'[11] Within one year of the introduction of the newsreel into Britain the weekly issue of newsreels was replaced by a twice-weekly issue, thus occupying a half-way position between the daily and the Sunday newspapers, a result largely due to the capital investment and technological inventiveness of the Pathé laboratories. Before the twice-weekly newsreel was one year old (1911), the Manager of the *Gaumont Graphic* gave this description of how he saw the immediate future: 'The *Gaumont Graphic* is quite ready to appear daily . . . The complete paper (*sic*) could be turned out in four hours. The early special trains which now leave the great cities at express speed for the delivery of printed newspapers may yet be called upon to carry small boxes of daily newsfilms for similar distribution.'[12]

The almost instant success of the newsreels as a remarkable approximation to a world newspaper was not due either to some startling improvement in film technology or to the invention of new techniques of news communication by pictures. The secret of the success of the Pathé newsreel lay in the business organisation evolved by that company, which became the model for all its successful competitors. Rationalising the more or less haphazard results of its export—import operations as a successful distributor as well as producer of entertainment films, Pathé evolved the prototype of what more recently came to be known as a 'multinational corporation'. An international network of nationally registered companies was created, each with a substantial measure of autonomy and native staff headed by a native editor in most cases. Each company produced its own national edition and was responsible for filming events in its own country. Through extensive use of telegraphy, the telephone and a highly developed transport organisation, each national office made known its own 'stories' and made copies of its own national film material available as 'foreign stories' to the others via a pyramid of regional headquarters. Paris was Pathé's European headquarters, New York the American, and sub-headquarters were established in St Petersburg, the Far East, South America and so forth. Although Pathé was a 'French' company, London was the 'world' headquarters owing to Britain's primacy in the development of the cable-based news agency system, an important factor, largely owing to Baron Reuter's initiative and to the Foreign Office's intelligent early recognition of the utility of Reuters for British foreign policy. Despite the retention of its uncompromising French name, Pathé was a genuinely international organisation in terms of personnel with an ethos which anticipated much of the good and the bad features of the present-day multinational corporation. There can be no doubt that the impact and acceptance of newsreels worldwide was fundamentally due to the worldwide approach engendered by this structure and that more than anything else was Pathé's contribution. National newsreel companies, such as the British Williamson News, Jeape's Graphic, Jury's and others, came into existence with a local viewpoint and conforming a good deal more to the insular approach of the British popular press, but they were all destined to fail, despite their often excellent work. The successful 'British' newsreels were in fact the 'national' editions of the multinational newsreels, such as the *Gaumont Graphic*, later *Gaumont British News* (known and advertised as *G.B. News*) and of course the evergreen *British Pathé*.

## The newsreels: the illusion of actuality

The motto of Gaumont, which when sound came thundered out at the start of *every* issue, 'This is the Gaumont British News presenting the world to the world', encapsulated and emphasised the approach which characterised the successful, mass-audience newsreel. Between 30% and 70% of the total content of each newsreel issue, in a normal week, carried foreign news. This was in striking contrast with the content balance of the British press as a whole, even more so in the case of the popular newspapers. It created amongst its audience a much more cosmopolitan outlook. The frequency of stories coupled with the immediacy of motion pictures as a medium made the boxing ring of the Madison Stadium in New York, the salons of Parisian couturiers, the floods of the Mississippi Valley, the sight of Unter den Linden filled with troops, the motor-race circuit of Le Mans, the capital ships of the world's navies, a common ingredient in the awareness of the ordinary cinema-going people. Projected on a screen in a cinema at Leeds they appeared as near, as real, as immediate as events in Norwich or Edinburgh, and so did the rioting strikers of Budapest or of the Rand in South Africa. But the same illusion of immediacy which broadened people's outlook also distorted. It obscured the relative relevance and importance of each event, for the particular people of each country.

The cosmopolitan coverage led to the absence of any in-depth analysis and the suffocation of developments in that direction. Towards the close of the pre-newsreel era there were attempts to move towards interpretative film journalism. The suffragette film of 1908 by the Jeape company was an illustration of this trend. 'A natural development from this could have been a type of film showing a greater interest in current social and political issues', but in the newsreel 'news-item petrified into formal disassociation from its context'.[13] This was primarily due also to the multinational structure of the newsreel industry, the obverse side of its achievements. To reach for deeper causes and to discuss motives and implications in depth can only be done in the case of subjects about which there is already an awareness and at least a minimal degree of information in the mind of the audience. That means, at the least, that it would have had to be a British problem which was analysed before a British audience. A detailed and thorough film of, say, the wave of strikes in Britain in 1911, would have certainly interested the primarily working-class cinema-goers in Britain, but would have been of little use elsewhere in the Pathé organisation. The commercial purpose of the multinational set-up was precisely that thereby each story could be used twice: once as a national story and then as a foreign story elsewhere. Moreover this necessarily longer treatment would have squeezed out the 'foreign' stories, already filmed and paid for by the organisation elsewhere – a double loss. And finally, such analytical journalism about current social and political events, by definition 'controversial', would have run into 'trouble', difficulties with the authorities in many countries – almost certainly including Britain. Thus the whole ethos of a multinational corporation was against this kind of journalism. Pathé did in fact cover some of the main strikes of that troubled year, but in the same snappy external manner in which it presented the Siege of Sydney Street, the visit of Kaiser Wilhelm to Austria or the Henley Regatta.[14]

World War I brought the newsreel official recognition as a medium of public persuasion of especial importance because it could reach precisely those sections of society which the written word could not and yet which supplied the soldiers and armament workers. The cinema had proved its power already as a recruiting medium as far back as the Boer War. Films designed to show the army and navy life in a favourable light, made with the co-operation and often sponsorship of the War Office and Admiralty, began in 1900, with Robert Paul's serial *Army Life*. By 1911 it was reported as a matter of historical fact:

> They proved immensely popular with the public and were far more potent as a means of inducing enlistment with the colours than the most glowing word pictures painted by the glibly persuasive recruiting sergeants. The idea has been copied by other nations and today the cinematograph is regarded as an indispensable weapon for attracting recruits to the land and sea services.[15]

At the same time the impact of the newsreel presentation of the Balkan Wars of 1912 and 1913 showed the potential of the newsreel as war propaganda.

Some sort of government control of newsreels in war was therefore inevitable in order to ensure that their potential was properly employed. The enervated conduct of the war which characterised the Asquith cabinet, however, delayed this step considerably. It was left to the newsreel companies themselves to form a committee for co-ordination and for the obtaining of suitable facilities for war coverage. William Jury, later knighted for his services, emerged as a natural leader amongst the newsreel owners. He was a man of some vision, and robust and simple patriotism, a man of the people with the common touch, as well as an adept at dealing with officialdom and looking after his own business interests. In the War Office there were by 1914 a few men who had witnessed the recruiting potential of film as well as had some experience in dealing with film companies. As a result it was through the War Office rather than through a more appropriate channel that the propaganda potential of newsreels came to be organised at first. Officially approved War Office cinematographers were appointed and the material filmed by them was shared by the newsreel companies. Overall control passed gradually into the hands of a joint government/cinema trade committee under Sir Max Aitken, Lord Beaverbrook. As the propaganda aspects of this by then worldwide war fought by conscripted soldiers were appreciated, the committee took over the Topical Film Company, one of the smaller native newsfilm establishments, and from 1 October 1917 an official newsreel was issued, *The War Office Topical Budget and Pictorial News*, mercifully abbreviated four months later to *Pictorial News Official*. By this time a central organisation for the conduct of propaganda as a whole was in being, albeit in ineffective control of the various agencies which had developed piecemeal and often by the drive of an individual, and this was raised to a ministry in the spring of 1918.

With some 4000 cinemas in operation, and a weekly audience which could be as high as twenty million on occasions, and with the recognition that the latter was predominantly working class, or at least the 'cheaper sort of people' as one report put it, the newsreel played an important role in maintaining morale. This was partly due to the awareness with which its producers approached their task. 'I have always tried to remember', wrote Geoffrey Malins of Gaumont, one of the first official war cinematographers, 'that it was through the eyes of the camera, directed by my own sense of observation that the millions of people at home would gain their only first-hand knowledge of what was happening at the front.'[16]

Although the excitement of war produced war melodramas and comedies which at first competed effectively, 'newsreel and official records [the War Office Topical Committee's and then the Ministry of Information's films] continued to exercise an irresistible fascination over audiences throughout the war, [while] military dramas enjoyed a comparatively short period of easy popularity'.[17]

If World War I brought the first official and general recognition to newsfilms as an important new medium of public information and persuasion, it was also during the war that the limitations of the silent newsreel came to be first recognised. As early as 1915 there were complaints, even within the cinema trade, that the newsreels were not doing justice to the war: their treatment, it was claimed, was bitty and too short and they whisked from subject to subject too quickly. There was little however that could be done within the format of the newsreel. Silent film with captions is a very slow medium for telling news stories if anything beyond the most superficial glimpse is required. The only way such coverage could be given was by devoting the whole reel to a single subject, and even then, it was usually necessary to over-run the limits. Such 'special' reels could not be successfully employed more than occasionally. An alternative approach was to select some long-running but essentially past event, such as the preparations for a battle, and to produce a weekly or fortnightly serial treatment of it. Both of these self-contained larger treatments, of subjects chosen by hindsight rather than news value, were the filmic equivalent to the 'magazine' technique rather than to the newsreels' 'tabloid' approach. They fitted in less well with the entertainment supplement place occupied by the newsreel in the cinema programme, and only the inability of the silent newsreel to cover at all satisfactorily a story of even minimal complexity forced the producers into them. Their introduction in fact signalled the failure of the silent newsreel as a journalistic medium to fulfil the very high expectations pinned on it. Its decline was rapid after 1918.

By the time F.A. Talbot's book came to have its second edition, in 1923, the author who wrote in such appreciative terms a decade earlier felt it appropriate to drop altogether his chapter on 'The Animated Newspaper'. Many newsreel companies collapsed or withdrew from this branch of the business after the war and the bustling newsreel scene of the pre-war days greatly subsided. It could no longer attract able journalists, for example. There were, in the first place, business reasons for this decline. The war had hit the Anglo-French cinema very hard indeed. The loss of the central European market for the duration of the war had led to the development of strong native industries. The recognition of the propaganda significance of the cinema in general and of newsfilms in particular resulted in a marked reluctance on the part of the governments of the defeated nations to do anything at all which would help the Anglo-French newsfilm industry regain its pre-war share of their market. The very important Russian market was irrecoverably lost and the Soviet Union as a source of news stories closed altogether. The heavy taxation of the industry and shortage of capital during the war drained European and British talent, production facilities and expertise to America and gave a starting advantage to Hollywood which proved irrecoverable. Within the news industry the multinational corporations alone survived long after the war, and the general shift of vigour to America was reflected in the internal shift of power within these corporations to their American branches. This led to an ever growing increase in the proportion of American 'stories' which made the news content of the reels ever more artificial, and for the first time British and French audiences too came to experience this artificiality.

But the fundamental reason for the rapid decline of the silent newsreel as a serious purveyor of news and as a journalistic medium was the lack of a sound track, once the great spectacle of war was over. The guts of 'news' has always been and can only be politics in the wider sense of the word. And, as Colin Seymour-Ure reminded us recently, politics is an essentially verbal activity.[18] A medium which can only communicate pictorially can make effective propaganda, but cannot effectively operate as a regular reporter of current political activity. Once the novelty of seeing Mr Churchill or President Wilson move their lips and gesticulate has waned, people want to hear what they were actually saying, or not bother with the pictures at all. Once they have become used to being able to see pictures of distant riots, they want an explanation of what is happening, why and with what consequences — in fact they want to have a *verbal* report with the pictures. So, silent films came to be driven after the war away from real news, and towards intrinsically spectacular rather than political events, coronations, state openings, civic ceremonies, military tattoos and the like. And increasingly they came to practise the substitution of manufactured news stories for real news stories, the vice of 'stunts', such as those featuring the exploits of their own daring cameramen, or those of cranks such as the eternally optimistic bird-men. In addition to featuring such 'news' in place of real news, visual stunts came to be introduced into real events which were too verbal for the silent reels, thus trivialising and further debasing their coverage. Instead of the hoped for 'animated tabloid newspaper', a filmic equivalent to the *Daily Mirror*, the silent newsreel evolved only into something akin to *Tit-Bits*, though in fairness never quite as much a non-news medium.

Entertainment, of course, is an essential element of popular journalism and the line between being an entertainment rather than a news medium is always somewhat uncertain, but there is no doubt that the silent newsreel after the war was forced on to the wrong side of that line. Owing to its inability to communicate verbally on any real scale, it became a branch of the entertainment business, as Professor Fielding has remarked in connection with the American newsreels. The silent newsreel did continue in the 1920s to render for each new generation of cinema-going youngsters the service of giving them a semi-artificial but still at least a world view, instead of the parochial one which had been the horizon of ordinary people in all previous ages, but its impact upon the polity grew less and less. Unless the newsreel could find access to verbal communication, it was dead as a branch of journalism, at least in peacetime.

It was thus no accident that while the cinema industry as a whole found little use for the synchronised sound film invented by Lee De Forest, it was *Fox News*, 'the world's largest newsreel', and its parent company, 20th Century Fox Corporation, who bought it and developed it into a practical system. On 21 January 1927, the first public performance of sound film (as distinct from experimental showings, of which there had been many going back to Edison himself) was held to announce the intention of issuing the *Fox Movietone News*. On 6 May 1927 Benito Mussolini addressed the camera directly, delivering a speech in English aimed at the U.S. public, in one of the very first recordings made in preparation for the regular issue of *Movietone News*. Having viewed the result, Mussolini expressed the opinion: 'Your talking newsreel has tremendous political possibilities, let me speak through it in twenty cities in Italy once a week and I need no other power.' With the Lindbergh flight (and the speeches thereat) to fire the public imagination, and with the work of converting the Fox chain of cinemas behind it, on 3 December 1927 the regular twice-weekly issue of *Fox Movietone News* commenced.[19] All the newsreel companies and most of the cinemas in the Western world had changed over to sound by the beginning of 1931.

The new age in mass communications and politics, expected for twenty years, had at last begun. The sound track gave the newsreels access to the life-blood of journalism, politics and the reportage of what politicians said, and they could report with much greater verisimilitude than either the press or the radio. Now they could also comment and interpret as freely as the press on any issue, whether or not it was pictorially self-sufficient. And most importantly, the soundtrack enabled them to offer or refuse to offer to politicians the services of a medium which was obviously of great value to all who strove to address and persuade the people. This power made the sound newsreel at once not only a fully-fledged member of the journalistic fraternity but a different and important member. Mussolini's appreciative comment on the potential of sound newsreels for his demagogic dictatorship was echoed in a practical way in the British context by the eagerness of the Conservative Central Office to obtain the rights of one of the sound film systems (Phonofilm) in 1928, and by the eagerness of the press barons to obtain control, or at least a share of control, in the sound newsreels. Lord Rothermere, then at the height of his powers and influence, bought a major share in Fox, when its British subsidiary was established. This gave him the right to nominate the editor, and he installed his secretary, Gerald Sanger, as the man in charge of *British Movietone News*. Lord Beaverbrook was too slow off the mark and in the end failed to purchase *Universal (Talking) News* in 1932, the only other company open to purchase, though he succeeded in establishing some co-ordination between it and the *Daily Express*. Beaverbrook proceeded however to project himself through sound film on behalf of tariff reform. The *Daily Express* by this time had substantially left behind Rothermere's *Daily Mail*, and became the largest circulation newspaper — it was food for thought, not missed at the time, that within three years *British Movietone News* reached a larger audience than either the *Daily Mail* or the *Daily Express*. Within five years it had an audience as large as the pair of them.[20] Journalists now came over to join or work on a free-lance basis for newsreels and such ballyhoo publicity occasions as the famous 'Fleet Street Shakes Hands with Wardour Street' mammoth dinner of 1932 merely publicised what was a real union.

But if there was a well-recognised analogy between newspaper and sound-newsreel journalism, there were also some fundamental differences which soon emerged. Politics is indeed a 'verbal activity', but it is as much or more a spoken activity as a written one. Oratorical persuasion was equally at the heart of the parliamentary spoken debate, the party-political campaign for the new mass electorate as pioneered by Gladstone's Midlothian campaign, and dealings at the caucus/pressure-group level as exemplified in the Carlton Club debate in October 1922. In communicating these essentially spoken forms of political activity the written and the audio-visual forms of journalism had very different powers. In the latter case it was not a written transcript of selected passages, for which the politician was obliged to rely on the journalist, by which it reached the public, but the speaker as well as the speech could be brought to appear before the public. If the newsreel editors agreed, the politician could directly address the public as a whole, in person yet simultaneously, and cut out the whole intermediary stage of speech—interview—transcript—report (and editorial comment) which lay in the newspaper age between him and the public. The manipulation of immediacy, the job of the newsfilm editor, whether in newsreels or in television news, is a different art despite the apparent similarities with newspaper editing.

As important was the difference between newspapers and sound newsreels on the level of reception. The chief characteristic of newspapers was 'the reader's ability to control the time, place, frequency and quantity of his exposure'.[21] That is, the fact that in newspapers, the *reader* decides which articles to read; when to read them; in what order to read them; when to stop and if necessary re-read a passage; and he can even compare side by side two different newspapers' versions. In the case of newsreels (and equally so in television news and radio news) it is the *editor* who determines *all* of these factors of reception. He and not the reader imparts a sequence — hence a sequential/causal connection if he chooses to do so — to the items, and determines the speed with which the reader is given the story without the chance of the reader omitting anything and without any opportunity whatever for either 'reading it again' or comparing it with another version, side by side. On the other hand, there was the fact that a newspaper could use virtually unlimited numbers of words, while the newsreel editor was severely restricted.[22] Balancing the effect of enforced brevity was the most fundamental difference of all between newspaper and sound newsfilm communications: the latter entered the recipient's mind through both channels of reception, while silent film and the printed word shared the limitations imposed by communicating only through the eyes. Sound film could talk while the eye took in the picture and thus at once distract and guide the mind in analysing what the picture meant; conversely it could flash pictures into the eye to reinforce the unhindered or unquestioning reception of what it was shouting into the ears. Loud volume for this reason was a design feature of the newsreel. The sound newsreel was also what the newspaper emphatically was not, a medium for *man-in-the-mass*, in the warm, communal darkness of the auditorium, rather than for the *individual* wrapped in his own very private copy of 'the paper'. As a medium for suggestion and direct persuasion rather than for putting an argument before critical eyes, it was in a different world altogether from the newspapers.

Partly as a result of these qualities, partly because of the simple point that it operated through the spoken word and the picture, the newsreel reached that very substantial lower section of the population which was by education or background not in the position to be an effective reader of the press, and in that fact too there was something new and different from the assumptions of the press as a whole. It was no longer a case of communicating to the literate but to the people as a whole.

It was not long before the originally claimed intention of merely recording what had been said or heard at an event took second place to the voice of the commentator/journalist doing his own direct persuasion instead. Whatever element of 'visual record' there had been in the silent newsreel was quickly submerged in the torrent of words which thereafter characterised the sound newsreel. Once the strident voice was there to tell the audience what they were seeing, there was practically no limit to the use of visual substitutes — the less distinct the shot the better, or at least almost so. The soundtrack also enabled the editor to utilise even better the holdings of the silent newsreel library in lieu of the 'real' footage, and then to utilise the rapidly building up sound-film library in a new and especially effective way. Inserting sound film of a person, for example, taken sometime in the past into a current story – entirely indistinguishable from film taken yesterday – gave a new edge to the time-distorting element inherent in any form of audio-visual communications. The novelty and impact of this technique upon the audience of the 1930s should not be underestimated in itself, but its chief significance lay in the additional power it gave to the editors to talk about anything whatever, irrespective of whether there was any direct film material at all. It also allowed them to produce extraordinarily effective (or confusing) compilation/montage pieces out of edited past footage, as arguments of current validity. Hence, the importance of 'the library' grew even greater. Newly established newsreels had virtually no chance of competing without a library, which, by the definition of being a new company, they did not possess. No newcomer lasted therefore longer than a few months. The result was a tight oligarchy of five newsreels covering the whole of Britain and substantially integrated with the equally tight oligarchy covering the U.S.A. – a position radically different from the British press and even more from the 14,000 U.S. newspapers.

The oligarchy of five companies shared a regular weekly audience of 18.5 million in 1934, and slightly over 20 million in 1939 in Great Britain, excluding Northern Ireland. This meant well over half the population between five and sixty-five years of age. Some 80% of the working class during their most formative and effective years, between fifteen and thirty-five in particular, received the newsreels as an absolutely regular part of their life at least once weekly.[23]

The five companies were Pathé, Gaumont British, Universal, Movietone and Paramount. Gaumont British and Pathé were the two survivors of the original Anglo-French enterprise in this area, now substantially British-owned and controlled. Gaumont British had the largest circulation by a short head, and it also editorially controlled Universal News, which was American-owned. Movietone, next in circulation, remained a part of the great Fox multinational network which, in addition to a host of South and North American reels, included the second largest German newsreel, *Deutsche Wochenschau*, which in turn dominated much of central Europe. Despite the position of partnership by Rothermere, Fox continued to exert a strong influence on the day-to-day running of the *British Movietone News*,[24] and its editorial policy reflected the American orientation as much as the Rothermere line.

Paramount, much smaller than Gaumont or Movietone in circulation, was a wholly American-owned subsidiary of Paramount Pictures Incorporated and it drew its foreign material almost exclusively from its U.S. parent company. Pathé just held its own in fourth place at home but with substantial exports to British colonies and dependencies, past or present. Gaumont British also exported and was particularly strong in Burma and Ireland. For their European and world coverage both Gaumont and Pathé depended on their American contacts,

## The newsreels: the illusion of actuality

Gaumont almost entirely on Movietone and Pathé very largely on its own American offices. Thus American-based multinational corporations in effect dominated all the British newsreels during their politically most effective period, after 1931, until the end of the Second World War.

Apart from the influence exerted by the multinational corporations through their ownership upon content balance – such as the continuing predominance of American over imperial stories for example – the newsreels operated relatively freely. They were accepted as part of the press rather than of the film industry and were therefore exempt from the extraordinarily comprehensive political censorship exercised over all other kinds of films. What did they make of their opportunities as the most effective new medium of journalism and political persuasion?

The opinion generally expressed in the writings of contemporary American observers has been well summarised by Professor Raymond Fielding. It amounted to the view that they were wholly given over to trivia and sensation-alism: 'a series of catastrophes ended by a fashion show', as Oscar Levant re-called them in 1965. This view could be paralleled from British writings, even if they tended to put it less picturesquely. It is true that a proclivity for 'stunts' survived into the sound period; and so did a fondness for all-in wrestling, panda bears, and the like. An irritating flippancy of tone in the 'commentaries' is also often remarked upon. True, this was as much a reflection of the conversational conventions of the 1930s as it was an adaptation to the new medium of the old journalistic need for being entertaining. Nevertheless it was in stark contrast with *The Times*, though not all that far away from the style adopted by the *Daily Express* or the *Daily Mirror*. It is also true that the newsreels' width of coverage was much smaller than that of the newspapers, just as news broadcasts cover far fewer news stories than the many thousands of words employed by 'quality' newspapers. Yet it is difficult altogether to justify the comments of contemporary authors, such as John Grierson or Graham Greene, against the records and above all the actual newsreels in the archives. Much detailed research has yet to be done. Preliminary analyses do not bear out the charge that the newsreels ignored the vital issues of their time. In 1933, for example, Paramount presented a total of 778 'stories' (self-contained news items corresponding to the 'articles' of the press) in its 104, twice-weekly 'issues'. Of these 112 were 'political' stories, ranging from de Valera's stand on 'no dictators in Ireland' to the U.S. recognition of the Soviet Union and the British Medical Association's report on the nutrition of the unemployed. No fewer than twenty-three dealt with Nazi Germany, from a report on Hitler's appointment to the chancellorship released on 2 February 1933 (issue 202) to the return of the British journalists arrested by the Nazis, released on 9 November 1933 (issue 283). Mussolini appeared in fourteen issues, while events even in Eire received five stories. Internally, Mosley's call for Britain to become the next country to take the Fascist road to salvation, as well as Lansbury's peace rallies were presented; and

113

unemployment was covered extensively, from the angle both of Jimmy Thomas and of the Archbishop of Canterbury. On such unpopular subjects as rearmament, Paramount gave both Lord Trenchard and Sir Roger Keyes the opportunity of a direct address. Of course such topics as the Budget — direct addresses again — the Geneva Conference, and other international and imperial conferences were covered both by speeches and comment. In terms of proportion — 112 out of 774 stories — there can be no doubt whatever that the proportion of column inches given to serious political issues by the popular press was far *less* than the 1/6 of space devoted to them by this newsreel. In fact, by the time we deduct the Sports, Society, Magazine, Review, Stock-Exchange and other such sections of *The Times* itself, the newsreels do not compare all that badly even with that quintessentially serious political organ of the upper middle classes in terms of the proportions of coverage.

If we look at what the newsreels actually told their huge lower-class public, for example, about the significance of Hitler's assumption of power, the newsreels compare very well indeed. While the pictures showed a Nazi rally after Hitler's appointment, Paramount told the viewers: 'Militarism long quiet in Germany has been rekindled by the dynamic Hitler, founder of the Nazi legions who acclaim him leader . . . nightmare visions of warring armies rise up before us. Only wise statesmanship can save the world from war, now.' Not at all bad for 1933! Nor was Gaumont's opening sentence a year later: 'German militarism is alive today: make no mistake. Under this hypnotic man Germany is on the march again.' Many newspaper editors of much more 'responsible' papers wished a few years later that they had printed that in 1934. For these years, this line was consistently pursued by Gaumont, and consistently though more optimistically by Paramount.

No balanced conclusion can be drawn until we have detailed studies of all the newsreels' policies and news content and also of those of both the B.B.C. and the popular press for the whole period, 1932–9. But *prima facie* there is evidence to suggest that we are dealing with a medium which had a lot to say and in an exceptionally direct and persuasive way to that very large and particularly susceptible portion of the public which went to the cinemas. It is well worth serious consideration. The policy adopted by the government towards the newsreels, during those vital years of facing up to both unemployment and yet another mass war, also deserves a closer study. The newsreels were the medium of the unemployed and the men of military age — and of the teenagers who grew to military age during those years.

The unwisdom of allowing American-based multinational corporations to dominate British newsreel communications began to dawn upon the government by the late 1930s, as a result of some undignified episodes of which Paramount's Munich escapade is the best known.[25] The internal effect of this domination had been to substitute American stories for imperial ones, which was bad enough. But the international implications of American domination were disastrous, especially because they were not perceived until it was too late. For practical purposes all the foreign distribution of newsreels was kept in the hands of the American parent companies, for both Gaumont and Pathé had lost most of their former international outlets during World War I. This meant the virtual elimination of that powerful influence which Britain had enjoyed before World War I, through her control of Reuters in the negative and through the predominance of British and imperial newsfilm stories all over the world in the positive sense. This loss occurred at precisely that point, in the years after 1927, when Britain needed more than ever to be able to project an image of strength, wealth and resolution, both imperial and national. But it was only at the outbreak of war in September 1939 that the full consequences of this erosion of the British capacity to project herself abroad came to be fully realised. It was left to the head of the Films Division of the newly re-established Ministry of Information to report that, despite the great urgency of the matter, it was quite impossible to produce again an official British newsreel for presenting Britain's own case overseas. He reported that: 'without the active co-operation of the [American] newsreel companies the work of foreign distribution of news items favourable to Britain is almost impossible'. It was small consolation that 'these large American distributing companies are sympathetic to us and would almost certainly be willing to offer all possible facilities provided however that *the editorial policy and make-up* of the newsreels that their companies released in neutral countries *remained with them*'.[26] Which is precisely what had to be accepted willy-nilly, resulting in the projection of Britain's struggle and image as Hollywood wanted it to be projected.

During World War II, the newsreels were regarded as the front-line troops in the battle for morale at home and for the projection of Britain abroad. Attempts to build up the documentary film in their place were defeated by the Select Committee on Estimates in the summer of 1940, and until the end of the war the newsreel companies received priority in the allocation of film stock and personnel.[27] In areas other than visual, the B.B.C. came to rival and exceed the importance attached to them on the Home Front and, of course, radio waves, which, unlike newsreels, could be infiltrated into occupied Europe, gave it complete priority in European propaganda. In neutral countries the newsreel retained its importance and a sort of official version also came into being through the system of commissioning each company in turn to produce a selection of stories from its own and other companies' output, called *British News*. The selection was made by the British Council under the guidance of the Foreign Office. It was of little importance, for its distribution was very limited.

The price the newsreels paid for their high priority in the war effort was heavy. At the beginning of the war they were remarkably popular and well-liked. A survey conducted by Mass Observation, whose personnel was far from devoted to the ethos of the popular press or the newsreels, nevertheless found three-quarters of the respondents actively pleased with the newsreels, an unusually high percentage amongst Britons. By the end of the war they had lost their popularity and respect to an alarming degree. In the first place they were subject to heavy-handed and none too skilled dictation from the Ministry of Information to hammer home constantly, and in the most obvious manner, the propaganda messages of the day — many of which especially in the early days were hopelessly misconceived. Second, there was faulty thinking on the part of the government not only in imposing upon the newsreels an over-tight censorship — every frame of film had to be submitted to examination and every word in every script vetted — but also in forcing them into a rigid 'rota' system. Each front and each event came to be assigned to one company's cameramen only, who had to supply a copy of the resultant film to all five companies. The editors were often at their wits' end in trying to make something of the material which did not make it immediately obvious that it was but a single 'official' footage, especially because what each company could say about the identical material or make of it by cutting it differently was also pretty well determined by the Ministry of Information. Either the newsreels came to be depressingly similar or the audience was treated to a lesson in the art of editing, by seeing identical sequences made to tell a slightly different story, neither of which could do anything except instill distrust and even irritation. In any case the newsreels were overloaded with a heavy, centrally inspired, commentary, often pursuing a line which the newsreel men knew would not convince. The government should have either nationalised the newsreels for the duration of the war and made them into an 'official' issue, like the B.B.C. news bulletins were, if shortages of film stock etc. made single coverage unavoidable, or left them more room to create their own versions and follow their own lines, at least a little, as in the case of the press. As it was, the 'five' reels looked like a propaganda sham which annoyed and irritated the public.

But perhaps nothing could have saved them from at least a substantial loss of popularity. From May 1940 until November 1942 they were the bearers of bad news only. They paid the price of the bearers of bad news. The very immediacy and impact of sound film made the presentation of defeats more upsetting and unpleasant for the audience than either reading or hearing about them.

The fact that they operated in an entertainment context made it worse for them. People could not help hating the fact that when they went to the cinemas in order to escape and relax after a hard and cheerless day, the first item with which they were faced was a realistic film portrayal of some depressing news.

By the time victories started to come the newsreels had lost too much of their precious credibility. The audience had become distrustful and had learned too much, thanks to the rota system, about the propaganda possibilities of 'the camera which cannot lie'. They came to distrust also the commentator's voice which they had once trusted and enjoyed. There came also a change in the composition of the audience. During the war for the first time the middle classes began to attend the cinema regularly. The old homogeneity of a lower-class audience which made it relatively easy to set the right tone had disappeared, and to find the right tone became virtually impossible, as if the *Daily Mirror* had to cater suddenly for both its own previous readership and that of the *Guardian* as well. Whatever had happened after the war, a fresh start would have had to follow it, and the newsreels would have had to find some way of reflecting the social-class differences of Britain, emphasised by her educational system.

Instead of the development of new kinds of newsreel parallel to the social-class-oriented stratification of the newspapers, new technology replaced the cinematic newsreel altogether, with television news. Once it became technically possible to transmit newsfilm over the air directly into people's homes, there was no room left for a news medium in the cinemas. Of course, the same development transferred the role of mass entertainment from cinema films to television programmes, making the cinema primarily an artistic medium, or at least a minority as opposed to a mass medium of specialised entertainment.

Paramount News, the last to open, was also the first to close down on 1 January 1957. Gaumont British/Universal followed it on 28 January 1959. Pathé, in a much modified form, survived until 1970, but as a cinemagazine rather than as a newsreel, and largely because it could be made in colour while television was still only black and white. Colour television finished off the pioneer of the newsreels. Movietone is still in production on a government contract as the supplier of the current version of *British News*, for consular and British Council use in countries where television is not yet dominant. What still survive are the libraries of all the newsreel companies (except Universal). In them there is to be found the record material for studying what the British public had been told about the world in which it lived, and for which it fought, by the first medium of mass communications which had successfully crossed the age-old frontiers of insularity and education as far as the mass of the ordinary people was concerned. For all those who are curious about the 'common thoughts of common people' during the period which began when Maitland died, those archives are a treasure house.

NOTES

1. Other methods, based either on the principle of flicking a pack of cards before the eye or on viewing frames directly on a moving film or paper base, although capable of producing similar effects, suffered from major and incurable faults. The first was drastically limited in the length of time it could run, the second in the size and definition of the image. See C.W. Ceram, *The Archaeology of the Cinema* (London, 1965).
2. F.A. Talbot, *Moving Pictures* (London, 1911), p. 40.
3. Birt Acres had already opened something called Picture Palace on Piccadilly — according to his own notes — which might have been the first 'cinema' in the sense of a place for the exhibition of moving pictures for an entrance fee. No corroborative evidence has been found, however. According to Acres, it burned out soon after opening: if so, its place in history is as the first of the dreadful 'cinema fires'.
4. Robert Paul has the extraordinary distinction of being the first man to retire from films on the ground that all their technical possibilities had been realised already, in 1900.

5. The classic case of this was Georges Méliès' splendid film of the *Coronation of Edward VII*, completed well in advance owing to the unforeseeable illness of the king, which in fact delayed the actual coronation by several months, and many weeks after Méliès' newsfilm was already in the can.
6. R. Fielding, *The American Newsreel 1911–1967* (University of Oklahoma Press, 1972), chapter 3, 'Faking the Early News Films'.
7. *Optical Magic Lantern Journal and Photographic Enlarger*, January 1900, p. 30. Cf. *National Film Archive Catalogue*, part 2, *Silent Non-Fiction Films 1895–1934* (London, 1960).
8. *The March of Time*, for example, regarded by such eminent men as John Grierson and Edgar Anstey as the model of what the newsreel ought to have been, used re-enactments as a standard technique.
9. *National Film Archive Catalogue*, part 1, *Silent Newsfilm, 1895–1933* (London, 1965), p. 16, no. 166.
10. Fielding, *op. cit.*, pp. 74–5.
11. Talbot, *op. cit.*, p. 278.
12. *Ibid.*, p. 281.
13. R. Low, *The History of the British Film 1906–1914* (London, 1949), p. 151.
14. Whether silent film was really suitable as a medium for this kind of analytical journalism is questionable. Whether the audience would have preferred their minds and emotions more heavily engaged on their night off at the 'pictures' – including the need to read the endless captions such treatment calls for – is even more open to question. Miss Low appears to ignore this aspect of the problem, as has indeed become the fashion among the intellectual critics of the newsreels and of television.
15. Talbot, *op. cit.*, p. 317.
16. Quoted in R. Low, *The History of the British Film 1914–1918* (London, 1950), p. 160.
17. *Ibid.*, p. 30.
18. C. Seymour-Ure, *The Political Impact of Mass Media* (London, 1974), p. 159.
19. The foregoing account is largely based on Fielding, pp. 159–65.
20. Direct comparison of newspaper sales and cinema admissions needs to be made with caution, for more than one person may have had access to a newspaper bought by a member of the household, while on the other hand some people may have bought more than one newspaper. Nevertheless, with an audience figure in the region of five million for *Movietone*, 2.2 million for the *Daily Express* and 1.5 million for the *Daily Mail*, there is little doubt about the general position.
21. Seymour-Ure, *op. cit.*, p. 159.
22. The B.B.C. Television News staff handbook attempts to bring this fact home by asking trainee editors 'to realise that they have to present the whole of the day's news in a length of just two short columns of a newspaper'.
23. N. Pronay, 'British Newsreels in the 1930s', part 1, 'Audience and Producers', *History*, 56 (1971), 411–14, for references and statistics.
24. It should also be noted that Movietone's British leaders, Gerald Sanger, Sir Gordon Craig and Sir Malcolm Campbell, were of Conservative sympathies and that Movietone co-operated in many ways with the Conservative Central Office under Sir Joseph Ball. For example, it provided projection personnel for Conservative election candidates. These links were not advertised at the time. Gaumont British was also of Conservative sympathies. Its production system was different, however, from the other newsreels, inasmuch as its commentator and editor were the same person, the talented E.V.H. Emmett. This system enabled the Gaumont reels to become the most effective medium of political news communications, because the synchronising of sound and picture montage was thus particularly sophisticated and unobtrusive.
25. In the wake of the Munich Agreement, the government decided that it was imperative that no sentiments to the effect that Britain would have to fight Germany one day, and the sooner the better, should be conveyed to the world at large at home. Paramount decided to do just that, and flatly refused to obey a government order to the contrary. In the end the Foreign Office found itself obliged to ask the U.S. State Department for

help, and through that assistance the offending item was removed from newsreels already distributed to cinemas, upon a telegraphic order sent by the (American) president of the Paramount Corporation, who, as it was reported, 'was fortunately on our side'.

26. Public Record Office, INF. 1/194. Memorandum by Sir Joseph Ball in response to questions in Parliament put by Lord Strabolgi, October 1939 (my italics).

27. This does not of course mean that there was not produced a large number of excellent documentary films, but the attempt to supplant the newsreel with a documentary, such as *Canada Carries On* or *World in Action*, had to be abandoned, and the documentary confined largely to non-theatrical distribution, reaching a mere 350,000 a week, at the most, as against the 23–4 million a week newsreel audience.

# Part IV
# Film in the interpretation
# and teaching of history

# 6. The historian as film-maker I

ROLF SCHUURSMA

The timetable of primary schools is to a great extent filled with the arts of read-ing and writing, and evidently children need many hours to learn how to use their abilities for these in fact very intricate skills. However, almost nowhere is the art of observing part of the timetable, and in fact not one hour is really reserved for that equally difficult subject. Nevertheless, especially since modern civilisation sometimes includes hours of looking at the television set daily, it would be better to teach children at a young age how to get on with pictures and how to handle them with the same skill that they are taught to use when reading a book or writing a letter.

Especially for the student in contemporary history, the lack of training in how to look at pictures is a handicap now that film documents are part of his sources and television will be of ever more importance. If only because of the lack of a more basic education in this field, it will be necessary to train future undergraduates in the faculty of history in how to work with film and other audio-visual media and to give them an opportunity to acquire what Professor Thorold Dickinson described as 'a sense of what I can only call cinemacy' (*Screen Digest*, September 1973, p. 135).

In fact the 'traditional' historian is very well acquainted with 'cinemacy' when it is a question of written documents. A critical approach, not restricted to the surface of the source but going also into the background and the political, social and economic context of the document, is basic for his work. It is only natural that this critical method should also be valuable and in fact indispensable in the case of audio-visual media, and it is therefore to be expected that contemporary historians will become ready to apply their methods of research to the new media as they are accustomed to do with more traditional sources. So one day

121

'cinemacy' must be part of their job, and it will then be only normal that they will educate their undergraduates in the same way. For that kind of education, however, the historian has to have among other things expedients and tools. Eventually he must even become a member of a team of film-makers, in order to help create some of these tools himself in accordance with the aims of his trade.

Although there are many ways open of using the new media actively, like making and evaluating videotape recordings of historical scenes 'played' by pupils and the recording and evaluation of discussions in the classroom, these are evidently sidelines of the hitherto more important use of newsreels, documentaries and feature films with essential information for research and teaching. I shall mainly deal with the latter application of the media and then restrict myself to film as indicated by the theme of this book.

One way of getting along with documents is to stare at them in the hope that they will eventually talk for themselves and tell their own tale. However, such a passive approach is usually very unpromising, and the teacher in particular knows very well that he has to explain what is essential in the document and what not, and which ties connect the document with its historical surroundings. Film documents also require much more than a performance in the cinema where the pictures move over the screen rapidly without really telling what they are doing there and what connection they have with their original context. Unless we are dealing with a feature film made to tell its own story, a more active approach is very much needed in order to become fully alive to the meaning of records from film archives.

It is even better to let undergraduates work on the document themselves. This is a well-known fact in the case of written records, which are frequently the subject of seminars and prove to be excellent starting-points for a thorough discussion of their historical significance and context. As we have seen, film documents are not fundamentally different from traditional written records when we are looking at them as subjects for research and as tools for educational purposes. But then it is necessary to remove them from their original setting in the movies to the viewing table, where we are able to handle them in every conceivable way and where analysis is really possible.

A film is made of sixteen or twenty-four (for television twenty-five) frames per second. Each frame is a still which can be interesting in itself because it may contain important information different from the contiguous frames. Groups of frames make a shot in so far as the camera was working uninterruptedly. It is worthwhile to inspect the position of the camera during the shot, the angle of its lens and its movements, because these data not only reveal to a certain extent the aims and procedures of the director and the cameraman, but also are the factors which literally narrow down the point of view of the onlooker in the cinema or the student in front of the screen of the viewing table.

Groups of shots make sequences which to a much greater extent reveal the aims of the maker of what eventually proves to be a document of historical value.

## The historian as film-maker I

By editing the shots and by putting them behind each other the film-maker
expresses what is to be his message, and in many cases this expression is more
important than the objects taken by the camera. But understanding that message
requires a careful analysis of the elements of which it is compiled, and here the
viewing table provides an excellent means to look at each frame separately, to
study the manipulations of the cameraman, to follow the transitions from one
shot to another and from sequence to sequence and also to compare the document with other records, like sound recordings and printed sources, relating to
the same event.

In the future the viewing table will certainly prove to be disadvantageous in
comparison with the video cassette player. Documents are naturally rare and
have to be kept in the archive under optimal circumstances. It is understandable
that most film archives never let their records leave the premises, and since the
production of copies on acetate film and their transport prove to be an ever
more expensive affair, copies on video cassette are preferable. They are handy
and easy to dispatch, while the recording can be erased after the analysis is
completed. However, the choice between the two systems is a technical affair
which need not trouble us in this connection.

By using the viewing table or the video player the historian is able really to
work on film documents and to use them as a medium for teaching in a very
active way. But the document is then only useful for small groups of students
who can sit around the viewing table or the television monitor and may do their
part of the analysis as medical students do during so-called bedside teaching.
Besides, even the most energetic teacher has trouble in getting what he wants
from the archive during the few hours left to him for the collection of material
to work on in the classroom. From these points of view it may be worthwhile to
use the medium of the compilation film to provide teachers and students alike
with a selection of records in such a way that the film takes the place of the
printed edition of selected documents.

A compilation film is in essentials a combination of (parts of) film records,
put together in a production usually of twenty to fifty minutes' duration and
linked with each other by a commentary. Photographs and maps may be added,
pictures of written sources can come in and graphics may help to give better
understanding of what it is all about, so that the complete product is really a
kind of restricted textbook, telling its own story as much as possible.

This certainly does not mean that the compilation film could eventually take
over the role of the teacher or could even serve as a handbook of twentieth-
century world history. Before going into the making of the compilation film it is
therefore best to define to a certain extent its possibilities as well as its limits as
a means for expression and communication in the classroom or in the much
wider framework of television.

Film is a lively medium, sometimes much more interesting and exciting than
any other way of expression. It stands alone when it is a question of the record-

ing of movement of living beings and things. Film is unique in that for the first time in history it became possible to register historical processes for play-back purposes. Never, before film came into being, was the behaviour of man and his relationship to nature put on record in so precise and detailed a way. Even in the beginning of cinematography the technical facilities were so much developed that directors like Griffith were able to record big scenes of the maximum of movement and action and make them ready for play-back on the screen everywhere in the world.

Nevertheless, film cannot be more than very concrete unless the maker is able to stage the scene and to direct the players in order to suggest an expression of more abstract feelings and ideas. Newsreels especially tend to be registrations of the outside of the world around us, because the camera is seldom capable of penetrating behind the façade of life. What seems to be the utmost of reality in fact is only the surface, where we can perhaps see the expression of deeper feelings and reactions, but usually no entrance to the human mind is to be found. Film is fragmentary as well because it is an expensive medium and the celluloid is running through the machine at great speed. And lastly film is restricted in its expression by the limits of the angle of its lens and the relative slowness of its movements, where the human eye looks around easily and with greater adaptability.

The conclusion is not that film is a second-rate medium useful only as a (rather expensive) addition to the so much more easily handled traditional printed and written sources. If film had been there to make recordings of daily life in ancient Rome or to put on record the ways things were done in the general assembly of Athens during Pericles' time, every historian would have been very glad to look at it and to let the pictures deeply influence his mind. Nevertheless, the compilation film seldom seems to be effective as a substitute for what really belongs to the realm of the word. However lively, it can never replace a good teacher, if only because it is a one-way traffic system. And however exciting, it will not do as a complete replacement of the textbook which will always be more complete and easier to handle. Film has to be considered as an unsurpassable medium for the play-back of movements, processes, actions and everything else which in the first place needs looking at in order to be understood.

With these restrictions and possibilities in mind the compilation film, with other tools, is an excellent medium for the teaching of history. Whenever enough documents are available it can be used for pictorial biographies or for the depiction of political movements like Fascism, where show is an essential element of propaganda. It is a useful medium for the explanation of battles in World War II where the combination of authentic film extracts and stills with maps, interviews and shots of the battlegrounds made afterwards proves to be effective in telling the story with more impact than a book could do. The compilation film also can be an interesting instrument for the comparison of different ways of human behaviour and expression, fields where history and cultural anthropology seem to meet.

Since a compilation film consists to a great extent or even exclusively of documents, the first thing to do after the subject of the film is established is to travel to the archives and find the records. It is not my task to go into the troubles which the historian may encounter on his way through the film vaults. They are different from country to country and from office to office but not easy to handle in any instance. The historian who undertakes the job will find that he is obliged to make a complete list of all the documents which have to do with the subject of his film, and that he has to view them all. Only then can he be reasonably sure of the starting-points from which to begin the composition of his film. The research into the available records, including if possible the accompanying written notes as well, always proves to be a time-consuming, sometimes tedious and not always rewarding job, fully comparable with the equally tiring work of going through traditional archives.

After having completed the first stage of making a compilation film the historian must try to make a choice from the documents he has studied. Several criteria are within reach to help him with this task. In the first place history itself provides him with a synopsis of the subject and by following the historical timetable he is at least able to make a classification of the records. He then has to think of the impact and significance of the documents he has seen. They must express visually perceptible phenomena, which are characteristic and do really enlarge the existing knowledge of the subject. It is, for instance, no use to show more than once Winston Churchill stepping out of a car and going into a building, shaking hands and making the V-sign; but looking at the man while delivering one of his famous speeches gives an impression which no other medium can provide. It is equally useless to have shots of soldiers running through unknown pieces of land; but showing the horrible circumstances in the trenches along the river Lys during part of World War I can help one to understand more of the muddy misery of those days than many books together.

In the third place our historian has to make sure that the documents he wishes to use are really what the card-index says they are. One cannot be too careful about that aspect of the compilation of film documents, unless one is prepared to use every possible piece of film in order to let the compilation look 'realistic'. To my mind this is no matter of childish obstinacy but a point of salutary reserve. Nobody is asking historians to make films, but when they do they are at least expected to do a proper job in full accordance with the principles and rules of their trade. Therefore the research into the reliability of the documents which may become a part of the selection for the compilation film is as necessary as it would be in the case of printed documents.

Lastly there is the matter of the composition of the film from the point of view of the historian. Naturally the selected documents have to be in some balance as to their place in the historical timetable, their significance for the subject of the film, the amount of authentic sound which could be of value (I return to that subject later on), their eventual length in comparison with the total duration of the film and other aspects which may differ from subject to subject. If in the end there is some scheme for a more precise composition along chronological or thematic lines there has to come a decision about which documents can be taken into the film completely and from which ones extracts have to be selected. The next step is to establish in broad outlines the limits of these extracts. Then it is high time to start working with a team of film-makers who will be responsible for the last stage of the production of the compilation film.

Unhappily it is not possible to tell in general how to find a team of film-makers ready to produce the film at low cost but with a high standard of quality, and willing to co-operate with the historian without submitting themselves too much to his inexpert views regarding their trade. In some cases there is an audiovisual centre in the university which can provide the people and the equipment at very low cost. In other situations the historian has no such help and has to ask for the co-operation of the commercial film industry. In any case the processing of the final product is the work of a commercial laboratory, which understandably likes to make at least some profit from the historian's project.

First, however, it is important to get some insight into the process of teamwork which is necessary for the production itself. In the case of film the author, comparable with the writer of an article or a book, is in fact made of two persons: the historian and the director, or — when the film consists only of extracts from documents — the historian and the cutter. While the historian brings in the selection of documents and the general lines of the eventual extracts, the director or cutter has to put these extracts together in such a way that the spectator does not get a feeling of aesthetic nausea. However interested in film the historian may be, it is my firm belief that the scientific approach and the composition are very different fields, each of which needs its own expert. It is only natural, then, that both of them have to agree on this point in order to avoid quarrels about matters of competence. Mutual respect and some care not to interfere with each other's responsibility are without any doubt at the basis of a good film.

Although representing two different aspects of the traditional author, the historian and the director tend to overlap somewhere in the middle. I can perhaps make this clear by defining the various stages they have to go through in order to get a sound and valuable product. It is definitely the historian who is fully responsible for the choice of documents, although also in that early stage he does well to consult the director about the technical qualities of the documents. Things like nitrate films, for instance, which are beyond saving are better left out of the scenario. The historian too is responsible for the broad outlines of the extracts he wants to take from the authentic documents, but here the director must certainly advise him about the precise limits of these fragments in relation to their connection with the adjacent parts. Even for those who know little or nothing about film it must be clear that the change-over from one extract to another asks for certain rules, which are self-evident for the director since he learned to master them in a film academy or in the everyday experience of the film or television studio. Although many outsiders may think that these rules are simple to handle, this is not the case.

Thereafter the discussion between the historian and the director will continue with the working copy as *pièce de résistance* on the editing table. Then the play of give and take, the search for a compromise, goes on until the cutting is completed. During this stage of production the historian naturally can stay away pleading lack of expertise or excusing himself because of more important work, but I do not think that wise. If it were a question of publication of extracts from written sources every editor would want to know precisely where to begin and where to end the 'takes' from the original documents. The process of cutting by the film editor is not different and is certainly also part of the historian's responsibility.

The production will be more complicated when maps are going to be part of it, if only because a map nearly always means animation. Here the historian is to a great extent at the mercy of designers and animation technicians, although here also he has the responsibility of making the decision as to what maps he wants to show. If there is good teamwork between the director and the people from the animation department the result will be in accordance with the overall standard of the film.

I leave aside the making of interviews for incorporation in the film. They seldom help to clarify things and mostly cost a lot of precious time. Their value is in the local colour and the enrichment with atmospheric elements, which may help to make an intricate and dull subject more lively. Parallel with these inserts are takes of surroundings made during the production of the film, because they may not only explain geographical factors but also give occasion for animation of for instance military movements in 'live' terrain, where authentic shots are unavailable. However, a compilation film usually prospers by careful and sober design, leaving out extravaganzas which are meant only to impress and not to explain.

Although one may think sound the less important part of a compilation film, it is in fact the very element which makes the film coherent and understandable. The pictures in themselves are fragmentary and limited in expression. Unless somebody explains their connection in the commentary they will fall apart like the accidentally found photographs of the members of an unknown family.

The sound in a compilation film consists of three sections. In the first place there is the authentic sound track of the documents. This may contain an interesting piece of commentary from the original newsreel it was part of and sometimes it is possible to use such commentary as well. Other parts may contain the 'real' sound of people speaking or shouting, the (faked) sound of machines or implements of war, or the music used for 'illustration' of the original newsreel. Especially when the music was carefully inserted for propagandistic reasons, as it was in newsreels and documentary films of the Third Reich, it is worthwhile to keep some of it in the compilation film.

The second section contains non-authentic music. I am not an admirer of directors who like to avoid mute sequences by using compositions of Beethoven or Bruckner, however beautifully played. In feature films music is sometimes a much more important element than most visitors of the cinema realise. It almost imperceptibly influences even unmusical people to a great extent and makes for part of the suspense. But in compilation films where information and explanation are somewhat more important than suspense and drama (although these elements are present very much in a carefully prepared scenario, because history seldom does without them), music added afterwards to fill up otherwise silent places may take away the attention from the more essential pictures on the screen. And apart from that, it costs a lot of money. Nevertheless, if music is to be included I would prefer a score specially composed for this purpose to the use of too well known classical pieces.

The third section of the sound track of a compilation film is that element where the historian again comes in as the main responsible person in the team. He has provided the synopsis of the film, he has chosen the documents and decided eventually about maps, other graphics and interviews. Now he has to produce a commentary which must explain the contents of the extracts whenever they are not understandable from observation only. At the same time the commentary has to make clear the meaning of the pictures in relation to the theme of the film. This seems to be self-evident, and in fact a compilation of extracts or complete (short) documents, as with an edition of written documents, cannot do without explaining why these records especially were brought together in the film and what aspects they illustrate. But whenever the extracts are illustrations of an historical narration, as will be the case in most compilation films, the commentator may easily forget to communicate the 'captions' of the illustrations because he is concentrating too much on the general lines of the story and on what then proves to be a kind of radio play more than a film. Unhappily, the commentary cannot have more room than is left over by authentic sound. It cannot go on for the total length of the film because then the spectators would be very soon tired. It must leave pauses to allow room for looking at the essential pictures and it must correspond to the pictures very precisely. In fact one cannot be too severe about the matching of words and pictures because otherwise the spectator will go astray.

But then the wording of the commentary has to be clear and open to one explanation only. Like good historical writing it has to be careful in its expression, but it must also be short and to the point. It must explain details about what is to be seen without leaving the main lines of the story. So it has to answer several needs in a film of, for instance, thirty minutes where no more than half of the sound track is available for our poor historian and his comment. From this it may be clear that one has to economise very much. Every word is eventually one too many, and only by reducing the long and intricate sentences of the average historical work to a sober and precise usage of words, as in a poem, will a commentary work as the accurate and simple tool it has to be.

Two members of the team then come in to disturb the historian, possibly a great deal. One is the speaker of the commentary. He will certainly have his personal approach to the native language and thus some discussion about the wording may result. But there is also the man in charge of the sound recording, who is more interested in his level indicator than in any other argument. Here the historian and the director have to sail between many reefs in order to get a sound track not only perfect in the technical sense but again up to standard in terms of the historical value of the compilation film.

Leaving out the frustrating experiences with the laboratory, where everything which has survived thus far may be wrecked (mostly because the producer is in a hurry and leaves no time for the technicians), there is still to come the accompanying booklet with additional information for the users of the film. Here also I omit comment, given that this stage of the production, however time-consuming, is in accordance with the more 'normal' production of books and articles.

Thus far I have written mainly from the point of view of the historian who tries to produce a compilation film for use in the classroom, and although production for television is not really different, there are nevertheless some points which deserve special attention.

Broadcast television is there to serve the general public with entertainment and mildly educational programmes — programmes which ought to be seen by a high percentage of the people at home in order to be respectable from the point of view of the management. Nonetheless in many countries it is possible to produce programmes of high educational value and at the same time very good entertainment value. And since history is 'in' judging by the success of part works, picture books and historical novels there is also a certain interest in compilation films on the channels.

However, here it is much more difficult to come in as a historian and deeply to influence the concept and contents of the production. Not unnaturally there is a mistrust of the scholar who, without having any knowledge of what film stands for, tries to impress his intellectual over-sensitiveness on experienced makers of programmes. Nevertheless, here also I prefer a close co-operation between the experts on both sides of the authorship: the historian and the director. Only by using both their capacities to the utmost will the television company get a programme in full accordance with the points of view of historical research and at the same time entertaining for a more general public. If, on top of this, the historian himself accidentally proves to be entertaining he may come in and join the production as an artist, introducing the programme with that kind of wit and intellectual mobility which seems to be the art especially of some Anglo-Saxon scholars.

*Rolf Schuursma*

Returning to more fundamental aspects of film and history, the new media and especially their combination in the compilation film are there to serve teaching as well as education in a wider sense. I want to stress, however, the point that in my view the compilation film is not a replacement of the textbook for complete periods of twentieth-century history. The film is there to show what must be seen in order to be understood and is too expensive an affair to be treated otherwise. But inside that limited field there are many subjects to cover and there are millions of feet of documents waiting in the archives. These documents, then, may serve as parts of audio-visual monographs where pictures and sound simply are indispensable elements in telling the story, or they may be used as parts of a group of extracts compiled like the editions of selected written documents.

Next to the re-edition of complete and unabridged newsreels, propaganda films and other documents of that kind, the compilation film is pre-eminently the medium to bridge over the gap between the archive and the classroom or — in the case of broadcast television — the general public. Highly effective cataloguing may open up the vaults for researchers, but film documents have to be seen in order to be believed and not everybody is able to go all the way to visit the archives himself.

This is particularly true for a category of document which I have touched upon very briefly in the previous pages: the feature film. As we know now, the feature film is not a product made without any connection with what goes on in the society around us. It is on the contrary a sometimes highly effective manifestation of the social and political standards of the establishment (although nowadays the feature film may also be an expression of the 'underground') and at the same time a means for influencing the general public with these standards. Although Kracauer in his famous book *From Caligari to Hitler* looked far too strenuously for Nazism in every German film of the twenties, he nonetheless set the tone for research into the social and political background and impact of the movies.

There is, however, no better tool for such research than extracts of feature films themselves. A fine and richly illustrated book like Jeffrey Richards' *Visions of Yesterday* (London, 1973) gives me the impression that we could profit even more by using moving illustrations, which let us look at the movements of the stars and let us hear their texts. Here too the compilation film is an excellent help in the classroom (if not for the general public) to explain by cleverly chosen extracts the values and standards of the film-makers and the sometimes subtle, sometimes obvious ways of propagating them through a romantic or thrilling story. This was very well done by Erwin Leiser in *Deutschland, erwache!* and his example deserves imitation in other countries where the movies are products of a substantial industry and where they are instruments of commercial sponsors, dependent on the censorship of the establishment and the taste of the general public.

## The historian as film-maker I

Thus far the educational technologist has been left out of the story. This is understandable when it is a question of television programmes for the general public. The *Fingerspitzengefühl* of most directors and the commercial instincts of sponsors and producers seem to provide sufficient guarantee for programmes to meet their objectives. However, trying to teach pupils or undergraduates can be done only on the basis of the specification of the starting-points and aims of the curriculum. Since the compilation film with other things may serve as a tool to reach the ends of the curriculum, it seems only natural to ask for the help of educational technologists in order to make films which can meet the demands not only of teachers who want to use film as a kind of 'extra' on the last day before the vacation gets under way, but also of those who really are willing to use film as an integrated part of their programme. I am very much aware of the fact that educational technologists may complicate the procedures of film-making unnecessarily. They may, however, also help one to understand better the impact of audio-visual media on the onlooker who, in the remarkable one-way traffic of the projection hall, is helplessly undergoing the treatment of the moving pictures on the white screen.

# 7. The historian as film-maker II

JOHN GRENVILLE

It is an extraordinary fact that until the late 1960s no professionally trained historian had attempted to 'write' history through the medium of sound films. Plenty of films existed dealing with historical subjects, but none were made by historians. The very competence of the historian to make his own films was challenged from two directions. The professional film producers argued that the predominant skill required in the making of a film was the craft of film-making itself and that the subject matter of the film was therefore of necessity subsidiary to it. When applied to films purporting to be contributions to history this meant that the historian, when consulted, had to fulfil a subsidiary role in the production of the film. He was consulted, sometimes even asked to submit a script, but his advice was not necessarily followed when it conflicted with the needs and views of the professional film-maker. The producer was in charge, and the producer was never a professional historian and according to the argument never could be, because professional historians lacked the necessary creative and technical skills.

The public appetite for history on film nevertheless was immense. Since the pioneering days of the *Great War* television documentary, British television has catered for it, though standards, judged from the historian's point of view, have been declining rather than improving. This is history, so called, intended to provide entertainment and to attract a mass viewing audience. It has to be simplified and the spoken introductions presented by stars of the media. It is often rhetorical in style and banal in judgement. A few programmes only stand out as exceptions to this general depressing trend, which inevitably will lead to audience surfeit, as viewers become familiar with the same or very similar shots being used over and over again in different combinations. The audience will tire, just as it tired of the traditional cowboy and Indian films, composed as they were of clichés and stock shots.

The historian who is determined to communicate through the medium of sound film has to meet another barrage of criticism as well: from his own professional colleagues who argue that what he is doing is not 'history'. The film which uses and interprets selected film and subordinates this to a general historical interpretation is frequently criticised for attempting any interpretation at all. Some historians have therefore expressed their preference for what they call simply a 'collection of film documents', without connecting commentary. Others condemn the historian's film as peculiarly 'propagandist', presumably because it utilises material in its making that was propagandist in origin; to use newsreel as 'historical evidence', it is argued, is suspect, because the newsreels were short stories and editorially compiled by men with a contemporary political bias; they therefore do not describe the events impartially as they appear to be doing. This, as will be later shown, is quite true but it is a powerful argument in favour of rather than against historians utilising and interpreting this particular evidence. Another reason put forward against the use of film by the historian is that as a medium it is too powerful and robs the student audience of the ability to bring critical judgement to bear on what they simultaneously hear and see. Finally the criticism is frequently voiced that the newsreel film recorded events so selectively that reliance on the availability of such a source would limit, if not dictate, the historian's own interpretation.

Exposed to this cross-fire, it is perhaps more surprising that a few historians have persevered in the making of film than that there are not more films available. There are other reasons too for the slow growth in the number of historians making film, though there never has been a shortage of critics. The incentives in material and professional terms have so far not been great. The historian can earn a great deal more writing a book, especially if it has few words and many pictures. Individuals will not buy film; only a few libraries do so. Although a successful academic film eventually may be seen by more than 200,000 students over a period of several years, this audience can be reached by some hundred or so film libraries and a sale much in excess of 200 films has not yet been achieved by anyone. Even this figure can be reached only by steady sales year by year and not all at once. The royalties to the historian author from the sale of copies are small; the profits from 'hire', where they exist, negligible. Since, moreover, few fellow historians will yet accept work in film as 'scholarship', and career prospects are therefore not enhanced, the disincentive is a powerful one indeed.

The historian when faced with the task of film-making confronts two further challenges, intellectual and practical. He starts with no acceptable models to follow. If he is an economic, political or diplomatic historian for instance, when he *writes* history in his chosen field, he follows a group of other historians though hoping to add touches of originality to the new work. The historian in other words usually does not have to start from scratch, which was very much the case in the making of films in the mid-1960s. Before the historian can properly use historical evidence its precise nature has to be grasped. This in turn can be achieved not by abstract theorising — and there were plenty of historians ready to teach others on the subject without ever actually investigating a single foot of film in the archives — but only by working with film directly. This seems so obvious now that it is surprising how many historians still have not accepted the need to study the nature of the evidence at *first hand*. The same historians, because of earlier 'models', would of course raise their hands in horror if anyone attempted to instruct others on the proper use of say the Colonial Office records or cabinet minutes in the Public Record Office without ever having examined them! Alas, academics are prone to sweeping self-confidence. An understanding of the nature of the evidence thus becomes a prerequisite for its utilisation by the historian, and this was not so easy to acquire to begin with, though by now much useful guidance is available in print and on film itself.

The practical difficulties might have defeated the aspiring historians had they realised their full extent *when they began.* It is possible to make a film for little more than the printing cost of an inaugural lecture provided the historian has access to a film and television unit such as several universities in Britain possess, where skilled help and a minimum of equipment are available. The quality of the staff involved is more important in this respect than their number or the sophistication of the actual equipment used. But even small sums of money are difficult to extract from a college or university administration which has no budget heading for film. The alternative of collaborating with a publisher or a television company proved impossible in the case here in mind, as neither was willing to leave absolute final control to the historian whilst footing the bill. Only within his own academic walls can the academic sometimes be king, and even then he first needs to reach an amicable understanding with his professional film colleagues in the university: a totally new relationship has to be evolved. The present writer has a document before him dated September 1966, written to persuade the 'Treasury' of the University of Leeds to allocate £200 towards the making of a film 'with an academic purpose in mind and not for entertainment value'. The document goes on to assure the university that these films 'when used in co-ordination with our lecture courses will greatly add to their academic value and [the university] . . . will be pioneers in this particular field'. Among the many attractions of the project here so starkly set out was listed the hope that knowledge of it would spread and attract students to the university (!). It is to the credit of the farsightedness of Leeds University that the £200 was forthcoming and the 'hard sell' was not really necessary. There was much interest and scepticism, but the co-operation of the university's Television Service guaranteed a measure of respectability. A further £120 each was promised by the history departments of the Universities of Reading and Nottingham, provided the film turned out to be usable — a reasonable precaution on their part. A total budget of £440 seemed the limit of what could be extracted for a new, unproven project. In the end twice that amount was spent on the first film, *The Munich Crisis* (Leeds University, Grenville and Pronay, 1968), and royalty payments had to be postponed. The equally far-sighted co-operation of Visnews, the owners of much film archive material, got this first pioneer film off the ground; happily reasonable royalty arrangements could be concluded subsequently as sales of the first film underpinned the costs of the second and so on in a chain of films.

Even today, the individual historian might have difficulty raising more than £500 from his own university. Books, wall maps, microfilm, original manuscripts, for such purposes universities are accustomed to sanction reasonable sums for purchase, but the new category of 'film' has no budget and the administration has no yardstick by which to assess 'reasonable' cost.

An inadequate budget is only the beginning of the financial problems involved. If film and sound evidence from the past is to be used, the rights of the owners of this property have to be respected and, where appropriate, copyright agreements negotiated. Without much goodwill and generosity for an interesting pioneering effort this might have proved the rock on which the project foundered. In 1966, there was no financial base available to the academic historian wishing to make film. Ten years later the position is much improved. The Open University and the British Inter-University History Film Consortium now provide the historian with the financial, artistic and technical assistance required to enable him to undertake the work of communicating history through the medium of sound film or videotape. In 1966, the historian needed, among other attributes, stamina and good health to surmount the various barriers even before he could actually begin to grapple with the problems posed by the evidence he wished to use. The historian wishing to start on his own today is still faced with the considerable problems of finding adequate money to make the film, access to equipment, and the knowledge and means to negotiate agreements covering all the copyrights involved. Only then can work on a film begin.

Such obstacles underlined the need to found a 'film-publishing' house with established procedures, legal and financial, within which the historian could then work, saving enormous time better spent making film. The British Inter-University History Film Consortium is in fact such a university film publisher. It was founded on the initiative of three university history departments, Leeds, Reading and Nottingham in 1967, and was subsequently joined by the history departments of the University of Wales, the London School of Economics and Political Science, the Universities of Birmingham and Edinburgh, Queen Mary College, London, and Manchester University. Obviously the pooling of financial resources and creative and technical staff (with the Television and Film Service of Leeds University and the Department of Film, Bristol University pre-eminent) alone can provide a strong enough base for continuing productions. In Britain, the 'co-operative' structure of nine universities helping themselves to enable their historians to make film has worked well. The quality of the films and the steady rate of continuous production is the best evidence that historians have found the 'consortium' an excellent means to fulfil their desire to communicate in film. Elsewhere in the world different solutions have been adopted. In the United States a few universities dispose of large enough funds on their own to provide their historians with the means and facilities for making film. Even here, however, historians have found it an uphill struggle. In Germany, provision of facilities has been comparatively on quite a lavish scale with part of an Institute in Göttingen devoted to the subject. In the Netherlands the Film Foundation established in Utrecht is wholly subsidised by the Dutch Ministry of Education. Coming back to Britain, it seems safe to preduct that any continuous university film production not only needs to be justified on academic grounds but will have to pay its way through sales of the resultant films. Fortunately for such academic films there is a growing market throughout the world. The British Inter-University History Film Consortium has achieved good sales of its film, thus providing adequate funds for new historical studies in film.

The way the Consortium operates is that each member university agrees on an annual financial contribution which now works out at rather less than the sale price to others of one historical study in film. This provides the basic budget for each film. Every member university agrees to nominate two historians to the management executive of the Consortium which meets annually and makes all decisions. A chairman is elected by the members. Since 1967 there have been three chairmen, J.A.S. Grenville, H. Hearder and N. Pronay, the current chairman. Each university has also joined the Consortium with the intention of providing the historian and being responsible for at least one film production. The committee of the Consortium decides on the order in which the films are made. Some member universities have technical film facilities, others have not – but the film is made in one or several studios of the member universities. As soon as a film is completed it is distributed to each member university without further payment. These days more than the basic budget is spent on each film by the Consortium and in some cases as well by the individual member university making the film. Sales to non-member institutions of higher learning provide the means for recovering the extra-budgetary expenses, first those of the Consortium then those of the individual university. The aim is not to make a 'profit', but rather to balance income and expenditure and to fund research and expanding productions. The Consortium casts its net widely for archival film material. Visnews, with its collection of the largest newsreel archives in Britain, is one very important source and has actively co-operated in several productions, but recently, for example, film was found in Finnish archives, unique sequences never before shown. With adequate finance, the availability and suitability of film for particular historical studies becomes the sole criterion of use. The Consortium aims at completing an average of one historical study in film a year. The first film, *The Munich Crisis* (Leeds University), was followed by: *The End of Illusions: from Munich to Dunkirk* (Birmingham and Leeds Universities, Grenville and Pronay, 1970); *The Spanish Civil War* (Edinburgh University, Addison, Edwards and Aldgate, 1973); *Introduction to Palaeography* (Reading and Leeds Universities, Pronay, Holt and Taylor, 1974); *The Winter War in its European Context* (Nottingham University and Film Department of Bristol University, Spring and Brandt, 1974); *Neville Chamberlain*, Archive Series (Leeds University, Dilks and Pronay, 1975).

The Universities of Nottingham, Wales and Birmingham have further film studies in various stages of production at the time of writing in the spring of 1975, and proposals from Queen Mary College (University of London) are under consideration. Experience has shown that from start to finish a film may take about two years, so completions tend to be 'bunched'. Distribution is a vital aspect if adequate funds are to be generated. The Consortium during its early years handled its own distribution successfully, but has now handed this over in the United Kingdom to the Longman Group.

Unless the historian is prepared to work with an existing organisation dedicated to the production of academic film, the negotiations necessary before he can begin are likely to occupy him for at least a year. Supposing these obstacles are overcome then intellectual problems need to be squarely faced. When the modern historian has such an abundance of written evidence at his disposal why bother with film evidence? Is this film evidence not trivial, showing little more than, for instance, people walking up and down stairways as some of the surviving film of the Paris Peace Conference of 1919 does? It tells us nothing worthwhile about the Peace Conference, any more than shots of ministers hastening into No.10 Downing Street tell us anything about the decisions that took place around the cabinet table. When the historian first comes to view film the banality of the information that can be derived from it about the actual event depicted is frequently a first disillusioning impression. As a generalisation it is probably true that relatively little film of the pre-sound era is likely to prove of great interest. As a means of communication, posters, pamphlets, the radio, and newspapers were far more important than silent film. With sound the propaganda potential of film was enormously enhanced. Provided film is studied and used as studies in propaganda, in the same way as newspapers have been studied and the radio is only beginning to be studied, the immense significance of film in the twentieth century becomes apparent. Film in sound and pictures tells a story. It is not the individual frame that is important but the total effect. No wonder that historians have begun an intensive study of the newsreels. They were a new and persuasive form of journalism seen by immense audiences in the 1930s. In their television form they now account for a principal influence shaping public opinion. The historian of the twentieth century cannot ignore the phenomenon of this shift from the relatively small reading public affected by propaganda in the nineteenth century to the mass sound and vision audience of the post-World War I era.

The criticism of other historians that newsreel is trivial or propagandist thus in fact becomes the very reason why it should be studied seriously. It rarely throws new light on the event itself, say the Munich Conference of 1938, but it is the prime evidence of how the events were presented, or misrepresented, to the public at the time. Without an appreciation of the nature of the evidence the historian cannot begin a work of scholarship based on film. He should therefore start by asking what questions does this film evidence answer. This will dictate the shape of his film.

In presenting film evidence the historian next has a broad choice similar to the choice he has to make when writing history. A collection of edited documents can be put together. Such a collection of course will reflect the ideas and judgements of the historian; a subject needs to be selected and then the 'film documents' which best illustrate the historian's view of that subject need to be put together. Alternatively the historian can present his views in a coherent story which utilises the new film evidence. But in either case, and this needs to be emphasised, the results are history in the sense that they represent the point of view of one historian. Film evidence, no more than any other historical evidence, provides a kind of pure account of an historical event that is adulterated only by the intervention of the historian. Film is not the answer to history without historians. There can be no history without historians. It is just as idle to argue that historians should not 'tamper' with the film evidence in the sense of selecting and editing it as it would be to argue that they should not select the evidence concerning nineteenth-century constitutional history. In the first place there are millions of miles of film evidence. Without selection it remains a mass of evidence in the archives. There is no more valid reason for arguing that the historian utilising film should use all the film as he finds it than there is for demanding of the biographer of Disraeli that he print in full all his evidence, that is every letter written to and from Disraeli and every other scrap of documentary material. Without labouring the point, it is not the function of the historian merely to copy the archives and leave the material as such, even if this were practicable, which it is not. A moment's reflection reveals that the rules for using film evidence are precisely the same as the rules governing the use of any historical evidence.

The necessity for the historian to control the making of films which are historical expositions is due to the obvious fact that the proper use of historical evidence requires the historian's training. We do not expect professional printers to write the books they print however skilled they may be at their craft. The film producer makes film of creative value; it is possible for him to become an historian too; but the use of 'historians' as advisers is no satisfactory solution. What a number of historians have now demonstrated is that they can learn the craft of film-making to the extent necessary to control this medium for communicating their ideas. Experience has shown that the traditional hierarchical function of the film world does not apply to these films. The historian has to supervise every stage which leads to the final film and so work with professionals in other fields.

The research does not begin with film. The first step is to gain a thorough knowledge of the subject of the film from more traditional historical sources, manuscript archival where available, printed documents, contemporary accounts, newspapers, secondary studies and so on. The film evidence has to be correlated by the historian with other available evidence; after all the only way to assess the value of any evidence is to compare it with other evidence. Where the film producer traditionally begins more or less with a script which is then 'illustrated' and adjusted to available film, the historian has no script when he confronts a new source of evidence, but knowledge and questions and ideally an open mind.

The film 'evidence' is then looked at. To do so it is necessary to study the way in which the film catalogues at the archives actually operate. They were not designed with the historian in mind but for practical contemporary use. What does this evidence add to our knowledge of the historical events being studied? That decides how the film evidence is used.

The sections of film which have been chosen are then ordered and copied and in due course arrive on the historian's desk. The next task is to assemble the film pieces in a rough order corresponding to the main structure of the 'narrative' and analysis intended. Working together with an editor, the editing of the film and the 'script' emerge simultaneously, dependent as they are on each other. This is perhaps the most fascinating and also arduous task. A number of questions calls for decision. How valuable to the points the historian wishes to make is the original sound track? In what precise proportions should the original sound track and the historian's own commentary be arranged? A piece of film can be cut to fit the length of the commentary, it cannot generally be 'stretched'. Precise timing is of the essence of academic film-making. There will be clashes between desirable artistic effects and the requirements of the historian. A creative film editor can aid the historian enormously but in the last resort artistic considerations have to take second place.

The historian's ability to interpret the film evidence requires imagination. In the making of a film dealing with the events leading up to World War II, there was a piece of film portraying the reception of President Lebrun on a state visit to England in 1939. It was a beautifully put together newsreel story. But what could the historian say about it? The reception ceremony at Victoria Station, the ride in the state coach of President Lebrun, Mme Lebrun, George VI and Queen Elizabeth through London, the Guildhall banquet, all these events were traditional, familiar and unchanged. As the historian looked at this film there seemed to be a significant point made, but what was it? After repeated viewings an idea emerged. The very tradition and familiarity of the scene *were* the point. This was 1939. The world had drastically changed since Edward VII had sat on the throne. Britain was clinging to the safe and comforting traditions of the past. Here tradition was being emphasised, the Anglo-French entente first formed in 1904, victorious in 1914–18, a close alliance still in the face of a new German dictator. This was Britain's answer to the vulgar military parades of the dictators. It was intended to reassure and probably succeeded in reassuring the British public in these desperate last months of peace. Once the idea was conceived, the commentary was soon written and carefully timed to the rhythm and changing moods of this piece of film.

To come back to the analogy of written history, the account has been given in the form of a coherent story with a balance of narrative and analysis. It is not totally composed of 'new evidence'. The new evidence rather affects the story as a whole and is set, as with quotations, into existing known facts. So it is with film. The new points which can be made with film evidence – for example the

139

contemporary portrayal of Chamberlain as a peace-maker after the Munich conference – have to be set into a known narrative of what the Munich crisis of
1938 was all about. To do this film may be used purely narratively. But there
may be no film available to make the particular points the historian wishes to
stress: a discussion in the cabinet, secret conversations and negotiations or the
nature of the changing balance of power. Because of the absence of film material,
the film producer may simply conclude such points will have to be omitted. The
historian of necessity takes a different view, a means has to be found. The solution to this problem of correlating meaningful visual non-film material which
would add point to the historian's commentary proved the most challenging
part of film-making. In practice, stills in sequence and animated frequently
support the historian's argument more precisely than film and so can be chosen
in preference even where film exists. Maps, documents and newspapers can be
effectively utilised. There is no limit to ingenuity but a visual imagination and a
skilful cameraman are essential. The preparation of accurate historical maps
demands the co-operation of designer and historian. If the film in the end is to
work artistically and technically the co-operation of designers, cameramen and
skilled technicians, all 'artists' in their own right, is essential. And despite the
historian's lack of technical knowledge they must accept that their function is
to express the ideas of the historian, not their own. This is why the historian
needs to be present at every stage to see whether his ideas are coming across,
and if not what changes need to be made. Such teamwork is no longer unique
though it had not been attempted ten years ago.

Students have been quick to appreciate the advantages of the use of film by
the historian. Not only does film provide a comprehensive view of an event in
the time in which a lecture could deal only with a fraction of the material, but
it also raises questions of historical and contemporary relevance. The importance of how far public opinion is influenced in its judgements by the way in
which information is presented to it on newsreel is not a difficult question to
grasp for the present generation which derives so much of its own knowledge
from television. The study of the nature of prejudice and propaganda is after all
central to history. Historians are also teachers and as such concerned to equip
students with the necessary critical tools to distinguish between propaganda,
interpretation and fact. In this respect too the historian's film has proved to be
a valuable contribution to the study of history in higher education.

There is a genuine role for 'historical novels', frequently conscientiously
researched and well written, just as there is a proper use for historical novels in
film form on television; and there are excellent reasons why the producers of
such programmes should gain the assistance of historians, at least to avoid mis-
interpretations. But the basic belief underlying the work of the historians in the
British Inter-University History Film Consortium is that what purports to be the
work of historians must in fact be their work. There is no such thing as a 'com-
municator' who because of his specialised skills must *of necessity* stand between

the historian and his audience. If anyone seeks to 'transform' the historian's ideas into film and sound terms that person, usually the producer, inevitably begins to stamp his own ideas on the work and since he is not an historian what results is the combination — so often criticised by historians — which wrongly claims to be serious historical work. Much better that the producer honestly stick to his craft and make no false claims for it. It is àn eminently worthwhile job he is doing and requires no more defence than the work of any other artist. But the historian cannot compromise on what is historical work — it is nothing but the work of historians. Not every historian needs to be able to communicate through every medium, spoken, written, or audio-visual. But what historians have shown during the last few years is that those who wish to can communicate their ideas through a medium unique in the twentieth century: the sound film. They will not be excluded from it despite the difficulties encountered by any new enterprise.

# 8. Film in university teaching

ARTHUR MARWICK

Film can be studied for itself as a primary source and aesthetic artefact, or it can be used as a teaching aid in the study of ordinary bread-and-butter history. This distinction, corresponding to the traditional one between the historian's primary and his secondary sources, has almost become a cliché in the discussion of the use of film to the university historian. It is a distinction which we forget at our peril, yet which, if applied too rigidly, can lead to a misunderstanding of the complexity and richness of film as a medium of communication, and to a neglect of what can be called the 'magic' of film. In practical classroom situations, university teachers use both compilations which are clearly 'secondary', and feature film and original documentaries and newsreels, which are clearly 'primary'; yet the latter are often, and quite properly, used as much as a basis for broader historical discussion as for narrower source criticism.[1]

However, let us start by establishing firmly the difference between whole archive film of various types, and specially made 'secondary' film, whether made by historians or by the professionals of the film and television world (at present, and for the foreseeable future, a fair proportion of films actually used in our universities have been originated by the broadcasting networks). Specially made films fall roughly into four categories: continuous narrative compilations, based on archive film, originally designed for mass television audiences (for example Thames Television's *The World at War*); continuous narrative archive compilation films made by professional historians for history students (for example the compilations made by the British Inter-University History Film Consortium[2]); archive compilation films (also made by professional historians) which set out to perform the functions of a collection of film documents (for example the Open University[3] *War and Society* series); and, finally, films (originated both by historians and by television and film professionals) which deal with those historical topics for which pre-existing archive film is largely or wholly irrelevant, for example historical methodology, or subjects (such as the Renaissance) which fall outside the brief period for which archive film exists. These different types of specially made film are all in use at our universities, though for the time being at least they very much take second place to the showing of complete feature films, and, in lesser degree, documentaries and newsreels. Once the use of the various sorts of film has become established in the basic undergraduate history curriculum, it is likely that attention will be given at senior undergraduate and at postgraduate level to the highly technical analysis of historical film at present being undertaken by Dr K.F. Reimers and his colleagues at Göttingen and Mr Karsten Fledelius and his colleagues in Copenhagen, and to the very detailed and subtle study of feature films being pioneered in Paris by Professors Marc Ferro and Pierre Sorlin. But in this chapter I propose to confine myself to a discussion of the possibilities for the integration of film into the mainstream of historical study at university level.

The many conferences held recently to discuss the uses of film to the historian have tended to neglect the fourth category of specially made films, those for which archive material is largely or wholly irrelevant. I propose, therefore, to start off with the non-archival historical film, partly, indeed, because this type of film, more directly than any other, raises the fundamental issue of the utility of film for any type of university teaching. A recent study of this very topic conducted by the Media Service Unit of the University of Sussex stressed the value of film as providing both *stimulus* and *insight*. In elaborating the latter point the report declares:

> The notion that film can provide insights which are of a qualitatively different order from those provided by other information systems relies on two factors: the content area of film and the expressive system of film. In the content area, the physical *reach* of film — temporal as well as spatial — enables it to reproduce visual information which would otherwise remain inaccessible. . . .
>
> The expressive system of film, on the other hand, provides insights of another order: insights into aesthetic information which is inseparable from its mode of presentation and which is thus untranslatable. Without calling upon such notions as the ineffability of film we can characterise these insights into aesthetic information as specific and unique in the sense that they arise only from the particular experience of viewing a film. They can add information to existing patterns of knowledge but ideally they can act as catalysts in restructuring or destructuring these patterns.[4]

This, perhaps, is a trifle pretentious. But it seems difficult to disagree that film *can* show students things they could not otherwise see in the classroom, and that film *can* break through the boredom of the traditional teaching situation, enabling important material to be presented in a novel and striking way. More than this, in a media-conscious age, film *can* communicate with the student in a manner which relates closely to his experiences outside the classroom. I say film *can* do these things, not that it necessarily *does* do these things, for a bad or irrelevant film is, of course, of no more value, and may well be of less, than the lecture or seminar it has partially replaced.

There is a long tradition in general service and educational broadcasting of making non-archival documentary films on historical topics. At one extreme we have the brilliant B.B.C. series presented by Professor W.G. Hoskins on the historical landscape, at the other the abysmal B.B.C. television series on the British

Empire. Having concentrated most of its energies on archive film compilation, the British Inter-University History Film Consortium has now also turned its attention towards the making of a film on palaeography, while the Open University has been responsible for quite a number of non-archival productions. Apart from films on historical methodology, Open University history films have tended to concentrate on one or more of the following areas: technological developments (e.g. the invention of printing or the lead chamber process in the production of sulphuric acid); particular locations of specific interest, as in industrial archaeology; visual sources, such as cartoons or maps; dynamic visual contrasts, as between maps and the real landscape or between existing buildings and older drawings of them; and geographical settings with which students are unlikely to be familiar (including, for example, film specially shot in New England for a programme on the Thirteen Colonies on the eve of the American Revolution). Many Open University history programmes have not proved entirely satisfactory when broadcast over B.B.C.2 to Open University students, and quite probably would not be useful to history teachers in more traditional types of university. Yet, while there is likely to be little stimulus and less insight in a film which does no more than that which a good lecturer could do in person with a few maps and other visual props, it is clear that certain specially made non-archival films can be of the utmost value in the conventional classroom situation. History of science is a sub-history which is gaining in importance in many universities. Some of those who have viewed any or all of the sixteen films which form part of the Open University course on 'Science and the Rise of Technology Since 1800' have wondered how it has ever been thought possible to teach history of science properly to non-scientists without film of crucial experiments and technological processes. Many specialists in Renaissance history, too, would agree that very few students in any university show any real grasp of the nature and significance of the invention usually, and probably very properly, attributed to Guthenberg. A visit to an old, or reconstructed, printing press would help: failing that, film of the process is the next best thing.

Historical methodology is another growth area in some universities, though many academics remain convinced that it is only through the direct practice of history that its methods are to be gradually acquired. For university teachers who do believe in starting off with a preliminary study of the basic principles and methods of history, film can be an invaluable tool. The Open University has produced four *Introduction to History* films as part of the Open University Foundation Course in the Humanities: *The Necessity for History*, *Primary Sources*, *The Historian at Work* and *About Trevelyan* . . . (basically a study of the strengths and weaknesses of 'pop history'). Obtaining systematic feedback, even at the Open University, is a laborious and very expensive business. However, a considerable amount of information, in relatively 'objective' form, was collected on student reactions to the Humanities Foundation Course. Students were asked to rate programmes as 'very useful', 'fairly useful', 'not very useful', or 'not useful at all', and through the same spectrum from 'very interesting' to 'not interesting at all'. With, broadly, something rather below an eighty per cent score for being fairly or very useful and fairly or very interesting, the *Introduction to History* programmes on the whole did less well than, say, art programmes. More evidence suggested that, particularly in the earliest years of the Open University, there was quite a strong segment of student resistance to the whole idea of trying to introduce history in this manner (though many came, later, to appreciate the contribution of this approach to their studies as a whole — something, of course, not recorded in the immediate 'objective' feedback). Further, rather more 'subjective' evidence (collected, for instance, at summer schools, and through tutors actually in direct contact with students) suggested that those students who were sympathetic to the approach to the 'Introduction to History' presented in the printed correspondence material felt that the programmes contributed to, and enhanced in a manner particular to visual filmic presentation, their understanding of that material. An early version of the *Introduction to History* programmes (the first was subsequently re-made, and the fourth was added later) was evaluated in the journal *History* by Professor John Grenville of the University of Birmingham.[5] He dealt sympathetically with the weaknesses which he detected in the programmes, and it would be fair to say that when they have been shown to conventional student audiences they have attracted mixed reactions. Yet even the limited experience so far obtained of showing these programmes in traditional classroom situations suggests that those university teachers who are keen to develop the study either of the basic principles and methods of history, or of more advanced topics such as palaeography, would find properly made films, properly presented, invaluable shortcuts to effective teaching. (Several history departments do use existing archive films as a basis for analysing source material — I return to this use below.)

But let us move back into the twentieth century, and into the world of genuine archive film. And here I must stress the sharp distinction between the opportunities open to my colleagues and myself at the Open University, and the opportunities open to the history lecturer in a traditional university. At the Open University our only means of showing film material to students is on the brief and infrequent slots allocated to us on B.B.C.2. In the Humanities Foundation Course (of which approximately one-fifth concerns history) students receive one twenty-five minute programme each week; in the multi-disciplinary second-year courses, 'The Renaissance and Reformation', and 'The Age of Revolutions' (in both of which, obviously, history plays an important part) there is one twenty-five minute programme every two weeks. In the third-year history course 'War and Society' there is also one twenty-five minute programme every fortnight (and this will be the case for other third-year history courses). For the fourth-year history course 'Great Britain 1750—1950: Sources and Historiography' there are only eleven programmes for the full thirty-two weeks of the course. The 'War and Society' course does have a summer school (attended by each student for one week), and at this we show complete feature films and complete documentaries; otherwise we can only show to students such film material as can be fitted into a twenty-five minute programme. In traditional university situations the tendency is to show complete (or almost complete) feature films and complete documentaries, as well as specially made compilations, which can include those originated by the Open University.

From the pages of *University Vision* (the journal of the British Universities' Film Council, which, of course, is concerned with all university disciplines) and from the pages of *Film and History* (the recently established American journal, whose very title attests to the great interest in film in university history teaching in the United States), it is possible to form a broad picture of the different types of film programme at present being presented by different university history teachers. First of all there are the courses whose centre-point really lies in cinema itself, whose connection with historical studies lies in the thesis that cinema is central to any understanding of the twentieth century and the emergence of our own age. The most committed proponents of this type of course argue for the incorporation of a strong 'workshop' element, students themselves being involved in the actual processes of film-making. This is urged by the Sussex Media Service Unit, and takes place at a number of American colleges.[6] A model for this type of course (without, however, the 'workshop' element) in Great Britain is the course on 'American Cinema' at Aberystwyth which was initiated by specialists in literature rather than in history.[7]

This first type of course, which really pertains to cinema, or inter-disciplinary cultural studies, rather than to history, merges into a second type, where the emphasis is still very much on film as such, but where a particular historical theme is stressed, such as, for example, 'Modern War and its Images'.[8] This approach seems to be more common in the United States than in Great Britain: Professors James C. Curtis and J. Joseph Huthmacher, of the University of Delaware, have developed a course on 'The American Dream on Film', and Professor William Hughes of Essex Community College, Baltimore, has proposed a syllabus for a course on 'Films and History'.[9] Perhaps most ambitious of all is the study of 'Film as Social and Intellectual History' established by Professors Stuart Samuels and Robert Rosen of the University of Pennsylvania. In effect there are two one-semester courses, a lecture course involving nearly five hundred students, and a seminar course involving twenty-five. In the lecture course the 'two weekly lectures sketch out in both theoretical and specific terms the relationship of film to social and historical developments . . . Tapes are made available to the students. Readings are geared to the lecture topics.' Films are screened every day — sometimes two a day.

> We screen over 120 feature films in chronological order during the semester; for the silent films presented in the course we have our own professional piano accompanist. A study guide for each film is provided and in some cases film showings are followed by a general discussion . . .

146

Written work for the course consists of a detailed research paper on a problem dealing with the relationship of film to social change chosen primarily from a broad list of topics distributed to the students, a short 3—5 page review of a film the student has seen outside the course that explicitly relates to social concerns and a final exam.

In the small seminar class students do not have regular screenings, but make use instead of the facilities of local film societies, private collections, and the Museum of Modern Art in New York.

Students read the standard works of film history (Jacobs, Leyda, Kracauer, Knight, Bazin, etc.), study theoretical works on the sociology of knowledge (Mannheim, Merton, Sartre, Berger, etc.) and review some general surveys and significant monographs on European and American history. During the semester students write and present a detailed research paper on widely ranging topics: film during the McCarthy period, the role of propaganda films in Nazi Germany, the presentation of class in French and British films, the changing presentation of ethnic groups, and the persistence of the mythology of the Western represent a typical cross-section.[10]

The characteristic feature to be stressed about all of these courses is that film forms a central part of them, with students being assessed (a crucial point) on their grasp of the film material. In the United Kingdom the most fully comparable courses are those on 'Communications and Politics in the Twentieth Century' initiated by Nicholas Pronay at the University of Leeds, and on 'Film, Sound and Historical Analysis' organised by Ken Ward of the New University of Ulster.[11] Characteristically the British courses place a strong emphasis on historical methodology and include other media as well as film. The Leeds course contains a strong 'workshop' component, and both courses fit into the honours history syllabuses offered at their respective universities.

The third use of film is that to be found in courses which cover a much broader historical topic but which include the study of film as a vital ingredient (the modern European history course at the Queen's University of Belfast is a good example, as are the programmes being developed at the Cambridgeshire College of Arts and Technology and at Westminster College, Oxford — non-university higher education colleges here giving a lead that more venerable institutions might well follow). 'War and Society', as a broad historical topic, is becoming fashionable in a number of universities, and some of them are making use of the Open University *War and Society* programmes as well as using the great wealth of original feature films and documentaries relating to war. The Open University course, itself, is perhaps a key example of the way in which film can be integrated into a much more general historical subject, in which a strong emphasis is placed on methodology and the handling of sources. The sixteen archive compilations linked to the course adopt the 'collection of documents' approach mentioned at the beginning of this chapter. Each film is accompanied by a 'supplement' (analogous to the 'study guides' developed by other users of

147

film and specifically mentioned by Professors Samuels and Rosen) which, apart from providing full scholarly apparatus for the film (full list of clips used and their provenance), and a discussion of editorial and production decisions, relates the film to the other teaching material supplied to the student, and, above all, to the primary written documents which he is studying. In addition to setting essay topics which require students to incorporate assessment of the film evidence we also set assignments (suitable for marking by computer) which call for a direct comparison of film documents and written documents. Here is an example (relating to a film about the social consequences of World War II for Great Britain):

> If you read what is said about the historical context in the supplement for this programme, you will see that broadly speaking there are two views about the way in which the British people reacted to the immediate impact of the war, the blitz, and its various ramifications. For the purposes of this exercise, let us speak of the 'optimistic' view, that morale strengthened, people rallied to the government, life went on as usual, etc.; and the 'pessimistic' view that people were deeply disturbed, that morale was adversely affected, that there was great resentment against the government and the authorities, etc.
>
> The following list of film items [all included in this compilation], as witting testimony, present only an optimistic view, though this is not necessarily the case if we treat them as unwitting testimony.

| | | | |
|---|---|---|---|
| A | 1 | War Comes to London | [Documentary] |
| B | 2 | London Fire Service Film | [Record film] |
| C | 3 | Coventry: The Martyred City | [Newsreel] |
| D | 4 | Pioneer Army for London Clean Up | [Newsreel] |
| E | 5 | Air Raid Victim | [Newsreel] |
| F | 6 | Reprisal Interviews | [Unissued newsreel] |
| G | 7 | Ordinary People | [Documentary] |

> The following relevant documents present both views.

| | | | |
|---|---|---|---|
| A | G(i) 1 | (Unit 18, p. 47) | [Emergency Powers (Defence) Act, 1940] |
| B | G(i) 2 | ( " " p. 47) | [Extracts from H. Hamilton Fyfe's diary of the years 1939–42] |
| C | G(i) 3 | ( " " pp. 47–8) | [Article from the *Psychiatric Journal* on the effects of the blitz] |
| D | G(i) 4(a) | ( " " pp. 49–50) | [Evacuation: extracts from *Our Towns*, 1943, XVII–XX] |
| E | G(i) 4(b) | ( " " p. 50) | [Evacuation: reminiscences by Mel Calman] |
| F | G(i) 7 | ( " " pp. 55–7) | [Council for the Encouragement of Music and the Arts, Report 1942–3] |

*Film in university teaching*

G  G(i)  12    (Unit 18, p. 66)    ['Industrial Disputes involving Stoppages of Work in the United Kingdom', 1939–46]

*Question QV1*
Which *documents* on the list confirm the optimistic view presented by the film evidence?
*Question QV2*
Which documents present a pessimistic view?
*Question QV3*
Which film clip(s), wittingly or unwittingly, *suggest(s)* a pessimistic view?

At a more elementary level, film has also been integrated into the sort of broad survey course more common at American than at British universities. Inevitably the role of film here is largely motivational, there being little time in first- or second-year courses for really serious detailed analysis.[12] The danger then arises, in my view, of the too-ready acceptance of film as a 'creative interpretation of historical reality' (to rephrase Grierson's tendentious definition of the documentary) more persuasive than the straight lecture. A better use for film in introductory courses is perhaps to be found in those universities (such as Birmingham and Warwick) which emphasise the importance of basic historical methodology. At Warwick an assessment of the value of film as historical evidence is an integral part of the compulsory first-year course 'History: Texts and Methods'.

Fourthly comes the type of film programme which can perhaps best be described as a systematic ancillary to a general history course or courses. The various programmes organised by Roderick Kedward at the University of Sussex, and analysed by the Media Service Unit ('Images of War', 'Images of Peace' etc.) seem to fall into this category (though brilliantly conceived as film programmes, they do not make an entire university course in their own right), as also do the film programmes organised by the Slade Film Department for history students at London University. Similar programmes were organised in the 1960s at the University of Cambridge[13] and by Christopher Seton-Watson and subsequently Charles Wenden and J.M. Roberts at Oxford. Finally, we come to what is surely the largest category of all, the occasional use of film as a support to a more traditionally conceived teaching programme. Already very many universities lay on from time to time a showing of feature or other films felt in some way or other to be related to their modern history courses. At worst these are just an optional extra, a light-hearted distraction whose relationship to the rest of a student's studies is left very unclear; at best their relevance is pointed up with a written or spoken introduction, and time for discussion is made available in tutorials and seminars. So far too few compilation films have been produced by the British Inter-University History Film Consortium for a complete course to be built around them; obviously they are intended, for the time being, to be

149

introduced in this occasional manner, though clearly they are best used if an opportunity for introductory material and for detailed discussion is also provided.

In concluding this bare factual survey of some of the uses being made of film in British and American universities, I want to return to the essential distinction of emphasis between courses whose core lies in the multi-disciplinary study of cinema, or some aspect of cinema, and courses whose core lies firmly in the study of history itself. No historian could possibly deny the intellectual and educational validity of a course on the American cinema (even if conceived by specialists in literature!), and many historians would think it possible both to contribute to such a course and to benefit from studying it. The authors of the report on *The Use of Film in University Teaching*, which is based largely on experience at Sussex in history teaching, argue that the use of film must proceed from the lower plane of mere history to the higher one of full inter-disciplinary work. Yet in a pungent quotation from a sociologist of the media the authors highlight a central problem in the teaching use of film: 'When one sets out to examine the media directly, one frequently ends up talking about something else.'[14] The seminar discussions associated with the Sussex film programme were in fact very disjointed, reflecting faithfully, their sponsors claim,

> the unordered ideas generated by the use of film. It is an important question whether our investigations should be directed towards illuminating this lack of order or whether in fact the crucial contribution of film to study is that it evokes unordered responses.
>
> It is this question perhaps more than any other which lies at the heart of all discussions concerning the use of film in education. It is fundamental to the whole of education for we are really asking whether society provides education for the continuation of that society (and its implied order) or whether society accepts that education is provided for the individual who is likely, given freedom to develop himself, to have ideas which compared with the order of society will be unordered and hence potentially destructive.[15]

Running through many university teachers' descriptions of their use of film, particularly in *Film and History*, is the sense that film leads on to new perceptions and intuitions which cannot be pinned down, cannot be expressed verbally, cannot, presumably, be assessed, but which are nonetheless valuable in taking students out of the rigidities of the traditional verbal education. The concept of intuitions of this sort is in fact deeply ingrained in many history departments in the older British universities; though unable to predict them in advance, the lecturer or tutor is confident of his mystical ability to divine them, when they can equally mystically be described as 'showing a touch of alpha'. One must be careful not to substitute an unduly authoritarian model of education for the too liberal model of the older ivory tower establishments, yet there surely are grave dangers in using film to perpetuate the notion that university education is concerned with vague, ineffable intuitions, ungrounded in any common framework

150

of basic methods and concepts. In this connection certain American reactions recorded at the American Historical Association session on 'The Historian as Film-Maker' held at New Orleans in December 1972 are significant. Dr Rolf Schuursma had argued the case for the austere and scholarly use of film in university history teaching; but some American historians 'felt that the film-maker must be much more of an artist than Dr Schuursma allowed and make films which in an imaginative way would enable students or other viewers to penetrate beneath the surface and gain a deeper understanding of the subject of the film'.[16]

Here again, I believe, lies dangerous ground. Talk, in a university teaching situation, of the 'imaginative penetration' of films can too readily degenerate into the soft option of smart cocktail chat or high-flown woffle unrelated to any hard analysis. Accordingly, I should like to venture to propose certain fundamental principles to be observed in using film material for university history teaching. The first (a good rule in any kind of teaching) is that, before introducing a programme of film material, the organiser of the programme should clearly state his aims and objectives in so doing: in other words he should say clearly why he is showing the film, and what sorts of thing he thinks his students ought to be able to do *after* viewing and analysing the film material that they could not do *before*. Second, and as a direct corollary, all film material should be integrated firmly into a specific teaching context: in other words the film should not be a mere optional extra, but, through examination questions or otherwise, its relevance to the students' course of studies should be made abundantly plain.

Now both of these propositions are controversial. Let me say right away that I recognise that a good university course can often stimulate responses and achievements in individual students which were not envisaged by the creators of the course. But it is far better to be clear about basic objectives; one can then go on very properly to allow that with film, above all, all sorts of additional and unforeseen objectives are likely to be achieved as well. On the second proposition, many distinguished historians, experienced in the use of film, would argue that film can serve a function analogous to books on the library shelves. This attitude is reinforced by modern technology which now makes it possible for students in some universities to consult video cassettes on their own. For a minority of able and dedicated students free range across the library shelves and through all the media resources, reinforced by high level face-to-face tuition of the traditional sort, will remain the finest form of university education. But experience shows that many students today find it increasingly difficult to carry out unstructured study on their own, and demand more and more to know the relevance of any work which they are expected to do. Nicholas Pronay has told a recent conference[17] that having made video cassettes available of the Thames Television series *The World at War* he then had the tapes wiped because students said they were of no use to them. Which brings me back to the central point that it is all a matter of 'use for what'. Examination questions discussing the use made of archive film material in a popular television series, or discussing the interpretation of National Socialism presented in this particular series (both, surely, important topics in their own right) would soon make students find the tapes very definitely 'of use'. What is no longer any good is to make available to students a rag-bag of miscellaneous extra materials which do not seem to be structurally related to the main body of their studies.

If there is 'magic' in film, there should be no mystery or mystique. A third proposition would be that any and every film, or piece of film, should be presented with the maximum of relevant information: provenance, who made the film, and why, how it was made, and, above all, why this particular film is now being shown to this particular audience. There is still a natural human tendency for those showing film (particularly if they also happen to have made the film) to seek as their reward nothing more than gasps of awe and admiration: the *prima donna* tradition among university lecturers dies hard and can readily reappear as that of cinematic impresario. Open University research shows that one of the biggest stumbling blocks we have had to overcome is that students sometimes do not know why they are being shown certain visual material, do not know what to make of it, or how to relate it to the rest of their studies. It seems highly probable that conventional students can be afflicted by similar problems, whatever facility they may have in reacting in a disorganised way to film material. Thus the best of university film courses already offer, at the very least, study guides or 'supplements' with each film shown.

How then have experienced university teachers summarised the value of film to themselves and their students? Two of the pioneers in the more systematic use of film have been Professor John Grenville of the University of Birmingham[18] and Nicholas Pronay of the University of Leeds. Both have laid stress on the following points: film has been a central medium of communication for an important part of the twentieth century, and therefore no study of that century could be complete without the study of film; film is a particularly potent agent in opinion-forming and propaganda, so that any study concerned historically with these topics must necessarily involve the study of film; film raises, in particularly potent form, all the issues of faking, distortion and bias in historical evidence, together with some special problems of technical analysis, the study of which forms one of the main justifications for the inclusion of history in the higher education syllabus (indeed, Professor Grenville has argued, the study of film evidence leads one naturally into the study of all types of historical evidence, and can suggest to the student that some of the obvious tricks of the film-maker may also have been practised, in a more subtle way, by the parliamentarians and preachers of the past). Furthermore, since film furnishes the historical researcher with a special kind of information on environment, life-styles, and 'received attitudes' and 'unspoken assumptions' (what a less cautious and more innocent generation of historians called 'the climate of the age'),[19] so too can it provide the history student with the same kind of information, simply not available from purely written and verbal sources. Nicholas Pronay has rehearsed the various arguments with great skill in the Historical Association pamphlet, *The Use of Film in History Teaching* (1972). But on one argument I part company from Mr Pronay. He writes:

> Film is particularly well suited to the exposition of arguments which involve a large number of related events, or a large number of threads running for a long time separately but all coming together in the end to cause a result which cannot be satisfactorily explained by singling out a few 'main' threads. The Munich Settlement of 1938 was one such event. We all know the difficulty of trying to keep each thread alive in the student's mind as we work through all of them. The natural tendency of the mind is to foreclose too early, that is, to jump to a conclusion. For reasons which are not quite clear, film seems to allow a long suspension of judgement. People seem to be able to follow a film longer, to stay within the unfolding threads much longer and thus acquire a much fuller understanding of a complex story.[20]

Mr Pronay, as an ex-professional film-maker, has unique qualifications among British academics, and deserves to be listened to with respect. But I have to say that though fully in agreement about the implied 'magical' qualities of film, I find the particular view presented here unconvincing. Film, in my view, is not suited to the presentation of a complex historical narrative, and is most certainly unsuited to complex historical analysis. Yet there is no doubt that the kind of complex continuous narrative compilation film which Nicholas Pronay has in mind, can arouse a student's interest in a topic in a way in which a straight lecture might fail to do. Paradoxically, it seems that this use of compilation film succeeds best in areas with which students tend to be less familiar. The British Inter-University History Film Consortium film on *The Winter War* is an excellent case in point, since the Russo-Finnish War of 1939 is not usually given much attention in university history courses. It is doubtful whether most students would immediately grasp and retain all of the detailed information contained in this excellent compilation film; but the film does succeed admirably in presenting directly to them the dimensions of the historical problem, and the main issues involved; and in keeping the main outlines boldly in view, it serves as a stimulus to students to follow up some of the detail for themselves. Much the same is true of one of the Open University *War and Society* films even though it follows the rather different 'collection of documents' approach. The programme, *The Impact of the Second World War on Indonesian Nationalism*, presented for us by Professor Donald Watt of the London School of Economics, follows the very rigorous and austere principles laid down for the series. South-East Asia in World War II is only one element in a very wide ranging course. Yet experience in monitoring examination scripts shows that where students do choose to answer a question on this topic, much of what they know is derived directly from the film programme; here we do have a concrete example of the 'magic' of film, where the whole adds up to more than the sum of the parts, and where

153

the students, ostensibly presented only with fragments of film documents, together with Professor Watt's perceptive comments, in fact derive some understanding of the historical issues well beyond what they could possibly have attained from twenty-five minutes' reading or from a twenty-five minute lecture.

And so we move again to the question of feedback. As with the Open University Foundation Course, there is a fair amount of 'objective' feedback on the *War and Society* films. However, apart from providing invaluable general encouragement for the belief that on the whole the programmes were properly conceived, and were being used as intended by students, much of the more specific feedback scarcely provided positive guides to future action. We found that the least popular programme was one entitled *The Organisations of Peace*; but since we could not in all honesty see that this was a less well devised or well made programme than most of the others, we could only take this as evidence (incidentally confirmed in the University of Sussex report) that on the whole (as far as film is concerned anyway) students are more interested in war than in peace. A rather small sample (the course was nearing its end) gave a very enthusiastic verdict on a programme which we had already decided to remake because we felt the rather stiff presentation by the academic concerned to be a potential barrier between students and his quite excellent film material and commentary. The possible indication (I can put it no stronger than that, though there is some confirmation from other sources in regard to other programmes) is that students, if they find the content of a film satisfactory, pay less attention to the professionalism or otherwise of the presentation than might be expected of this television-reared generation. But the best feedback is that arising directly from the implementation of the propositions which I announced earlier. Devise aims and objectives, construct an integrated course, set essays, assignments, and, if you will, examination questions directly related to that course and designed to see whether the aims and objectives have been achieved, and you have devised the most nearly perfect of feedback systems: if students can answer the questions, you have succeeded; if they cannot, you have failed.

But for many university teachers the most compelling problems are simply those of physically setting up a film programme.[21] It is no purpose of this chapter to intensify the deterrent forces inherent in film as a technologically messy teaching medium. Nor do I wish to advocate what has been called the 'authority' model of education (an unfair description — it should be called the 'integration' model) against the 'freedom' model of unrestricted access to a library of audio-visual materials backed up by a plenitude of face-to-face contact. The fundamental point is that film must now be seen as central to certain important aspects of history teaching, as increasingly it is seen to be in certain important aspects of historical research. It is highly significant that film is already being most used in those university courses which in content are furthest in the van of contemporary developments in historical studies: methodological courses, theme courses ('War and Society', 'Film as Intellectual and Social

154

## Film in university teaching

History'), and courses on communications and popular culture. As the accounts
written by university teachers themselves show, the practical obstacles can be
overcome; and with a little forethought and planning the films themselves,
bought, copied, hired and projected, with such apparent difficulty, can be used
in a manner which both involves students in experiences which they can see to
be genuinely relevant to their world of study, and meets the exacting standards
which the historical profession has always sought to impose on itself.

NOTES

1. Those whose brains I have picked on this topic are too numerous to mention, so I list
   here only those who have provided direct help in the preparation of this chapter: Tony
   Bates, Clive Lawless, Helen Harrison and Tony Aldgate of the Open University; Yvonne
   Renouf of the British Universities Film Council; Frances Thorpe of the Slade Film
   History Register; Nicholas Pronay of the University of Leeds; Ken Ward of the New
   University of Ulster; Alistair Hennessey of the University of Warwick; Don Simmons of
   the Cambridgeshire College of Arts and Technology; and Ken Short of Westminster
   College, Oxford.
2. The Consortium consists of the history departments of the Universities of Nottingham,
   Leeds, Reading, Birmingham, Edinburgh, Wales, Manchester, the London School of
   Economics and Political Science and Queen Mary College, University of London.
3. The Open University was set up by the British government late in 1968, received its
   Royal Charter in the summer of 1969, and enrolled its first students in January 1971.
   Its 50,000 students are spread throughout the entire United Kingdom and are all in full-
   time employment (or are housewives). They are taught by means of correspondence
   booklets sent through the post and television and radio programmes broadcast by the
   B.B.C. backed up by a small amount of face-to-face tuition provided locally. They submit essays and assignments, also by post, to 'correspondence tutors' who assess and
   comment on these assignments. All assignments and examinations are monitored by
   external examiners from the older universities. The Open University awards its own
   degrees.
4. B. Chibnall, C. Rodrigues, and J. Collings, *The Use of Film in University Teaching*
   (Brighton, 1974), p. 3.
5. J.A.S. Grenville, 'History at the Open University', *History*, 57 (1972), 89–91.
6. See for example P.H. Griffin, 'The Making of a Documentary Film – "1900": A
   Montage', *University Vision*, 9 (1972), 25–31. See also Chibnall *et al., op. cit.*, p. 28,
   and William Hughes, 'Proposal for A Course on Film and History', *University Vision*, 8
   (1972), 14.
7. D. Clough, 'American Cinema: A Film Course at Aberystwyth', *University Vision*,
   9 (1972), 39–43. (Cf. David Adams, 'The Use of Film in American Studies',
   *University Vision*, 1 (1968), 15–18, and M. Gidley, 'Some American studies films at
   Sussex', *University Vision*, 6 (1971), 4–12.)
8. Eugene P.A. Schleh, 'Modern War and its Images', *Film and History*, 3/3 (1973), 12–16.
9. James C. Curtis and J. Joseph Huthmacher, 'The American Dream on Film', *Film and
   History*, 3/3 (1973), 17–19. William Hughes, *op. cit.*, 9–18.
10. Stuart Samuels and Robert Rosen, 'Film and the Historian', *A.H.A. Newsletter*, 2
    (1973), 35–6. See also Stuart Samuels, 'History through Film: Film as Social and
    Intellectual History at the University of Pennsylvania', *Film and History*, 2/3 (1972),
    14–17.
11. K.E. Ward, ' "Film, Sound and Historical Analysis" – A Course in Film and History',
    *University Vision*, 12 (1974), 50–6.
12. See, e.g., Richard S. Sorrell, 'Films and American Civilization at Brookdale Community
    College', *Film and History*, 3/1 (1973), 9–12, and Claire Hirshfield, 'History through
    Film: Film and American History at Penn State, Ogontz Campus', *Film and History*,
    3/2 (1973), 21–4.

13. C.H. Roads, 'A View of the Use of Film by the Universities', *University Vision*, 1 (1968), 9–14
14. D. McQuail, *The Sociology of Mass Communications* (1972), p. 11, as quoted in Chibnall *et al., op. cit.*, p. 21.
15. Chibnall *et al., op. cit.*, p. 17.
16. Peter G. Boyle, ' "The Historian as Film-Maker": A Report from New Orleans', *University Vision*, 10 (1973), 48–50.
17. 'Film and the Second World War', held at the Imperial War Museum, London, 23–7 September 1974.
18. See especially, John Grenville, *Film as History* (University of Birmingham, 1971).
19. Arthur Marwick, 'Archive Film as Source Material' in Open University, *Archive Film Compilation Booklet* (1973), pp. 1–5; and 'Notes on the Use of Archive Film Material' in Arthur Marwick, *War and Social Change in the Twentieth Century* (London, 1974), pp. 226–34.
20. N. Pronay, B. Smith and T. Hastie, *The Use of Film in History Teaching* (London, 1972), p. 14. The American Historical Association has also more recently published an excellent pamphlet perhaps orientated rather more towards schools than universities: John E. O'Connor and Martin A. Jackson, *Teaching History with Film* (Washington, 1974).
21. For teachers in the U.S.A. Martin Jackson's contribution to *Teaching History with Film* contains much practical guidance. Apart from *The Use of Film in History Teaching*, teachers in the U.K. can refer to the following lists: University of Birmingham, *A Survey of History Films for Hire* (1972); Imperial War Museum, *Film Loans*; and British Universities Film Council, *Films for Historians* (rev. ed., 1974). For a complete antidote to my views on the teaching use of film, see Mike Weaver and Mike Gidley, 'Film in the Context of American (and Commonwealth) Arts', in *Screen Education Notes*, 7 (1973), 21–3.

# 9. Film in the classroom

BRYAN HAWORTH

Most surveys of the use of film emphasise the far-sightedness of the pioneers of the 1890s and the continuing tradition of documentary evidence through the two world wars. Yet there is something of apology and special pleading in many of these and, admittedly, in this contribution. Why? While historical publications offering advice to teachers refer to film in various forms, it is only in the last few years that the Historical Association's journal, *History*, has begun to review films. In *Teaching History*, a magazine devoted to advice and experiment in that field, film reviews have been remarkable for their single appearance (vol. i,3). Furthermore the value of coins, 'simulation', drama and field work as contributions to history has been analysed — but not film. Again, why?

The most potent reason for the comparative neglect of what has been called 'the complete visual aid' over the years has been one of technical difficulty. Although 16mm projectors have long been standard equipment in secondary schools, their maintenance has been sadly neglected. The enthusiastic teacher soon becomes frustrated by simple faults: mechanical failure of the projector, a broken bulb and no replacement, inaudible sound from the amplifier and too much from an unserviced motor. For practical purposes the use of the projector can be beset by so many potential dangers that it is easier to rely on less complicated aids. There is a whole series of problems connected with this fundamental difficulty. The use of a specialised room, usually with inadequate blackout and screen, makes timetable and room changes necessary and this, in turn, is further complicated by the need for lengthy advance booking of the films required. If these are organisational difficulties which can be overcome with ingenuity and determination, more often the basic question of cost is the final stumbling block. With very tight school budgets it is, on occasion, difficult to justify even the return postage on free films. The hire charge for other films may be critical on a department's capitation and it is impossible to weigh the outright purchase of a film against that of essential textbooks. Little wonder that a personal survey of fifty secondary schools in Lancashire in 1968 showed that only twelve, of the twenty who replied, used films in their history teaching.

Yet, despite the undoubted disadvantages and difficulties, these twelve schools did use film, and there are many practical schemes where motion pictures of various kinds are an integral part of the history syllabus. The expense and disruption are obviously, in these cases, outweighed by the advantages, and teachers are increasingly aware of the value of film, television and video cassette. Is the teacher justified in battling with the apparently intractable problems outlined above?

The value of the film in the classroom will depend largely on the manner in which it is used; as with all audio-visual aids it is simply the tool of the teacher. History is so bedevilled by self-searching that the teacher is often uncertain of precise aims and thus any aid can be wasted. Without entering into the educational and philosophical questions involved, history in the classroom is largely concerned with response: an intellectual, emotional or imaginative response to something which happened in the past. (For a discussion of this question see D.G. Watts, *The Learning of History*, London, 1972.) In a world saturated by the visual image, this response can arguably best be stimulated by the visual. But the film, which is the instrument for this, is not a passive element: while imparting information, it can fire the imagination and yet carries a seductive authority which can paralyse the critical faculty. There is a tendency by teacher and taught to accept the flickering image where they would be more sceptical of the written word. This is particularly true of the use of contemporary film, newsreel or documentary, where, too often, it is simply used in the same way as a still photograph to illustrate dress, appearance or place, when the dynamics of the image are far more important. A wartime British newsreel can convey atmosphere, but, if looked at without insight, can convey little else. Turning down the commentary and analysing the visual content can show the important bias of the sound track; a discussion of the music and camera movements can reveal how subtly (or blatantly) the propaganda element is conveyed. Careful use of such a piece of documentary evidence can produce a fuller and more intelligent response than its use as mere illustration.

Only a proportion of any history syllabus lends itself to such treatment, however, and most of the films used in schools are more concerned with narrative or reconstruction. These have their place in the classroom, but must be treated with equal caution. Sir Arthur Elton claimed that a film is 'not a medium to teach statistic, date or place' (*Aslib Proceedings*, 7 (1955), 211), but all too often the film produced specifically for the classroom attempts just that. Although Elton's advice is, in the main, true, such a film can be of considerable value — if it can perform its informative function better than the teacher. With the aid of models, plans and pictures a history teacher can deal well with the development of castles, but a good film can cover the same ground in equal detail and more quickly and effectively. Animation, coupled with photographic resources the teacher cannot rival, can produce a reasoned and easily comprehended explanation of developments over a multiplicity of areas; the use of contemporary prints, paintings, newspapers and modern locations can recreate a distant age. It is in this latter sphere that film can 'miraculously illuminate and reveal', to quote Elton once more. Every teacher of history experiences the profound difficulty of stimulating intelligent sympathy with the past, and understanding of people and places within a particular time span. It can be done simply by the contagious enthusiasm of the teacher, by the stimulus of reading, seeing and visiting — and the film can provide an important element of all these experiences. Paris in 1848 is beyond recall but Daumier's sketches can recreate it, and twenty minutes of moving and evocative images and sound can provide a more immediate impression than a teacher, who would need to deal with the subject at much greater length. Whatever the doubts about dramatic reconstructions, the success of historical television and cinema films demonstrates their impact. Children can be educated into a true assessment of them by being exposed to a similar experience at school: at all levels pupils can enjoy Drake's dramatic exploits in the Pacific, the Pilgrims' voyage to the New World, Livingstone's mission to Africa. At a simple level such romantic stories can stimulate interest in further reading or, possibly, classroom dramatisation. At more sophisticated levels the film version can be compared with original accounts and details of contemporary conditions, and can lead to discussion of the validity of the interpretation and of historical reconstruction as a whole.

Here is the crux of the use of film of any description: the response, simple or sophisticated, it can produce, because history is concerned not only with the development of logical reasoning but also with that of emotional and imaginative maturity through the appreciation of other people in other ages. Films, whether dramatic, documentary or newsreel, can encourage identification and create atmosphere. To see and hear Martin Luther King, to watch the spectacle of a Nuremberg Rally, to follow the evolution of the written word, or to observe the ordered existence of a medieval monastery: all provide in different ways a necessary historical experience. Here the influence can often be in advance of the apparent stage of the child's development. Nicholas Pronay in *The Use of Film in History Teaching* (Historical Association, 1972) has pointed out how people can follow a complex story more easily in the cinema and can sustain interest in a difficult argument when it is integrated with the film. Young secondary school children can be introduced to the technical development of the internal combustion engine, the changing style of the motor car and its influence on transport and urban expansion in a single ten-minute film. Any one element in this would involve considerable difficulties for a teacher unaided — but such an introduction opens great possibilities for discussion, for imaginative writing, for model making. An intelligent and concerned appreciation of the life of a collier can be triggered by a study of documents and films amongst children whose experience and verbal ability are limited. Few children below the ages of fourteen or fifteen, and few even beyond that age, command the language skills necessary to deal with academic history, and it is with the majority of children of such restricted literary ability that teachers should be concerned. 'School history appears to be a satisfactory subject for the literate and verbal élite, but not for the remainder of the school population', wrote M. Honeybone in a survey of the development of formal historical thought (*Teaching History*, 2

(1970), 149). If history is to survive it must become a suitable subject for the whole school population, and, to ensure this, the history teacher needs to break out of the literary trap. The tyranny of the written word still dominates the teaching of history at a time when communication has become multi-dimensional. If we are to reach modern generations of children it is essential to overcome this preoccupation. Few historians regard pictorial evidence as valid to the same extent as documentary or archaeological; fewer still think in visual terms. One of the difficulties was indicated by J.F. Kerslake: 'the visual is not interchangeable with the written record; sometimes they support one another, but their interpretation requires quite different disciplines' ('Pictures as documents', *International Affairs*, 33 (1957), 459). While the training of historians neglects education in this interpretation there is little hope of making the break-through to the semi-literate and image-oriented youth in the schools. Teachers must learn how to 'read' the pictorial evidence, which, up to now, has largely been regarded as simple illustration of the text. For many children the picture is far the more important and informative element, more easily comprehensible than several pages of difficult wordage. The teacher needs to understand the implications of the visual evidence and how to educate the child's perception. Although this applies to all pictorial matter it is even more important when the picture moves, for here the dynamics of a moving image reinforced by sound can produce effects different from those anticipated by the teacher – and frequently from those intended by the film-maker. A trained historian brings to the film a fund of subsidiary information and visual impressions, an awareness of the meaning of word and image not shared by the child. On the other hand a pupil with a receptive imagination uncluttered by preconception may respond spontaneously to the stimulus of a film in a manner not anticipated by the teacher, but just as valid. A film intended to show the horror and degradation of war can, by its visual impact, produce a jingoistic and bloodthirsty response; only by careful analysis of the material is it possible to assess what the evidence really shows, as opposed to what we expect it to show. Close scrutiny of five minutes of film, analysing camera movement and the construction of the sequence, contrasting sound and image, identifying references, can, at once, be an important introduction to methodology and the prompting of a critical capacity for viewing other material. In this sphere the children in the schools are, potentially, as well equipped as the academic historian, because they have grown up in surroundings of visual communication, and the appeal to them is more direct than is the written word. But all film should not – and cannot – be used in this manner; just as some topics lend themselves to a close study and others to the broader sweep, so some films are to be used as a general survey, a background of impressionistic images. These, too, should not pass uncriticised but children should be encouraged to look, contrast and compare: if they are educated to an appreciation of technique they can quickly detect bias, misrepresentation or omissions. There is room therefore for the intensive study of pictorial evidence, but this should not be turned into a pedantic literary exercise; although the techniques are similar to those used in the study of documents, the stimulus and the response are different. The emphasis must remain on imaginative involvement in the past; the careful scholastic interpretation and dissection of history cannot come until the fifth and sixth forms. Film must not be made the excuse for further exercises in dull comprehension and tedious writing, it must be the springboard for discussion, dramatisation and sympathetic understanding.

Once accept that film is not only useful but essential for history teaching, what is available? The most widely used and easily obtained film is 16mm, although 8mm is being introduced into many film libraries, and the 16mm projector is normal school equipment. This width of film is usually available in various reel sizes, governed by length: one reel is approximately 400 feet in length with a running time of eleven minutes. The hire cost varies so considerably that the novice must do a great deal of preliminary research, but there are very good initial guides, such as *The Use of Film in History Teaching* (Historical Association, 1972) and the catalogues issued by the National Audio-Visual Aids Library. It is impossible to go into details of sources as they are so numerous, but there are several main categories of film which demand different assessment and treatment in history lessons.

The most obvious type is the 'educational' film, specifically made for the classroom. This can vary from the illustrated lecture, through the use of contemporary material, to the 'dramatic' reconstruction or a mixture of all these elements. The greatest fault of many of these is their intended simplicity: by aiming at a low common denominator they tend to underestimate the intellectual capacity of the children. Shortage of finance can also have dire effects, so that dramatic incidents may be reduced to a single actor on a galloping horse, or to uncredited clips from poor feature film. There is no easy way of judging the merit of such productions: a title gives little indication and the company's synopsis does not always indicate the actual material used in the film. Those distributors who aim at the educational market frequently indicate the age level intended but, despite no doubt expert advice, this is not always a good guide: the best films can be used with any age group, the worst with none. Each teacher will need to judge the film with his own pupils in mind, and can only do this ultimately by viewing it personally. Seeing one film from an educational series, or from a particular production company, will normally give an indication of the general quality, but individual directors or advisers can make considerable differences to the specific film; one good piece of work on, say, Norman castles, does not necessarily mean that one on the feudal system in the same series will be of equal value.

If specifically educational film has to be treated with caution, even more so must other categories, but here the field is very wide and apparently unpromising films can have a far-reaching impact. Many commercial firms and most governments produce films designed also for use in the classroom, but more are for

161

general information, entertainment or simple advertisement. Mainly from information centres, like the Central Office of Information, or from commercial distributors comes the straightforward documentary, aiming at giving information about an event, or communicating a particular point of view. The range here is from the detailed use of contemporary prints, as in the French *Napoleon III*, to the authentic dramatisation of the B.B.C.'s *Culloden*, or the compilation of material in a biography of Leverhulme. All are documentaries and all need to be treated with care. Reconstructions are more easily seen to be 'angled' and historically biased, whereas there is a temptation to take the films of contemporary material at face value. It is useful to know the source of the documentary and to have some knowledge of the reasons for its production: whether it is a personal project, a piece of special pleading, or an example of commercial or government publicity. That a film on the development of the helicopter is produced by a petroleum firm does not make it less valuable as a visual aid, nor more biased than if it were produced by an educational foundation — provided its source is taken into account. Industrial firms obviously concentrate upon their own products and inventions, but do not necessarily take a narrow view of their province: animal feedstuffs leads into a consideration of eighteenth-century farming; drilling for oil raises the problems of palaeontology; modern cotton is linked with ancient Egypt. Government agencies offer a varied selection of historical documentaries of equally varied technical quality and, once more, there is need to distinguish between those based firmly on original contemporary material, whether painting, print or cinematography, and those which illustrate by re-creation. There is special need for caution — and visual education — because the use of later feature films without citation in the context of a particular event can be misleading. Eisenstein's *October* has appeared many times, uncredited, as apparently authentic footage of the 1917 revolution, and the history of 'faked' newsreel is as old as the cinema itself (see J. Leyda, *Films Beget Films,* London, 1964).

Often the feature or entertainment film is quoted as useful in the history lesson and some teachers find it valuable, but its very length is against it. It would be impossible to show a full-length film in lesson time, and hardly justifiable if possible. There is no reason why a feature film should not appear as an integral part of the syllabus if it is relevant, but it must, of necessity, be shown out of school time and be expensive for school funds. The most practical way to deal with the problems of length and cost is to come to an arrangement with the school film society, if there is one: if not, it may be difficult to justify the expenditure of from £8 to £20 for one showing. The temptation is to see the film for its content rather than its relevance. It is difficult to think of any 'historical' film which does not tell more about the society and circumstances in which it was made than about those which it is supposed to represent. The most valuable role of the entertainment film is to give insights into the attitudes and preconceptions of the makers and of their social values — but it might be difficult for schoolchildren to see it in this light. This is not to deny the importance of the good motion picture; the visual images, the dynamic impact and the historical assumptions and arguments can contribute to class discussion and lead to important and original work. But historical films are the equivalent of the historical novel, rather than textbooks or select documents: for example, the film of *The Grapes of Wrath*, although nearly contemporary with the events it portrays, is one stage further removed than the novel and not to be compared with the photo-reporting of James Agee's *Let Us Now Praise Famous Men*. Besides the full feature film there are also 'study extracts' of ten to twenty minutes' length available for the more noteworthy productions. Although aimed at aesthetic appreciation rather than historical analysis, they are of interest to the teacher. They can be useful in the consideration of technique, which is so important in assessing the overall influence of the visual image. A close look at how effects are created by camera angles, cutting and montage in a fictional film can help in analysing the documentary or newsreel. Where the meaning to be conveyed is obvious through its immediacy and contrivance, the technique involved in creating it can be more easily seen than where it is less obvious because, in some cases, less conscious. The fiction film is an important educator of the senses if used correctly, but its appreciation is not necessarily a part of the historical process; it helps to sharpen an instrument which can be used in that process.

The final group of films, as yet not widely used in schools, consists of those which can be classed as original documents. Although many documentaries contain much archival footage, it is edited to a particular view and treated as illustration rather than evidence, the commentary is, at times, at variance with the material, and this material is not always as originally presented; to watch such a film is like reading a presumably scholarly work with documents abbreviated, misquoted, altered and uncited. However, this misuse of evidence does not necessarily detract from it. It is not possible always to use unedited or unchanged documents in the classroom; they need to be transcribed and translated, yet the teacher accepts that it is important to preserve the elements of originality and contemporaneity in them. Thus with film, editing, shortening and sometimes translating will be necessary, but the resulting product should be judged in similar terms to a document, though as a document which has an immediate and total emotional as well as intellectual appeal. The stark reality of a single baby crying in the midst of the utter demolition of a Shanghai air raid can, at once, convey the desolation of that child and the impact such an image would have on the cinema-goers of the time. The magnificence of the Delhi Durbar, the violence of the 1911 strike in Liverpool, the death of Emily Davidson on the Derby race track, the Ascot fashions and the solemn funeral of Edward VII communicate the atmosphere of pre-war England, but also tell much of the attitudes of the film-makers and of the society of the time. Nor is this appreciation of the evidence confined to those with great ability in verbal reasoning and maturity;

163

where primary school children may find it difficult to be plunged into the parish records, local newspaper files or contemporary diaries, they can listen to parents and grandparents and see the events which concerned them. Later the sixth-form student can analyse the depth in which these events were covered in the various media, the suppressions and omissions, and contrast them with what has been learned since. For this approach, however, there is as yet little material — what is available has to be quarried from longer compilations or children's attention has to be drawn to television coverage. The Open University makes great use of this archival material, but it is not available in its original form to schools. The Historical Association Film Committee has planned the production of suitable film 'kits' for use in the classroom, but in the film world the questions of copyright and finance are very complex and it is more difficult to get the 'raw' film material to the student than it is the equivalent written evidence. Until it is more readily accessible the teacher will have to remain the magpie he has long been forced to be, making use of such sections of documentary or educational films as he can obtain.

The way in which a film is used in the classroom, whatever its nature, will depend upon what is expected of film and pupils. A short documentary could be the starting-point for discussion, the subject for analysis or the inspiration for imaginative work; and in each case the preparation and development will be different. First the teacher must secure his film and this is not always easy. It is sometimes possible to book a film at short notice of two or three weeks, but more often it is essential to order a whole series at least one term ahead. Having decided on the films required and their position in the term's work, it is better to offer the library or hiring firm alternative dates, so the syllabus should be sufficiently flexible to allow for this. It is important also to book the films for a later date than anticipated to allow for the inevitable disruptions in the school timetable which delay arrival at a given point in the curriculum: it is easier to put off a topic than to hurry it forward. For practical purposes the film often arrives a week in advance and so can be used then, provided the conditions of hire are not infringed. In this area the primary schools have obvious advantages over the secondary as their timetables are less rigid.

Having chosen and ordered the film, and presuming it arrives on time, it must be viewed before being shown to the class. The teacher not only needs to know its content, but to make sure that the sound track is audible, the film really appropriate and the equipment in working order. It is disastrous to present a supposedly modern visual aid to a class, only to discover that the film has not been rewound, or the commentary cannot be heard: check the film and all the equipment immediately before use. If the school is lucky enough to have a technician he should be relied upon, if not, the teacher intending to use film regularly should attend some course in the operation of a film projector. Most local authorities organise such courses, and some film libraries request that film and equipment should be handled only by trained members of staff. On the technical side many things can cause difficulties, but this is not the place to deal with them — the National Committee for Audio-Visual Aids in Education printed a useful introductory article to this in *Visual Education*, November 1972.

The first viewing of the film will determine its best use and the teacher will have to judge whether his original intention was the correct one. Almost any type of film can be used as an introduction to a topic, or for summing it up. In considering the film as an introduction, the first criterion is its factual content, and the teacher needs to note carefully the relevant sequences, so that the children will benefit most from them. The preparation will depend entirely upon the ability of the group: a questionnaire is a useful guide to the main features and it can be a detailed appraisal, requiring written answers at the end, or simply a series of suggested highlights to prompt subsequent discussion. The film should be seen by the class as a whole, otherwise it loses its impact as a film, but where necessary it should be stopped and discussed with, possibly, only one relevant section studied in any detail. Ideally it should be shown twice, but this is the counsel of perfection in an imperfect world: a twenty-minute film cannot be gone through more than once, even in the standard double period. However, it is often possible to run a short sequence for further comment, after the first viewing. A word of warning here — it is not advisable to switch the projector bulb on and off at short intervals as the bulb will 'blow' and a replacement is expensive. With this proviso, a teacher should never be afraid of stopping a film when the lesson demands; there is a tendency to regard the moving image as sacrosanct, and those who would happily use only six frames from a long film strip feel it necessary to comment upon all 800 feet of a film. Where the emphasis is on facts, then the whole lesson should be structured around them and, although more can be communicated in a short time by film, it is important not to over-estimate the capacity of the children. Above all the follow-up work should not be a mere comprehension test on the information, but a development of the visual points made — if possible a development along practical and visual lines. For example a film on medieval castles can lead from its own treatment of the subject to sketches for improvements in castle design, a film script or dramatisation of a siege, models of the various types of castle and drawings of medieval warfare. If interest has been aroused in life inside the castle, similar work can be done on various aspects of this. What emerges will be governed partly by the teacher's preparation, but mainly by the children's responses. A specific element or line may be emphasised and studied, and this will be more stimulating than a vague and generalised wander through the variety of points raised by the whole film.

This same film could provide the end of such a study, instead of a beginning, and here attention will be directed to aspects dealt with by individual children. Criticisms should be encouraged of what is left out of the film or what is insufficiently covered. In this way the film becomes more than a pulling-together of class activities — it acts as a reinforcement of what has been learnt and, incidentally, stimulates a critical assessment of word and picture. Thus the information contained in the film is not just important for itself — such information can be learnt in other ways — but in the manner of its presentation and in its stimulus to the children. With carefully drawn oral or written questions, the faults of a bad film can be as illuminating as the virtues of a good one. If the children have studied the subject beforehand and the film is dealt with section by section, most of the class will be able to see and comment on its shortcomings. The discovery of error in an adult and seemingly authoritative account is a profound encouragement to the young historian: someone whose general educational achievement is low is not often in the position to recognise and correct, from superior knowledge, the mistakes of authority.

In a slightly different category and calling for a different approach is the film used for the creation of atmosphere and sympathetic understanding. The import of a film may be factual, but its prime function in the classroom may be the stimulation of imaginative and emotional response. There seems to be a distinct fear of arousing emotions in the history lesson, but this side of a child's development should not be neglected: the people of history cannot live until they arouse the emotions. Anger at the treatment of shiploads of slaves, anguish over the boy chimney sweep, tears over the death of Mary, Queen of Scots, laughter at the defenestration of Prague, all are essential historical responses, however they may be frowned upon by the academic. A teacher, unaided, may find it difficult to arouse the involvement of the children, a film by its impact can — but so few of those produced for schools attempt to do so, and here the committed documentary and the vivid re-creation, or the original film are the most valuable. The child's interest and appreciation can be involved by an impressionistic montage of Elizabethan England, the combination of visual image and correct music and words can evoke a past age for those who will never read Shakespeare or hear a madrigal. Genuine sympathy is invoked for the plight of refugees when their position is graphically explained, and this in children whose horizon does not normally extend beyond the immediate vicinity. Where less attention is being paid to factual presentation, then different preparation is necessary: in an exceptional case the showing of a film without introduction or explanation can have a profound effect. The Polish film *Ambulance* — a reconstruction of the liquidation of children in an ambulance — has a stunning effect on older students, without any preliminary build-up. In most cases it will be sufficient to set the film or subject in context; a formal questionnaire can be a disincentive to this approach, because children will become preoccupied with finding detailed answers and miss the point and impact of the whole. Nevertheless the film cannot be allowed simply to wash over inert spectators; it should be followed up by directed questions and the children encouraged to express their views. There can be no easy guide-lines here for each film must be treated as a whole, and the questions should be prompted by the film itself, not by preconceptions of what

166

to expect from the children. A difficult balance has to be managed between making capital out of the immediate impact and giving the pupils an opportunity to think out their responses. In some cases the instant reaction is silence which prodding destroys without stimulating, and the real discussion and benefit will not emerge until the following day. The average secondary school timetable is a grave disadvantage in this case — too often history appears only once per week and follow-up work can only come when the effect has largely faded. All the more reason, if at all possible, to see the film, or parts of it, more than once: first for the initial impression, then to reinforce and rekindle that impression. If this can be done in separate lessons so much the better, but this depends upon the availability of the film and very few schools can afford to possess their own copies. Failing this double viewing, the development could centre around further visual material; the after-image should not be dissipated but restimulated by the study and discussion of much relevant and related material. It is fatal to aroused emotional involvement to be faced by yet another exercise on 'Imagine you were . . . '

Film in the classroom can be used for information, recapitulation, discussion or imaginative stimulation — in these cases it is an instrument to be used in the encouragement of historical experience. It should be used more frequently as the object for the exercise of that historical experience. That this can be done with university and college students is obvious. The showing of a compilation film has triggered many of the obvious and necessary questions; how much of this was seen at the time; what was the original commentary; how does the film reporting compare with other contemporary evidence? Consideration of the limitations of documentaries as truthful record of the past has led to a greater interest in the original material and the way in which it was collected and put together. There is no reason why a similar process cannot exist in schools: a newsreel of the 1930s will, at first, arouse amusement, but then curiosity as to why certain items were included and treated in a particular way. Here careful preparation and structured questioning is essential. In showing, say, a documentary made for the Silver Jubilee of 1935, it is not enough simply to point to the changing fashions and incidents, but the children must be encouraged to look for genuine 'archive' material and acted scenes, to list what was shown and find out what was not. It is fairly easy for them to see the obvious dramatisations, and with guidance to analyse how a sequence is put together to give a particular impression. This is 'textual' criticism of quite a high order and possible of achievement by those who could not understand the complexities of written evidence. This approach demands greater use of the film, certainly one quick run through and a general chat are not enough, but it teaches far more of the attitudes, preoccupations and prejudices of the time. This might be followed by a discussion of what might have been included in the film and the preparation of a script for the treatment of the next Jubilee. If this is applicable to one film, the technique can be used with many: a ten-minute compilation on the Suffragettes, propaganda films of the two world wars, Ministry of Information films of the same period, or the extensive newsreel coverage since the beginning of the century.

The film opens up new areas for the history teacher and can help communicate with those whom the normal approach does not interest. Not only does it inform and stimulate imagination, but it can be used as direct evidence and introduce historical method. The impact of film may never again reach that of Lumière's train arriving at the station, which sent the audience fleeing in terror, but unless we can instil some of that originality and vitality and, even, that terror into our history teaching, Henry Ford will have been justified.

# 10. History on the public screen I

DONALD WATT

A certain experience of conference-going where historians and professionals of the media, film and television, congregate has taught me that there are a number of fundamental 'false problems' that have to be cleared out of the way before any intelligent discussion, let alone co-operation is possible.

That this process should be undertaken is, I take it, self-evident. For, at least on television, history has become big business. The Thames Television series *The World at War* was an enormous success both commercially and in its public reception. The B.B.C. series *The Mighty Continent*, though received with mixed feelings by television critics (of whom more anon) and professional historians, was also a considerable success. The degree of the success of these two series can be measured in the immense sales enjoyed in each case by the book of the series. On the other hand one has such monstrosities as the B.B.C.'s series on the British Empire, which was even denounced on the floor of the House of Lords, or its equally appalling *Churchill's People*, a series of historical playlets supposedly based on Winston Churchill's *History of the English-Speaking Peoples*, in which central episodes of English history are re-enacted as seen through the eyes of the 'common people'.

The first of these false problems (indeed the first two) can best be expressed in opposed propositions as follows:

The historian's main concern is accuracy: the producer of film and television is concerned with entertainment. The unspoken premise of the first proposition is that to be accurate is to be dull. The unspoken premise of the opposed proposition is that to be entertaining it is necessary to distort or misrepresent. A good lie, so it is maintained, is always more entertaining than a dull truth.

The second set of propositions, in some sense, complements the first. They may be stated as follows:

The historian (or more properly the academic historian) is concerned only with words. Given his preferences he will lecture, and all the audience will see is a 'talking head', that bogey of producers. The producer by contrast, is really interested only in what appears on the screen, the visual impact of the medium. Given half a chance he will go after anything provided that it is 'good vision' (or good television), irrespective of its relevance to the chosen topic. He will always prefer *art nouveau* 'wall-paper' to the plausible, credible narrative.

To call these 'false problems' is not to deny that they can exist. There are always unimaginative historians just as there are always irresponsible rating-bound producers. Indeed, when collaboration between historians and makers of documentary films for educational or television purposes began, one could collect encyclopaedias of horror stories wherever proponents of either camp could be found in Britain. But in the last decade there has grown up, as a result of mutual experience, and a sequence of conferences, a convergence of minds and a mutual comprehension of the technical problems, at least at the level of the producer and the historian. The problems the historian faces with the media at the time of writing are usually created by the administrators and policy-makers, not by the producers and the cameramen.

The subject of this essay, then, is to be the problems the historian faces with the media in the making of historical films of a non-fictional kind. This, of necessity, excludes all film but the purely educational, much of which is made for sale to public service or educational television anyway. Examples will be drawn mainly from the author's own experiences, in so far as these can be discussed without risking action for libel. But like most if not all of the other contributors to this book, the author feels that it is intensely important that the new media should be made use of and understood in all their aspects.

It is, of course, self-evident that the making of a non-fictional film or television programme on a historical theme is as much an exercise in historiography as the composition of a learned monograph, the editing of a collection of historical source materials, the writing of a historical best-seller or the composition of an article for an illustrated part-work designed for a mass audience. All of these present their own problems of composition and presentation, from the precise form a learned footnote or the citation of a source should take in the first, to the problem of how much one can compress of, for example, the first Moroccan crisis into two thousand words, in the last example.

It is equally self-evident that a historical statement made audio-visually is different from one made in writing. The tempo is different, there can be no re-call, no flipping-back of the page, no elaboration of parallel themes by footnotes or parentheses. Then there is infinitely more written evidence than visual material. Paradoxically this is least true of ancient and medieval history where the paucity of written material must be made up by the wealth of artefact and archaeologically-obtained materials. A series such as the B.B.C.'s recent *The Roman Way* illustrates how effectively this material can be used to enlighten and entertain (the use of Hollywood silent film of classical epics was a barely pardonable gimmick which neither added very much to nor subtracted very much from the total impact of the series). It is however characteristic of the problems presented by the visual evidence even here that it is at its richest for social history, and at its weakest on the political side. The impact of certain film however can be out of all proportion to its factual value. I know of few more effective ways of communicating the losses suffered by the front line combatants in World War I than the panning shots of the military cemeteries employed, for example, in the much criticised B.B.C. series, *The Mighty Continent*. The real difficulty arises always in audio-visual historiography when the attempt is made to make a statement for which no visual material is available. This is a problem all historians and producers must face repeatedly and for which there is no universal solution.

The problems the historian faces with the media may best be described under the heading of curses. *Curse No.1* arises because the media are administered by men of considerable sophistication, often highly educated, but of an education that in contemporary and recent history is usually a combination of out-of-date views and prejudices. It is embodied in the phenomenon of the amateur historian whose views were formed by the Left Book Club, an animal not tolerated for a moment in professional circles, who is rendered doubly intolerable by his mon-opoly access to the viewing audience conferred by the limited choice of tele-vision programmes. One of the hardy perennials resulting is Paul Rotha's *Life and Times of Adolf Hitler*; another, equally objectionable, was the series on the Third Reich, *The Rise and Fall of the Third Reich*, made on the basis of William Shirer's best-seller on the same theme, a book severely criticised for its restate-ment of old myths by every professional historian who reviewed it. I have written elsewhere of the combination of tendentious statement with verifiable inaccuracies exemplified by these two series[1] and do not need to repeat myself here. The B.B.C.'s action in rescreening the Rotha series showed a remarkable insensibility to criticism. Rotha's reputation as a maker of documentaries was, and is, considerable; but this should not be adequate excuse for reshowing, without comment, a documentary film of a historical rather than a contempor-ary nature, the only valuable historical contribution in it being the reproduction of Rotha's viewpoint, one forever imprisoned in the populist prejudices and half-truths of the British film-makers' popular front.

*Curse No.2* arises from the element of finance. The budgets for the great his-torical television series such as I.T.V.'s *The World at War* and the B.B.C.'s *The Great War* and *The Mighty Continent* run of necessity into hundreds of thou-sands of pounds. The B.B.C. has attempted to deal with this by dividing the cost with foreign agencies such as West German Television or the *Time–Life* agency. This, in itself, already arouses problems of audience, since there is little experi-ence or knowledge that a producer can assume to be common to British, American and West German audiences. But the anxieties of the financial auth-orities can lead to other difficulties, such as, for example, the setting of a time limit for the making of the series that makes originality of thought or approach simply impossible. Four months was all that was given in one celebrated series for the unit responsible to produce the first programme. A solution to the time-limit question recently produced is to engage a multiplicity of producers and writers, giving each a random allocation of programmes from the whole, as it might be programmes one, five, eleven and sixteen, irrespective of their having anything to do with each other, so that instead of a single conception designing and unifying the various programmes in the series, the series degenerates into a succession of individual programmes united only by a title or possibly an outlook.

A third set of problems which the heavy cost of historical series creates is the dissipation of know-how. The standard unit responsible for a historical film or television series consists of producer(s), writer(s), editors, musical contributors, cameramen etc. It may or may not include a historical adviser. But much of the most essential work, the actual discovery of visual material, is the task of the lowly and underpaid researchers, often, too often, bright graduates fresh from university with degree qualifications only vaguely relevant to the subject of the series and only the remotest of indications as to where to go for material. By the time they have finished the series they probably have amassed between them a very considerable body of knowledge of the available material. But with the end of the project the team is broken up and its members scattered to the four winds. So that when, four or five years later, a Granada mogul or a B.B.C. deputy director or whatever strikes the desk with his open hand and says it is time for another historical epic, the whole process has to be begun again with a new team which has to learn the business from the beginning. The temptation, the necessity almost, of using again the same familiar material, is obvious. Only the expertise, acquired on a shoestring, of the professional film archivists (which must include the invaluable catalogue of the Slade Film History Register), with their international connections, can save them from banal repetition or, most heinous of all faults, the misuse of material to illustrate something which it does not in fact depict.

*Curse No. 3* of the media is the battle for ratings and the competition between the channels. The B.B.C. is particularly open to accusation here. One remembers the deliberate placing of its highly publicised exercise in voyeurism, *The Family* (a slavish copy of an American original), so that it conflicted with the last five or so programmes of Thames Television's *World at War* series; the reshowing of *The Great War* on a Sunday afternoon; the pre-emption of the normal time slot of the Tuesday documentary for *The Mighty Continent*, which gave gratuitous offence to the fairly sizeable audience of auto-didacts and 'concerned' who regularly watched the displaced programme.

*Curse No. 4* is the straitjacket of time. If a multiple programme series is envisaged then it must for programme-planning purposes consist of six, seven, nineteen or twenty-six programmes since programme planners always work on three months at a time, or rather on quarter years of thirteen weeks each. Within this each programme has a fixed running time, usually of forty-five to fifty minutes or so (shortened on commercial television by the necessity of allowing for the insertion or addition of advertising material). This is not always too serious a problem for the producer, though it may offer a temptation to visual padding, and it certainly sets problems of balance over the series as a whole. The worst sufferer is the Open University whose time slot is severely limited to twenty-four minutes, far too short to deal adequately with the chosen subjects.

172

Anyone who has participated in making films on historical subjects for the Open University will remember the agonies of cutting what seems an excellently balanced forty minutes or so down by half its length.

The worst curse of the media, however, is the contempt shown by the top brass for the taste and judgement of their audience. Despite the abundant evidence of their own statistics of the existence of an enormous television audience for mildly educational material, especially on subjects connected with recent and contemporary history, war history in particular, they are petrified by the fear that if anything intellectually above the Noddy history book market is shown on their screens there will be a mass rush of viewers into alternative channels. The success of highly specialised general knowledge programmes such as *University Challenge* or *Mastermind* ought to have persuaded them that the large lay audience which they know to exist for films and series on historical subjects is intelligent enough to deserve respect. But the fear remains, to be expressed in such gimmicks as the introduction into serious historical programmes of showbiz personalities carefully talking down to the audiences,[2] or the metamorphosis of a collective historical view into that of a single personality as in Alistair Cooke's *America*, itself a gorgeously produced exercise in amateur and myopic pontification by a writer—journalist whose ideological view of Anglo-America is one to which few professional historians would subscribe today.

This perhaps is the point to bring in another curse with which historians and media men alike have to contend: the absence of any serious and well informed criticism of historical films and television programmes. Television criticism itself is confined to the dailies, the Sundays and the occasional weekly. Each paper or magazine usually employs only one critic who is expected to cover everything from documentaries to drama, from *University Challenge* to *Top of the Pops*, from *Yesterday's Men* to *Tomorrow's World*. What respectable journal would expect one book reviewer to cover everything from *Winnie the Pooh* to Winston Churchill's *War Memoirs*? Yet this is what the television critic is supposed to do. Only one critic, Philip Purser of the *Sunday Telegraph*, has to the author's knowledge displayed any interest in the debate between producer and historian.[3] Alone among the weeklies, *New Society* has employed a leading professional historian, Douglas Johnson, to review series such as *The World at War* or *The Mighty Continent* on the basis of having seen more than two random selections from the entire series at a preview. It is the lack of a solid body of informed criticism which is most felt by the practitioners in the field of historical documentary. The *Journal of the Society of Film and Television Arts* is too much of a trade journal to supply this lack.[4] Nationally perhaps there is too small an audience or readership to keep a journal devoted to this field alive, but room might be found for something on an international scale if funds were forthcoming. At the moment those who choose to use film or television for the making of historiographical statements have only the praise or censure of the ignorant or the appraisal of audience research as a guide to their success or failure. The first is

173

only of use or disadvantage when they are seeking to convince the bureaucracy of the feasibility or desirability of their tackling another historical theme. The second may be in addition a gratifying reward for the effort spent and the tension generated by the making of the programme. But it tells them little or nothing in answer to their questions in detail, as to variation in style and technique. With a multi-producer series like *The World at War* such mass approval is of little help to the individual producer.

In this it is easy to be cynical about the lot of the historical adviser. In many series he simply acts as a consultant: that is to say he is consulted by the programme researchers or the producer whenever they feel the need to do so but takes no responsibility for the final product. The historian who is inveigled into such a relationship is well advised to insist that his name be left off the credits or he may find himself held responsible by his professional colleagues for all the points on which he ought to have been consulted and was not. In some cases he simply functions as a means of internal persuasion. He will be asked to write a paper or a historical memorandum on suggested approaches or treatments, with which an ambitious aide may convince a reluctant departmental director to embark on a new enterprise or entrust it to him. He will often be lured, if unwary, into giving much unrewarded time and effort to the guidance of the plausible and ambitious, only to find in the end that the finished product incorporates all the received historical error against which he has given so careful a warning. He may find too that his name in the credits is being employed as a kind of British Standards Kitemark, a guarantee of the historical acceptability of the view to which the series or programme on which he is advising is dedicated.

It is to this latter case that the remainder of this essay must be directed. The historian's criteria for judging a programme from a professional viewpoint are three in number. The subject must be completely covered, within the limits the length of the programme and the material allow. Secondly the view presented of the subject must be objective within the acceptable definition of that term as understood by professional historians. It must not be *parti pris*. It must not be anachronistic, ascribing to the actors sentiments alien to the time and culture or condemning them for not recognising values dear to the producer. It must not be ideological or slanted for purposes of propaganda. There must be no recognisable and obvious bias. It must seem to understand rather than to condemn. Thirdly, the events described, the 'facts' outlined, must be accurate, that is, in accordance with the present state of historical knowledge. Hypothesis, reconstruction, inference are all legitimate but only if they are presented under their own colours.

To ensure this the historian rash enough to take on the post of historical adviser must insist on the right to vet the finished article in adequate time for alterations to be incorporated and distortions of statement or balance removed before showing. He must vet scripts before the film is dubbed. It would be advisable for him to be familiar with the shooting script and the producer's proposed manner of treatment. It is his job to be the conscience of the unit, to keep an eye on continuity and coverage, to stand back from the myriad and one day-to-day problems of T.V. shooting on location, or of putting the film together in workshop and studio. He will find he has to be diplomatist as well as heavy gun, the producer's ally in dealing with intervention from above. He must, if possible, deter the producer from using modern film to illustrate the past or film from fictional reconstruction as if it were actuality. He must have an accurate ear and memory for the kind of misstatement that creeps in through a commentator's ad-libbing. Lastly he has to realise that it is an adviser's job to advise and that final responsibility lies with the producer. If he does not establish as early as possible where final responsibility lies, he is in for trouble later. (He would be well advised to keep a diary of his actions towards and arguments with the producer.) In the end he will still be regarded by those who notice his name among the credits as responsible for all with which they disagree. And he will long for the chance of making his own film to show how it should be done.

This is perhaps where another false problem arises; who should be dominant, historian or producer? Those who despair of ever getting the media to treat history responsibly tend to gravitate towards the British Inter-University History Film Consortium, an enterprise which conjoins the subscriptions of a number of university history departments so as to enable one of their number every so often to make its own film on a historical subject. Inevitably there is an element of home movie about the final product, even where it has been made in conjunction with a university department of film. The historian as amateur producer is no more satisfactory than the producer as amateur historian. And the pressures of academic life do not normally allow those who have made one film to make another within the time span in which they might learn from their own mistakes.

The producer-dominated series on the other hand leads directly to disasters such as that of the B.B.C.'s *British Empire* series with its glaring omissions of central facts, its facile anti-imperialist prejudice, its reconstructions of the siege of Cawnpore and the demise of Ned Kelly on the cheap, its distraction by the contemporary televisual and its general catalogue of 'awful warnings' for the future. The true relationship between historian and producer must be a kind of partnership, shading into symbiosis where each understands, even if he cannot practise, the craft of the other. Audio-visual historiography is a bimedial art, like ballet or opera.

This ideal state has been most closely approximated by the producers of the Open University whose profession it is to work with historians who co-operate by writing the script and selecting the material they wish to see incorporated into the film. This body of expertise is now being dissipated in turn since the Open University's budget will not allow new series to be made: the constriction of the very limited time slot allotted by B.B.C.2's programme planners is a source of constant frustration. Even here, the producers have to unlearn their B.B.C.-instilled terror of the switch-off or switch-over. Early programmes wasted valuable minutes establishing a locale, cameras panning around an archaeological site for example.

With that the historian and producer still face the abiding problems of audio-visual historiography. What material is available? Is it to be used to illustrate a lecture or should it be made into a silent film with a 'voice-over' commentary, talking head or mobile wall-paper? How do you make an essential point where no material exists? Do you use interviews with eye witnesses or participants in the events you are describing? There was an excellent two-part series on Austria in World War II shown on West German television made up almost entirely of selected eye witnesses telling their story, cut cleverly into each other so as to preserve the proper chronology. Can you avoid 'bang-bang film' of the kind that might have been shot anywhere from Brest to Brest-Litovsk? Can you spot faked-up film (as the B.B.C. documentary on the General Strike of 1926 most notoriously did not)?[5]

Each set of problems can only be resolved on the job itself, usually on the floor of the cutting room. There are enough and to spare without having to cope with the biggest problem of them all, the state of mind of those who direct the media, who cannot believe that waiting in front of their sets there is an educated, interested, mass audience, people unsure of their knowledge and avid for more, particularly if it will help them understand their own lives and lifetimes, and for whom there is no conflict between learning and entertainment, only between bad and good, pretentious and honest programmes. It is this amorphous and not easily defined lump of bureaucracy in the media that has created the present unsatisfactory state of audio-visual historiography in Britain with its three equally, if differently, unsatisfactory types of material, the media epics, mutilated before birth by the top brass, the home movies of the British Inter-University History Film Consortium or the straitjacketed expertise of the Open University, forever trapped in its twenty-four-minute time slots and starved of money to develop from its present level of expertise.

NOTES

1. In *History*, 55 (1970), 214–16; 58 (1973), 399–400.
2. For example, see *The Times*'s television critic's reaction to Mr Benny Green's pictorial history of London, a two-part series made for Thames Television under the title *London – the Making of a City*: 'looked splendid . . . a script which when it did not drown every fact in cliché, was plain straightforward vulgar . . . an opportunity not lost but determinedly rejected by the producer who was his own writer; a deliberate and coldly calculated decision to ruin a good idea by trying to slice it so as to serve everyone'. *The Times*, 12 February 1975.
3. See his entertaining account of a *rencontre* at Cumberland Lodge in the *Sunday Telegraph*, 28 April 1974.
4. See for example vol. 2, nos. 9–10 (1974), on *The World at War*. *History* carries reviews of films, but does not seem to be read at all in television circles.
5. See the letters of Frank Hardie and Paul Rotha in *The Times*, 22 April 1974, and the reply of Elizabeth Sussex, *ibid.*, 3 May 1974.

# 11. History on the public screen II

JERRY KUEHL

Relations between academic historians and producers of television documentaries have always been uneasy. Historians are maybe offended by the superficiality and incompleteness of programmes made without their active collaboration; while producers resent efforts by academics to impose their standards and concerns in a field which may, they think, lie outside their area of competence. What lies behind this mutual unease is, I think, a serious failure in communication between the two professions. Each misapprehends the job of the other; makes wrong assumptions about what the other can or should do; and as a result is unable to appreciate fully either the other's achievements or his limitations. In the previous chapter Donald Watt examines this problem from the standpoint of the professional historian: I write as a producer of historical documentaries for mass audiences.

Let me say right at the beginning that what seems to me to be at the heart of the matter is the question of the commentary which is an integral part of every documentary: who should write it, how should it relate to the film, to whom should it be addressed, and above all, what should it contain?

Most television documentaries are fifty minutes long. So let us consider just how much can be said in fifty minutes. B.B.C. newsreaders, who are professionally trained to speak rapidly and comprehensibly, talk at about 160 words a minute; which means that by talking *non-stop* they could deliver, in fifty minutes, a text not twice as long as this chapter. But in fact, as a rule of thumb, competent documentary producers begin to worry when a commentary takes up more than about a quarter of a programme's length. In other words, a commentary of between 1000 and 1500 words is quite long enough; any more, and the film is liable to become a kind of illustrated radio programme. It will appear to viewers as dense, overstuffed. They will be repelled, not informed. The consequence of this may be quite sobering to an academician: it is that whatever the writer wishes to say ought to be said in the equivalent of a single-page *New Statesman* article, or a *fifteen-minute* lecture. There is no way around this. If he tries to say more his audiences will understand less. They will, in time, simply switch off — figuratively or literally.

Once this point is taken, it is easy to see how inappropriate much academic criticism is. Consider for a moment the persistent academic complaint that historical documentaries invariably omit significant details, or even major themes

177

of matters which they touch. To take a particular instance, from Thames Television's *World at War* series: the introductory programme, which dealt with domestic events in Germany from 1933 to 1939, was reproached, both in public and in private, for not dealing with events in Germany from 1918 to 1933. It was also reproached for not dealing with international affairs from 1933 to 1939, and for not dealing with international affairs from 1918 to 1933, and for not dealing with British domestic affairs from 1933 to 1939, and even, by one earnest correspondent, for not having examined the United States' government's 1938 contingency plans for the mobilisation of American industrial production in the event of war breaking out in Europe. All this in a programme lasting fifty minutes.

The historian who wonders tartly why we omitted Stanley Baldwin from our account of pre-war Germany should pause to consider what he would have included and what left out, in his own 1500-word comprehensive account of the Third Reich (even if he were not limited by the necessity to confine his exposition to subjects about which film was available). That is, by misunderstanding the nature of the activity, the academic may find himself applying to it assumptions and expectations which have no hope of being fulfilled. Small wonder that professional television producers, for their part, so often think of academic historians as behaving like small children, helpfully offering their services as referees or peace-makers to Mummy and Daddy because they have not quite grasped that their parents are not really *wrestling*.

What I should like to do here is, first, to elaborate on what I think conscientious producers of historical documentaries do try to do; on how and why academic historians are liable to misunderstand both their intentions and their achievements and on what the consequences of their misunderstanding may be; then finally to offer a suggestion about what academic historians and documentary producers in fact should be able to offer each other.

First, what is it that television producers try to do? The first thing the good ones learn is that what they make are television programmes; that is to say, works which should follow the rules of *television* – which are not at all the same as those which govern the production of learned articles, or, indeed, purely literary works of any sort. The second thing they learn is that their audience is a mass audience – never fewer than several hundreds of thousands of viewers, and sometimes more than twenty million. Now these two points, that television is television and not something else, and that television is a mass medium, may seem self-evident; but their implications are often misunderstood even by many who earn their living in television. It is hardly surprising that academics may fail to appreciate them.

One characteristic of television as a communication medium is that it offers its audience virtually no time for reflection. It is a sequential medium, so to say, in which episode follows on episode, without respite. This clearly means that the medium is ideally suited to telling stories and anecdotes, creating atmosphere and mood, giving diffuse impressions. It does not lend itself easily to the detailed analysis of complex events; it is difficult to use it to relate coherently complicated narrative histories, and it is quite hopeless at portraying abstract ideas.

The reason is simply because there is no stopping *en route*, no feedback between audience and programme maker; which means that the viewer's interest in any programme is no more than the curiosity any audience has in the performance of a story-teller, who invites his listeners to attend to what he says, tries to hold their attention by all manner of devices, but does not invite, or even tolerate, interruptions. It is, of course, true that there is no opportunity for feedback in literary works, either; but it is possible to stop midway, to re-read, to reflect at leisure. It is also true that much effort has gone into trying to minimise or overcome television's defective feedback mechanisms, but none of the attempts made by such admirable agencies as the Open University are very relevant to the problems of programme making for general audiences.

It is not the fact that the skills the historians prize most are precisely those which television can use least that is surprising, so much as the idea that anyone should ever have thought otherwise — although it does become less puzzling as soon as one takes into account the intensely literary and verbal background of so many people who commission, produce, and publicly evaluate historical documentaries.

A second point about the uniqueness of television as a medium relates to commentary writing, and I have already touched on it. Commentaries are intimately related to the images which they accompany, point up, explain, call attention to, make sense of. Because of their brevity, they cannot be in any real sense exhaustive or comprehensive. They need not even be coherent, in the sense that they need not unambiguously argue that one thing or another is the case. They do not lay down the line: they evoke. The one thing they cannot do with any hope of success is to use as their models such literary forms as the learned article, the public lecture, or even the popular journalistic review. They are not an independent literary form.

Moreover, since a great many significant events, processes, decisions were never, could never, be filmed, the gaps in commentary may be dictated, not by the writer's conscious decision — as would be the case if he or she were writing a brief article for a part work — but by what is or is not available on film. An example again: relations between Church and State were very important to the leaders of the Third Reich, and, it goes without saying, to ordinary Germans too. But very little film was ever made which even showed National Socialist leaders and churchmen together, let alone doing anything significant. So considerations of Church and State were virtually omitted from our films on Nazi Germany — and from our commentary.

A third point focuses on commentary as well, but really involves the totality of the programme: how much should it try to say, or at least mention? How much dare it leave out?

## Jerry Kuehl

Historical documentaries do not exist in a vacuum. Nearly forty years after regular broadcasting began in this country, and with three channels transmitting over a hundred hours of programmes a week, it is highly unlikely that a subject will be done for the first or last time ever. Yet just this kind of awesome prospect seems to brood over the producer and academic critic alike as they approach major undertakings. No one would seriously reproach Hugh Trevor-Roper for not including in his *Last Days of Hitler* a comprehensive account of the organis- ation of the N.S.B.O. or of the Reichswehr (though if he were thought to be particularly knowledgeable about those topics, his admirers might well be dis- appointed if he never turned his attention to them). Yet this kind of reproach is regularly directed against documentary series, and even single programmes, and it is more than just a quarrel with the producer about the relative importance of various elements in a story. From the producer's point of view the fear is that *this* is the only chance there will ever be to do something — so everything possible must be done. It is this desperate last chance to catch the moving train attitude which accounts for the presence of a great deal of bewilderingly super- ficial elements, as for instance the brief mention of the Polish question in episode 25 of *The World at War* — not long enough to be informative, yet long enough to be controversial and, almost certainly, offensive to those with know- ledge of the matter, and there simply because it seemed inconceivable that a twenty-six part series should totally omit any mention of Poland once it had been conquered by the Germans in the first reel of the second programme.

Turning now to the second general consideration, that of television as a *mass* medium, a number of other special characteristics are apparent. The very num- bers involved in programming for mass audiences are daunting. Any competent university lecturer alters the style and the content of his presentations, depend- ing on whether he is dealing with a class of 150 first-year undergraduates, twenty-five third-year specialists or a postgraduate seminar. And he also shapes his manner and matter depending on whether his post is a permanent one, totally free of student pressures, or whether he is teaching in an institution where stu- dent assessment of his performance has a bearing on whether he continues in employment. Academics assume, and rightly, a high degree of professional mo- tivation on the part of their students. They are articulate and sociable; they expect to work in a systematic and sustained fashion, guided, if not positively directed, by their instructor or supervisor; they are verbally relatively skilled. They are young.

The audience to which a television producer addresses himself is not like that at all. A television producer has no students. The proportion of viewers who watch television as a part of their work is statistically trivial; the rest watch it to relax, to entertain themselves, only sometimes consciously to inform themselves. They are under no obligation to watch; they are not a captive audience in the sense that a university class or seminar is. They are unlikely to be highly edu- cated — most of them in fact have had no more schooling than is required by law. Some are young, some middle-aged, some are old age pensioners. Many are not articulate, they are all individuals and there are twenty-four million of them, at least.

It is insulting and wrong to think of this mass audience as uniform, homogeneous, ignorant; but it is equally unrealistic to think that its members will be or ought to be interested in a programme intended to entertain or instruct a highly literate, highly educated minority. A producer making a documentary for such an audience could legitimately make assumptions about its cultural furniture which would leave a popular audience utterly bewildered. (Producers know that it is as dangerous to overestimate a mass audience's knowledge as it is to underestimate its intelligence.) To take a homely illustration: any serious account of the early years of National Socialist Germany must deal with the Roehm purge. To understand this, it is obviously necessary to describe the internal organisation of the S.A., its relations with Hitler and its relations with the army. This background is not difficult to acquire from a handful of appropriate scholarly works. But it is quite unrealistic to expect that a Lewisham school leaver, now working on a building site, should have an intimate knowledge of the intricacies of National Socialist infighting in the years before Hitler's accession to power. I cannot pretend that any of the films in our *World at War* series made luminously clear what the *Sturmabteilung* represented to the life of Germans living in the Weimar Republic, still less the transformation it underwent when the government fell into the hands of the National Socialists, but I suspect that had we been better at our jobs, we could have made such things clearer; and moreover that it was our job to make such things clear. Now admittedly, there is an element of running with the hare and hunting with the hounds in what I am saying: claiming on the one hand that it is beyond the capacity of mass television to explain intricate relations between events and institutions, and on the other hand reproaching myself and my colleagues for being unable to do it *better*. So perhaps it would be more accurate to say that television's capacity to portray abstract notions is strictly limited, and depends on striking a series of very fine balances between simplicity and precision. Believing that, I have little patience for producers whose film may have failed to impress viewers because they assumed that their audiences would be so intimately familiar with the persons and events that they need no more than say 'S.A.' or 'S.S.', and their entire audience would instantly grasp who they were, and what their significance was.

There is a vulgar way of putting this: it is that a television producer has one bite at the cherry of audience interest. If he fails, then he loses his viewers, and that is the end of the song. The academic has repeated chomps at the fruit. If his audience fails to follow him that is its own hard luck. If it does not understand, *it* is deemed to have failed, not the 'producer': professors do not get the sack when attendances at their lectures start to fall off. So the obligation that a responsible television producer has is to make his thoughts comprehensible to an audience about which he can assume nothing, so far as its degree of specialised knowledge is concerned. What he can rely on — and it is a pity that more producers do not take advantage of the fact — is a high degree of shrewdness, worldliness, and common sense. To put it in a slightly different way: to make a programme for a mass audience is to make a programme for an audience whose ordinary mode of apprehension is not literary. People who watch a great deal of television do not as a rule read many books; viewing and reading are for them mutually exclusive, not complementary, activities.

That means that for most of the audience *The World at War* was not a complement to the memoirs of Albert Speer, the learned volumes of Captain Liddell Hart, or the speculations of Mr A.J.P. Taylor; it was *all they had*. Many of my colleagues are inclined to dismiss or simply not understand those whose education does not equip them for the task, or the pleasure, of translating Alan Taylor's flights of fancy into sober assessments. They, I believe, fail utterly to understand what their own job should be. It is not to furnish pictorial counterparts to the knowledge that their audience has acquired through its reading; it is to tell, and show — in a word, to *do* history for — people who do not, as a rule, read very much.

I confess that this understanding came late to me. An American ex-serviceman in his fifties told me after a projection of one of our programmes how, through it, he had come to understand how his own job as a stoker on an American troop transport in the South Pacific helped shorten the war, and so helped save Dutch Jews from extermination. My initial harsh reaction was to think, aghast, how if he had bothered to *read* even one popular account of the war in the past thirty years, he would not have needed the film to reveal that to him. But a moment's reflection showed how wrong I was to think that way. The point was precisely that here was a man who did *not* enjoy reading books for pleasure or instruction, but who was pleased to use his eyes and his ears instead. No books about the war had struck his fancy — our films did. And our films were not made for book-lovers who wanted more; they were made for film-lovers who had little else.

If I am right about this characterisation, then a great deal about the soured relations between academics and producers becomes clearer. Academics often think that their talents are ignored or misused, because they have such a lot of knowledge at their fingertips (or in their file cards) which television producers perversely refuse either to acknowledge, or to make use of. An academic views a documentary and asks its producer, 'Who was your historical adviser?' The answer, 'I was myself', he finds an insult and an outrage. Yet, I would argue, there is no reason why it should be felt as such. No one forces producers to deal with historical subjects. If they do choose to make films about the past, it is because they want to, and the idea that historical studies are in such a state of anarchy and confusion that none except a professional historian has the qualifications necessary to thread his way through conflicting accounts of, or make public judgements about, the past seems to me to be arrogant and wrong. And even if it were true, it would not change matters at all. Because, as a matter of logic, a producer incapable of making sound judgements about historical events because of his own inherent defects must also be incompetent to judge between the claims of rival historical advisers — unless of course the competitors were to speak with one voice, in which case there would be no problem in the first place. And the producer who knows enough to decide which of two or more competing advisers he is to trust clearly knows enough to form his own judgements without the supervision of any advisers at all.

What he does is to turn to the same sources which academic historians turn to: standard historical works, conversations with knowledgeable friends, learned articles, his own researches. Where the professional academic goes wrong is to think that the point of the producer's labour is to produce a work which will win the esteem of fellow historians: if it does not break new ground, if it does not contain new insights, then it is not worth doing. But this is simply not the case. Because it is the popular history that it is, television history is unlikely to be innovative. Let me give examples, once again, from our own series on World War II. I cannot think of a single programme which contained doctrines unfamiliar to any competent practising historian, though a great deal of what individual writers said and producers endorsed was novel, and offensive as well, to large sections of the viewing public. I do not simply mean — though it is true — that numbers of young people were surprised to learn that the Soviet Union fought on the side of the Allies during the last four years of the war, or that Britons of all ages were surprised to learn that Japanese troops had to acclimatise themselves to fight in the Burmese jungles just as British troops did. What must have been incredible, judging from the correspondence generated by the programmes, were, among others:

1. Our remarks about the contribution the *Luftwaffe* made to its own defeat in the Battle of Britain. Popular belief in this country has always been that the R.A.F. defeated the *Luftwaffe* against all hope and expectation; not that the *Luftwaffe*'s attempt to secure air supremacy over southern England was a desperate gamble, almost inevitably doomed to failure from the start.
2. Our judgement about the magnitude of the Soviet contribution to Allied victory. Few viewers knew that at least twenty million Russians died, or that the bulk of Germany's forces fought on the eastern, not the western, front. Still less did they know that the Soviet Union was probably capable of defeating the Germans single-handed.
3. The idea that Hitler was a social reformer, whose destruction of the political power of the Prussian aristocracy and the military establishment made possible the emergence of a stable parliamentary democracy in post-war West Germany.

Now, none of these notions is incontrovertible, but no one could claim that any would outrage the sensibilities of conscientious professionals. They are the commonplaces of routine contemporary historical exposition; it hardly takes any special expertise to be able to grasp them or their significance. The expertise, it seems to me, comes in making them understandable to the mass audience. And that is not an historian's expertise.

There is another, less obvious point. Historians see one of their principal tasks as that of conveying information (those with literary skill, of course, delight in conveying information pleasurably). But producers of programmes for mass audiences – and in this they do differ from producers for adult education programmes, or for schools – must be more concerned to convey their own *enthusiasms*. The form that their best efforts take is not: 'Here are some things you all ought to know about the Battle of Stalingrad', but rather 'We are passionately concerned about the Battle of Stalingrad. If you will watch our programme, we will try to share with you some of our passion and some of our concern'. This is not a sentiment which, in my experience, informs the pages of the *English Historical Review*.

I have not said anything so far about the producer's use of historical evidence, a matter of evergreen concern to academics. This is because I think it is of only peripheral interest. If producers were making films for an audience of professional historians, they would work in quite different ways. But their films are not densely packed arguments; and they neither need nor use the kind of *apparatus criticus* obligatory in scholarly articles, or even textbooks. If there is a literary analogy, it is not the doctoral dissertation but the reflective essay in which nothing is said recklessly, but in which the flow of the text is not burdened with a scholarly apparatus either.

It ought to be self-evident that competent producers are scrupulous in their use of film. They do not try to pass off feature films as newsreels, nor an interview made in 1960 as a faithful representation of the interviewee's views in 1970, but that is not because either the film or the interview is 'evidence'. 'Evidence' is something used in arguing a case. If all films argued a case then the elements incorporated into them could properly be called evidence. But many documentaries do not argue a case – they explore possibilities, or they present alternatives, or they tell true stories. To misuse film in such contexts is not to fudge the evidence; it is simply to use film and interview less than honestly.

So far, I have been muddling prescriptive accounts with descriptive accounts – talking as if all producers were good and all good producers behaved the way I said they did, and as if all historians were on another side of a sharp dividing line. But perhaps this is the wrong kind of distinction to make. Some producers do make films (indeed whole series) which are based on literary models, deploy arguments as if they were trying to convince a sceptical donnish audience, and contain indifferently selected and irrelevantly deployed visual material. And, equally, some academics do exhibit a lively awareness of the limitations and resources of the television documentary; are careful not to confuse genres; are capable of communicating with large audiences. In other words, the distinction is not between dons and academics on the one hand, and professional producers on the other; but between those who are sensitive to the points I have raised about the world of the past and those who are not.

A final point. That there is academic discontent with the state of historical documentary seems to me to be obvious: I have tried to account for some of its causes and consequences. What seems to be unfortunate is one form in which academic discontent has crystallised. Dissatisfied with what they take to be the superficiality, triviality and incompleteness of popular accounts, concerned historians have begun to produce their own works. They have done so under difficult conditions with the help of devoted collaborators and on very small budgets. Their enterprise, and their ingenuity, deserve praise, but I fear that they have mistaken a profound characteristic of the medium for a simple defect in execution on the part of existing practitioners. So their work, far from breaking new ground, has only reproduced the worse faults of the kind of documentaries it has sought to replace. Films need a high ratio of visual material to commentary, and a low ratio of information to noise. In other words, trying to say too much is a recipe for not being understood at all, whether the subject is the Potsdam conference or the Spanish Civil War. But this should not be construed to be a claim that there is no place for historical documentaries made by academics for academic audiences. What it does mean is that very careful thought ought to be given to what those documentaries ought to be like. Academic film-makers ought to think not twice but three times before embarking on expositions of diplomatic encounters, analysis of abstract concepts or complex narrative histories. I hope I have shown why. What they might consider instead is to produce films about historical topics which do not have wide popular appeal, and of which no non-partisan accounts yet exist: the internment of aliens in the U.K. during World War II, for example; or the persistence of British working-class hostility to Winston Churchill.

But in any event, I think that the universities would never wish to become major centres of documentary film production. Their efforts would be more valuable if directed to making filmed records of persons or events which would otherwise go unrecorded, and above all, to doing the sorts of thing they do best, traditionally; not to despising and dismissing popular television for being what it is, still less to trying to replace the mass television history of our day by their own mandarin versions, but to doing their jobs as historians as well as they can, so that the history they write will be as good as it can be, so that the popular accounts which we provide will be as true as they can be.

# Select bibliography

The bibliography has been compiled by the Slade Film History Register. It makes no pretension to completeness in the areas which it covers (especially in languages other than English), and it omits some areas altogether. The output of literature on all aspects of film is enormous. A large proportion of it is of some potential interest to the historian who wishes to work on or with the medium, but the greater part of it must be disregarded here. The aim of this bibliography is simply to provide a guide to literature relating specifically to the use of film by historians or for historical purposes. It therefore omits all consideration of film theory, aesthetics and criticism, sociology of film, and film history in the narrower sense. It also leaves out discussions of particular films, with one or two exceptions

## General

Aretin, K.O. von 'Der Film als zeitgeschichtliche Quelle', *Politische Studien*, 96 (1958), 254–65.

Bateson, G. 'Cultural and thematic analyses of fictional films', *Transactions of the New York Academy of Sciences*, series 2, 5 (1943), 72–8.

Bawden, L.-A. 'Film and the historian', *University Vision*, 2 (1968), 32–6.

Billard, P. See Chevalier, L. and Billard, P.

Bokor, P. 'Geschichte und Fernsehen', *Rundfunk und Fernsehen* (1967), 3–8.

*Bulletin of the International Committee of Historical Sciences*, 1 (1926–8), 352–4, 733–5; 2 (1929–30), 335, 361–4, 452–6; 3 (1931), 45–9, 283; 4 (1932), 467–74. Papers and discussions on film and history and film archives. Principal contributors: A. Depréaux, M. Fauconnier, R. Fruin, M. Hankin, M. Lhéritier.

Burns, E.B. 'Conceptualizing the use of film to study history: a bibliofilmography', *Film and History*, 4/4 (1974), 1–11.

Chevalier, L. and Billard, P. *Cinéma et civilisation*. Paris, 1968.

Conference on the use of audio-visual archives as original source materials, *The History Teacher*, 6 (1973), 295–323. Contributors include J.L. Jellicorse, E.B. Burns, S. Kula, M.A. Jackson, D.L. Parker, R.A. Venables, R.A. Weinstein.

Coultass, C. 'Library material and the historian', *Journal of the Society of Film and Television Arts*, 41 (1970), 10–12.

## Select bibliography

*Cultures*, 2 (1974), issue on 'Flashback: Films and history'.

Dickinson, T. 'Inside view: Film and the historian', *Screen Digest*, (1973), 135–7.

Dickinson, T. and Thorpe, F. 'Film and the historian', *Social Science Research Council Newsletter*, 10 (1970), 22–4.

Elton, Sir Arthur 'The film as source material for history', *Aslib Proceedings*, 7 (1955), 207–39.

Ferro, M. 'Le film, une contre-analyse de la société?', *Annales*, 28 (1973), 109–24.

Ferro, M. 'Société du XX$^e$ siècle et histoire cinématographique', *Annales*, 23 (1968), 581–5.

*Film and the historian*: Proceedings of a conference held at University College, London, in April 1968. London, 1968. Reprint of the above together with *University Vision*, 1 (1968). London, 1969.

Furhammer, L. and Isaksson, F. *Politics and Film*. London, 1971.

Grenville, J.A.S. *Film as History: the Nature of Film Evidence*. Birmingham, 1971.

Griffin, P. 'Film, document, and the historian', *Film and History*, 2/2 (1972), 1–6.

Houston, P., 'The nature of the evidence', *Sight and Sound*, 36 (1967), 88–92.

Hubatsch, W. 'Probleme des geschichtswissenschaftlichen Films', *Geschichte in Wissenschaft und Unterricht*, 8 (1953), 476–9.

Hughes, W. 'Proposal for a course on films and history', *University Vision*, 8 (1972), 9–18.

Isaksson, F. See Furhammer, L. and Isaksson, F.

Isenberg, M.T. 'Historians and film', *The History Teacher*, 7 (1974), 266–72.

Isenberg, M.T. 'A relationship of constrained anxiety: historians and film', *The History Teacher*, 6 (1973), 553–68.

Jackson, M.A. 'Film as a source material: some preliminary notes toward a methodology', *Journal of Inter-Disciplinary History*, 4 (1973), 73–80.

Kuiper, J.B. 'The historical value of motion pictures', *American Archivist*, 31 (1968), 385–90.

Leab, D.J. 'From "Sambo" to "Superspade": some problems in the use of film in historical research', *University Vision*, 10 (1973), 41–7.

McCreary, E.C. 'Film and history: some thoughts on their inter-relationship', *Societas*, 1 (1971), 51–66.

Marwick, A. 'Archive film as source material', in *Archive Film Compilation Booklet*. Open University, 1973, pp. 1–5.

Marwick, A. 'Notes of the use of archive film', in *War and Social Change in the Twentieth Century*. London, 1974.

Matuszewski, B. *Une nouvelle source de l'histoire: création d'un dépôt de cinématographie historique*. Paris, 1898.

Select bibliography

Moltmann, G. and Reimers, K.F. *Zeitgeschichte im Film- und Tondokument.* Göttingen, 1970.

Mowat, C.L. *Great Britain since 1914.* London, 1971, pp. 163–70.

Mura, A. *A Study of the Value of Film as an Historical Document.* Rome, 1963.

Murphy, W.T. 'The National Archives and the historian's use of film', *The History Teacher,* 6 (1972), 119–34.

Muth, H. 'Der historische Film: historische und filmische Grundprobleme', *Geschichte in Wissenschaft und Unterricht,* 6 (1955).

O'Connor, J.E. 'Historians and film: some problems and prospects', *The History Teacher,* 6 (1973), 543–52.

Pontecorvo, L. 'Aspects of documentary and newsreel research', in *Archive Film Compilation Booklet.* Open University, 1973, pp. 6–14.

Reimers, K.F. 'Göttinger Filmdokumente zur Zeitgeschichte, Bericht 1966', *Vierteljahreshefte für Zeitgeschichte,* 14 (1966), 334–9. See also Moltmann, G. and Reimers, K.F.

Roads, C.H. *Film and the Historian.* Imperial War Museum, London, 1969.

Roads, C.H. 'Film as historical evidence', *Journal of the Society of Archivists,* 3 (1966), 183–91.

Roads, C.H. 'A view of the use of film by the universities', *University Vision,* 1 (1968), 9–14.

Rosen, R. See Samuels, S. and Rosen, R.

Sadoul, G. 'Photographie et cinématographie', 'Cinémathèques et photothèques', 'Témoignages photographiques et cinématographiques', in C. Samaran (ed.), *L'Histoire et ses Méthodes.* Paris, 1961, pp. 771–82, 1167–78, 1390–1410.

Samuels, S. and Rosen, R. 'Film and the historian', *A.H.A. Newsletter,* 2 (1973), 31–7.

Schuursma, R.L. 'Film and history in the Netherlands', *Film and History,* 2/4 (1972), 10–16.

Small, M. 'Motion pictures and the study of attitudes: some problems for historians', *Film and History,* 2/1 (1972), 1–5.

Smith, P. 'Historians and film: a progress report', *University Vision,* 4 (1969), 36–9.

Sorlin, P. 'Clio à l'écran, ou l'historien dans le noir', *Revue d'Histoire Moderne et Contemporaine,* 21 (1974), 252–78.

Terveen, F. 'Der Film als historisches Dokument: Grenzen und Möglichkeiten', *Vierteljahreshefte für Zeitgeschichte,* 3 (1955), 57–66. Condensed translation in *University Vision,* 1 (1968), 22–5.

Terveen, F. 'Historischer Film und historisches Filmdokument', *Geschichte in Wissenschaft und Unterricht,* 12 (1956), 750–2.

Thorpe, F. See Dickinson, T. and Thorpe, F.

Treue, W. 'Das Filmdokument als Geschichtsquelle', *Historische Zeitschrift,* 186 (1958), 308–27.

Vanderwood, P.J. 'Hollywood and history: does film make the connection?',

## Select bibliography

*Proceedings of the Pacific Coast Council on Latin American Studies*, 2 (1973), 53–9.

Waugh, W.T. 'History in moving pictures', *History*, 9 (1927), 324–9.

Wilson, D. 'Historical hindsights', *Sight and Sound*, 41 (1972), 202–3. Report of a conference on the use of film in the study and teaching of twentieth-century history.


### Film in its relation to particular historical periods and themes

Albrecht, G. *Nationalsozialistische Filmpolitik – eine soziologische Untersuchung über die Spielfilme des Dritten Reiches*. Stuttgart, 1969.

Amengual, B. 'Vichy entre le réel et l'iréel', *Ecran*, 8 (1972), 5–8.

Baldelli, P. and Filippi, A. *Cinema e lotta di liberazione*. Rome, 1970.

Barr, C. 'Projecting Britain and the British character: Ealing Studios', *Screen*, 15 (1974), 87–121, 129–63.

Becker, L. 'Inside view: a German view of history on film', *Screen Digest* (May 1973), 71–4.

Becker, W. *Zur politischen Ökonomie des N.S.-Films*, Band 1: *Film und Herrschaft*, Band 2: *Film und Kapital*. Berlin, 1973.

Berghoff, G. and Eder, K. *Der Kampf gegen das nationalsozialistische Deutschland· Filme aus der U.d.S.S.R. und aus den U.S.A*. Oberhausen, 1973.

Bergman, A. *We're in the Money*. New York, 1971. American films of the thirties.

Bodenstedt, A. *Sonderbericht der deutschen Wochenschau vom Überfall auf Jugoslawien und Griechenland*. Hamburg, 1958.

Bramsted, E.K. *Goebbels and National Socialist propaganda 1925–1945*. Michigan, 1965.

Brooks, C.W. 'Jean Renoir's "The Rules of the Game" ', *French Historical Studies*, 7 (1971), 264–83.

Brunetta, G.P. *Intellectuali, Cinema e Propaganda tra le Due Guerre*. Bologna, 1972.

Burns, E.B. *Latin American Cinema: Film and History*. U.C.L.A. Latin American Studies, 26, Los Angeles, 1975.

Burns, E.B. 'The Latin American film, realism and the historian', *The History Teacher*, 6 (1973), 659–74.

Burns, E.B. *The visual dimension of Latin American social history: student critiques of eight major Latin American films*. U.C.L.A., Department of History, 1973.

Cadars, P. and Courtade, F. *Le Cinéma nazi*. Paris, 1972.

Coultass, C. 'The German film 1933–1945', *Screen* 12 (1971), 38–41.

Courtade, F. See Cadars, P. and Courtade, F.

Cripps, T.R. 'Birth of a race company: an early stride toward a black cinema', *Journal of Negro History*, 59 (1974), 28–37.

## Select bibliography

Cripps, T.R. 'The death of Rastus: negroes in American films since 1945', *Phylon*, 28 (1967), 267–75.

Cripps, T.R. 'The myth of the Southern Box Office: factors in the perpetuation of white supremacy in films 1920–1940', in *The Black Experience in America*, ed. L. Gould and J. Curtis. University of Texas, 1970, pp. 116–44.

Cripps, T.R. 'The reaction of the negro to the motion picture "Birth of a Nation" ', *The Historian* 25 (1963), 244–62.

Cripps, T.R. 'Movies in the ghetto B.P. (Before Poitier)', *Negro Digest*, 18 (1969), 21–7, 45–8.

Cripps, T.R. 'Paul Robeson and black identity in American movies', *Massachusetts Review*, Summer 1970, 468-85.

Croizier, R.C. 'Chinese movies and modern Chinese history', *Journal of Asian Studies*, 32 (1973), 501–5.

Daniel, J. *Guerre et cinéma: grandes illusions et petits soldats 1895–1971*. Paris, 1972.

Demeter, K. 'Die Filmpropaganda der Entente im Weltkriege', *Archiv für Politik und Geschichte*, 3/8 (1925), 214–31.

Drozdowski, B. 'Historia rewolucji i legenda rewolucji', *Kino* 7/7 (1972), 37–43. The history and legend of the October Revolution in the modern Soviet cinema.

Durgnat, R. *A Mirror for England*. London, 1970. On British films, 1945–68.

Eder, K. See Berghoff, G. and Eder, K.

Fernandez, C.C. *La guerra de Espana y el cine*. Madrid, 1972.

Fielding, R. 'Mirror of discontent: the "March of Time" and its politically controversial film issues', *Western Political Quarterly*, 12 (1959), 145–52.

Filippi, A. See Baldelli, P. and Filippi, A.

Fleming, A. 'The cinema and the second world war: the Resistance', *University Vision*, 8 (1972), 37–40.

Fofi, G. 'Cinema of the Popular Front in France (1934–38)', *Screen*, 13 (1972–3), 5–57.

Freiwald, H. 'Filmdokumente über die Jugend unter Hitler und ihre Bedeutung für die Politische Bildung', in *Beiträge zur Erziehungswissenschaft: Festschrift der Pädagogischen Hochschule Oldenburg*. Oldenburg, 1966.

Friedman, N. 'American movies and American culture 1946–1970', *Journal of Popular Culture*, 3 (1970), 814–23.

Gili, J.A. *Fascisme et résistance dans le cinéma italien (1922–1968)*. Paris, 1970).

Grunberger, R. *A Social History of the Third Reich*. Harmondsworth, 1974, pp. 475–91.

Habryn, A. 'Przed Wiertowem: O narodzinach radzieckiej publicystyki filmowej', *Kino*, 8/11 (1973), 41–3. Early Soviet newsreels of the October revolution and the civil war.

Hull, D.S. *Film in the Third Reich: a Study of the German Cinema 1933–1945*. Berkeley: Los Angeles, 1969.

## Select bibliography

Johnston, W. *Memo on the Movies: War Propaganda 1914–1939*. Norman, Oklahoma, 1935.

Jones, K.D. and McClure, A.F. *Hollywood at War: the American Motion Picture and World War Two*. New York, 1974.

Jowett, G. 'The concept of history in American produced films', *Journal of Popular Culture*, 3 (1970), 799–813.

Kiselev, G.F. 'N.K. Krupskaia i pervye ispolniteli roli V.I. Lenina v teatre i kino', *Voprosy Istorii*, 4 (1966), 203–8. Krupskaya's involvement in plays and films of the 1930s depicting Lenin's role in history. Includes details of primary materials held by the Central Party Archive of the Institute of Marxism–Leninism.

Klaue, W. *Sowjetischer Dokumentarfilm*. East Berlin, 1967.

Klaue, W. and Lichtenstein, M. *Filme contra Faschismus*. Staatliches Filmarchiv der D.D.R., East Berlin, 1965. Twenty-one articles by international writers.

Kracauer, S. *From Caligari to Hitler: a Psychological History of the German Film*. Princeton, 1947.

Leab, D.J. 'From "Sambo" to "Superspade": the black in film', *Film and History*, 2/3 (1972), 1–6.

Leab, D.J. 'The gamut from A to B: the image of the black in pre-1915 movies', *Political Science Quarterly*, 88 (1973), 53–70.

Leglise, P. *Histoire de la politique du cinéma français: le cinéma et la IIIe République*. Paris, 1970.

Leiser, E. *Deutschland erwache!: Propaganda im Film des Dritten Reiches*. Hamburg, 1968.

Lévy-Klein, S. 'France 1940–4: le cinéma de Vichy', *Positif*, 148 (1973), 51–5.

Lichtenstein, M. See Klaue, W. and Lichtenstein, M.

Loy, J.M. 'Latin America through film: problems and possibilities', *Proceedings of the Pacific Coast Council on Latin American Studies*, 2 (1973), 39–52.

Lyons, T.J. 'Hollywood and World War I 1914–1918', *Journal of Popular Film*, 1 (1972), 15–30.

McClure, A.F. 'Hollywood at war: the American motion picture and World War II', *Journal of Popular Film*, 1 (1972), 123–35. See also Jones, K.D. and McClure, A.F.

McDonald, J. 'Film and war propaganda', *Public Opinion Quarterly*, 4 (1940), 519–22; 5 (1941), 127–9.

Manvell, R. *Films and the Second World War*. London, 1975.

Nichols, W. 'The American Photo League', *Screen*, 13 (1972/3), 108–15.

Noble, P. *The Negro in Films*. New York, re-issue 1972.

Oehling, R.A. 'Germans in Hollywood films' parts 1–3, *Film and History*, 3/2 (1973), 1–10; 4/2 (1974), 8–10; 4/3 (1974), 6–10.

Opgenoorth, E. 'Analyse eines historischen Filmdokumentes – Kundgebung im Berliner Lustgarten 1. Mai 1933', *Research Film*, 7 (1971), 320–7.

Ozimek, S. 'Cytat dokumentalny', *Kino*, 8/5 (1973), 30–3. Newsreels from

## Select bibliography

World War II and their use in Polish feature films.

Ozimek, S. *Film Polski w Wojennej Potrzebie*. Warszawa, 1974.

Pevsner, M. 'Les actualités cinématographiques de 1940 à 1944', *Revue d'Histoire de la Deuxième Guerre Mondiale*, 64 (1966), 88–96.

Pevsner, M. 'Les thèmes de la propagande allemande avant le 22 Juin 1941', *Revue d'Histoire de la Deuxième Guerre Mondiale*, 64 (1966), 29–38.

Pontecorvo, L. 'Film as a record of British industry and social life: an appeal for help', *Business Archives*, 30 (1969), 25–6.

Prédal, R. *La société française (1914–1945) à travers le cinéma*. Paris, 1972.

*Propaganda und Gegenpropaganda im Film 1933–45*. Österreichisches Film-museum, Vienna, 1972. Eight articles on propaganda, bibliography and list of films shown at the Museum's seminar, 1972.

Reimers, K.F. 'Der Führer als völkische Erlösergestalt: die Berliner N.S.-Weih-nachtskundgebung 1933 im offiziellen Filmbericht', *Geschichte in Wissen-schaft und Unterricht*, 3 (1968), 164–75.

Reimers, K.F. 'Das 20. Jahrhundert im Film- und Fernsehdokument', *Film Bild Ton*, 10 (1968), 11–16.

Richards, J. *Visions of Yesterday*. London, 1973. The cinema from the point of view of mythology and ideology.

Rubin, B. 'International film and television propaganda: campaigns of assistance', *Annals of the American Academy of Political and Social Science*, 398 (1971), 81–92.

Schoenbaum, D. 'Brecht's "Kuhle Wampe": an expression of Communism in the Weimar Republic', *Film and History*, 2/2 (1972), 11–17.

Simcovitch, M. 'The impact of Griffith's "Birth of a Nation" on the modern Ku Klux Klan', *Journal of Popular Film*, 1 (1972), 45–54.

Sloan, W. 'The documentary film and the negro: the evolution of the integration film', *Journal of the Society of Cinematologists*, 5 (1965), 66–9.

Stafford, J. 'Films on the second world war', *University Vision*, 1 (1968), 19–21.

Stott, W. *Documentary Expression and Thirties America*. New York, 1973.

Stumpf, V.O. 'Film propaganda and British history', *Film and History*, 3/3 (1973), 8–11. Report of a conference on 'Film propaganda and the historian' held in London, 1973.

Taylor, R. 'A medium for the masses: agitation in the Soviet civil war', *Soviet Studies*, 22 (1971), 562–74.

Tumler, K. 'Zu den Traditionen des Sozialistischen Films in Deutschland', *Beiträge zur Geschichte der Arbeiterbewegung*, 11 (1969), 993–1008.

Waley, H.D. 'British documentaries and the war effort', *Public Opinion Quarterly*, 6 (1942), 604–9.

Wegg-Prosser, V. 'The way we were', *Sight and Sound*, 43 (1974), 145–6. Review of the National Film Theatre season 'Britain in the thirties'.

Wulf, J. *Theater und Film im Dritten Reich: ein Dokumentation*. Gütersloh, 1964.

## Select bibliography

Zeman, Z.A.B. *Nazi Propaganda*. London, 1964.

### Historical development of the film industry and of film types

Babitsky, P. and Rimberg, J. *The Soviet Film Industry*. New York, 1957.
Barnouw. E. *Documentary: a History of the Non-Fiction Film*. London, 1975.
Barsam, R.M. *Nonfiction Film – a Critical History*. New York, 1973.
Betts, E. *The Film Business – a History of the British Cinema 1896–1972*. London, 1973.
Bohn, T.W. and Lichty, L.W. 'The "March of Time": news as drama', *Journal of Popular Film*, 2 (1973), 373–87.
Fielding, R. *The American Newsreel 1911–1967*. University of Oklahoma Press, 1972.
Gili, J.A. 'Actualités et films de montage', *Etudes Cinématographiques*, nos. 78–81 (1970), 87–99.
Hughes, W. 'The propagandist's art', *Film and History*, 4/3 (1974), 11–15.
Leyda, J. *Dianying: an Account of Films and the Film Audience in China*. M.I.T. Press, 1972.
Leyda, J. *Films Beget Films: Compilation Films from Propaganda to Drama*. London, 1964.
Leyda, J. *Kino: a History of the Russian and Soviet Film*. London, 1960.
Lichty, L.W. See Bohn, T.W. and Lichty, L.W.
Low, R. *The History of the British Film*. 1: 1896–1906; 2: 1906–1914; 3: 1914–1918; 4: 1918–1929. London, 1948–71.
MacCann, R.D. *The People's Films: a Political History of U.S. Government Motion Pictures*. New York, 1973.
Murphy, W.T. 'The method of "Why we fight" ', *Journal of Popular Film*, 1 (1972), 185–96.
'Newsreel in wartime', *B.K.S. Journal*, 9 (1946), 17–27.
Phillips, M.S. 'Nazi control of the German film industry', *Journal of European Studies*, 1 (1971), 37–68.
Pronay, N. 'British newsreels in the 1930s', part 1, 'Audience and Producers', part 2, 'Their Policies and Impact'; *History*, 56 (1971), 411–18; 57 (1972), 63–72.
Rotha, P. *Documentary Diary: an informal history of the British documentary film, 1928–1939*. London, 1973.
Rotha, P. *Documentary Film*. London, 1952.
Snyder, R.L. *Pare Lorentz and the Documentary Film*. Oklahoma University Press, 1968.
Tallents, S. 'The documentary film', *Journal of the Royal Society of Arts* (December 1946), 68–85.
Wenden, D.J. *The Birth of the Movies*. London, 1975.

## Select bibliography

### Production of film studies of history

Aldgate, A. 'British newsreels and the Spanish Civil War', *History*, 58 (1973), 60–3.

Aldgate, A. 'The production of "Spanish Civil War" ', part 1, 'The archives and the newsreels', part 2, 'A film in the making'; *University Vision*, 11 (1974), 16–23; 12 (1974), 42–9.

Anon. 'The use and abuse of stock footage', *Film Comment*, 4 (1967), 47–53.

Aumont, J. 'Comment on écrit l'histoire', *Cahiers*, nos. 238–9 (1972), 64–71.

Besançon, A. See Kriegel, A., Ferro, M. and Besançon, A.

Boyle, P.G. 'The historian as film-maker', *University Vision*, 10 (1973), 48–51. Describes the session at the A.H.A. convention, December 1972.

Essex, A. 'The user's problems', *Journal of the Society of Film and Television Arts*, 41 (1970), 3–6.

Ferro, M. '1917: history and cinema', *Journal of Contemporary History*, 3 (1968), 45–61. See also Kriegel, A., Ferro, M. and Besançon, A.

Grenville, J.A.S. and Pronay, N. 'The historian and historical films', *University Vision*, 1 (1968), 3–8.

Griffin, P. 'The making of a documentary film – "1900": a montage', *University Vision*, 9 (1972), 25–38.

Griffin, P. 'The making of "Goodbye Billy" ', *Film and History*, 2/2 (1972), 6–10.

Hayward, E. 'Production Problems', in *Archive Film Compilation Booklet*. Open University, 1973, pp. 15–21.

Kriegel, A., Ferro, M. and Besançon, A. 'Histoire et cinéma: l'expérience de "La Grande Guerre" ', *Annales*, 20 (1965), 327–36.

Kuehl, J. See Wilson, D.

Pattison, B. 'Use of historical film in new productions', *B.K.S.T.S. Journal*, 52 (1970), 230–2. On making the compilation film *Australia at War 1914–18*.

Pronay, N. See Grenville, J.A.S. and Pronay, N.

Schuursma, R.L. 'De Slag om Arnhem', *Spiegel Historiael*, 10 (1967), 523–6.

Wilson, D. and Kuehl, J. 'The truth of film history', *Sight and Sound*, 43 (1974), 240–2.

'World at War', *Journal of the Society of Film and Television Arts*, 2/9–10 (1974). Complete issue on the Thames Television series written by members of the production team.

Yergin, D. 'Politics and autobiography: an interview with Marcel Ophuls', *Sight and Sound*, 43 (1973–4), 20–1.

### Use of film in teaching

Adams, D. 'The use of film in American studies', *University Vision* 1 (1968), 15–18.

## Select bibliography

Ball, G.H. See Foxon, G.E.H., Ball, G.H. and Duncan, C.J.

Buscombe, E. 'Hollywood and American studies', *Screen Education Notes*, 7 (1973), 3–7.

Chasko, L.V. 'Kino na Urokakh Istorii S.S.S.R. U VIII Klasse', *Prepodavanie Istorii v Skkole*, 5 (1964), 71–4. The use of film for teaching about the 1917 revolutions.

Chibnall, B., Rodrigues, C. and Collings, J. *The Use of Film in University Teaching*. Brighton, 1974.

Clair, G. 'L'enseignement de l'histoire par le cinéma', *Cineopse* (April 1929).

Clough, D. 'American cinema: a film course at Aberystwyth', *University Vision*, 9 (1972), 39–43.

Collings, J. See Chibnall, B., Rodrigues, C. and Collings, J.

Consitt, F. *The Value of Films in History Teaching*. Historical Association, London, 1931.

Cripps, T.R. 'Circumstances within our control: television as a synthesizer of multi-media teaching resources', *Film and History*, 2/2 (1972), 18–22.

Curtis, J.C. and Huthmacher, J.J. 'The American dream on film', *Film and History*, 3/3 (1973), 17–19.

Curtis, J.C. and Schwartz, S. 'Learning history through the use of media: an experimental course', *The History Teacher*, 6 (1973), 535–42.

Duncan, C.J. See Foxon, G.E.H., Ball, G.H. and Duncan, C.J.

Edlington, A.R. 'Some material for the teaching of history by television', *Educational Television International*, 1 (1967), 144–9.

Enstam, E.V. 'The case for electronic media in college history courses', *The History Teacher*, 6 (1973), 191–200.

Foxon, G.E.H. 'The use of films in teaching and research in British universities: some further remarks', *University Film Journal*, 22 (1961), 1–11.

Foxon, G.E.H., Ball, G.H. and Duncan, C.J. *The Use of Film in Teaching and Research in British Universities*. British Universities Film Council, London, 1959.

Franzel, E. 'Film im Geschichtsunterricht', *Film Bild Funk*, 1 (1948).

Gidley, M. 'American studies in schools: materials and methods', *British Journal of Educational Technology*, 3 (1972), 52–74.

Gidley, M. 'Some American studies films at Sussex', *University Vision*, 6 (1971), 4–12. See also Weaver, M. and Gidley, M.

Grenville, J.A.S. 'History at the Open University', *History*, 57 (1972), 89–91.

Grenville, J.A.S. 'The use of film in schools', *History*, 58 (1973), 397–9.

Gwynn, T. and Willis, I. 'The role of feature films in the teaching of history', *Teaching History*, 3 (1974), 204–8.

Hanke, L. and Loy, J.M. 'Films on Latin America: a project', *Film and History*, 2/1 (1972), 13–14.

Hastie, T. See Pronay, N., Smith, B. and Hastie, T.

Herman, G. 'History through film: making multi media lectures for classroom use', *Film and History*, 2/4 (1972), 17—23.

Hirshfield, C. 'Film and American history at Penn State, Ogontz campus', *Film and History*, 3/2 (1973), 21—4.

Hirshfield, C. 'Teaching history to the disadvantaged college student: a history through film approach', *Film and History*, 4/1 (1974), 4—11, 20.

Holmes, L. 'The history of civilization since 1660', *Film and History*, 4/4 (1974), 4—8. Outline of a course at the University of South Alabama.

Huthmacher, J.J. See Curtis, J.C. and Huthmacher, J.J.

Jackson, M.A. See O'Connor, J.E. and Jackson, M.A.

Kinross, F. 'Teaching history by television', *Educational Television International*, 1 (1967), 10—15.

Loy, J.M. 'Classroom films on Latin America: a review of the present situation with some suggestions for the future', *The History Teacher*, 8 (1973), 89—98. See also Hanke, L. and Loy, J.M.

O'Connor, J.E. and Jackson, M.A. *Teaching History with Film*. A.H.A. Discussions on teaching, no. 2, Washington, 1974.

Poinssac-Neil, J. 'La télévision et l'histoire', *Bulletin de la Société des Professeurs d'Histoire et de Géographie*, 216 (1969), 483—96.

Pronay, N., Smith, B. and Hastie, T. *The Use of Film in History Teaching*. Historical Association, London, 1972.

Raack, R.C. 'Clio's dark mirror: the documentary film in history', *The History Teacher*, 6 (1972), 109—18.

Raack, R.C. and Smith, A.M. 'The documentary film in history teaching: an experimental course', *The History Teacher*, 6 (1973), 281—95.

Rodrigues, C. See Chibnall, B., Rodrigues, C. and Collings, J.

Rubini, D. 'Western civilization and comparative revolutions at Temple University', *Film and History*, 2/1 (1972), 15—19.

Sakmyster, T.L. 'History and films of East Europe', *Film and History*, 3/3 (1973), 20—2.

Samuels, S. 'History through film: film as social and intellectual history at the University of Pennsylvania', *Film and History*, 2/3 (1972), 14—17.

Schleh, E.P.A. 'Modern war and its images', *Film and History*, 3/3 (1973), 12—16.

Schwartz, S. See Curtis, J.C. and Schwartz, S.

Smith, A.M. See Raack, R.C. and Smith, A.M.

Smith, B. See Pronay, N., Smith, B. and Hastie, T.

Sorrell, R.S. 'Films and American civilization at Brookdale Community College', *Film and History*, 3/1 (1973), 9—12.

Stults, T. 'World war two films as propaganda', *Film and History*, 2/2 (1972), 23—7.

Tardy, M. *Etude de la contribution d'un film historique composé à partir de métrages d'actualités à l'enseignement de l'histoire dans le second degré*. Centre Audio-visuel de l'Ecole Normale Supérieur de Saint-Cloud, Section

## Select bibliography

Recherches no. R.10, Paris, 1960.

Toms, V.G. 'The film archives of the Imperial War Museum and the teaching of twentieth century history in a college of education', *Education for Teaching*, 77 (1968), 65–9.

Turnbull, L. 'The use of film in the teaching of history', *Screen Education Notes*, 6 (1973), 9–20.

U.S. Department of Health, Education and Welfare, *The identification of criteria for the effective use of films in teaching history in the classroom, in a variety of teaching situations, grades 7–12*. Office of Education, Bureau of Research, Washington, 1968.

Vanderwood, P. 'History through film at San Diego State', *Film and History*, 4/3 (1974), 16–18.

Ward, K.E. ' "Film, sound and historical analysis" – a course in film and history', *University Vision*, 12 (1974), 50–6.

Weaver, M. and Gidley, M. 'Film in the context of American (and Commonwealth) Arts', *Screen Education Notes*, 7 (1973), 21–7.

Wenden, D.J. 'Films and the teaching of modern history', *History*, 55 (1970), 216–19.

Willis, I. See Gwynn, T. and Willis, I.

## Archives and their resources for the historian

Arbaugh, D. 'Motion pictures and the future historian', *American Archivist*, 2 (1939), 106–14.

Barkhausen, H. 'Zur Geschichte des ehemaligen Reichsfilmarchivs', *Archivar*, 13 (1960), 1–14.

Barry, I. 'Films for history', *Special Libraries*, 30 (1939), 258–60.

Bittner, R. 'Film archives as information retrieval systems', *Educational Broadcasting International*, 6 (1973), 216–17.

Butler, I. *To Encourage the Art of the Film: the Story of the British Film Institute*. London, 1971.

Chittock, J. (ed.) *World Directory of Stockshot and Film Production Libraries*. London, 1969. Covers 310 film libraries and lists type of film held and oldest document.

Cowie, P. (ed.) *International Film Guide*. London, annually. Contains guide to film archives and their holdings.

Culbert, D.H. 'The Vanderbilt Television News Archive: classroom and research possibilities', *The History Teacher*, 8 (1974), 7–16.

Ford, C. 'The National Film Archive', *University Vision*, 1 (1968), 36–41.

Ford, C. 'Universities and the National Film Archive', *University Vision*, 5 (1970), 11–16.

François, M. 'Les filmothèques', in C. Samaran (ed.), *L'Histoire et ses méthodes*. Paris, 1961, pp. 1179–83.

## Select bibliography

Glénisson, J. 'Les documents audio-visuels', *Manuel d'archivistique: théorie et pratique des archives publiques en France*. Paris, 1970.

Humphrys, B. 'The Rhode Island Historical Society Film Archive', *Film and History*, 2/2 (1972), 27–31.

Klaue, W. 'Das Staatliche Filmarchiv der D.D.R.', *Archivmitteilungen*, 11 (1961), 146–51.

Langlois, H. 'The Cinémathèque Française', *Hollywood Quarterly*, 2 (1947), 207–9.

Lauritzen, E. 'Studie- och forskningmöjligheter', in *Social årsbok*. Stockholm, 1949, pp. 75–84. Preservation of film records as historical documents at the Swedish Film Archive.

Lindgren, E. 'The selection of films as historical records in the National Film Archive', *University Vision*, 6 (1971), 13–23.

Murphy, W.T. 'Film at the National Archives: a reference article', *Film and History*, 2/3 (1972), 7–13.

'National Film Archive', *Journal of the Society of Film and Television Arts*, 39 (1970). Complete issue on the Archive with contributions by members of the staff.

Philip, A.J. 'Cinematograph films: their national value and preservation', *Librarian*, 2 (1912), 367–70, 406–9, 447–9.

Pontecorvo, L. 'Film archives and university research', *University Vision*, 1 (1968), 25–35.

Renting, R.A.D. 'Filmcollecties in Archieven', *Nederlands Archievenblad*, 3 (1967), 219–25.

*Rescue of Living History*. National Film Archive, London, 1969.

Roads, C.H. *Text of an address delivered to the XXIII Congress of the International Federation of Film Archives in East Berlin on 9th June 1967 on behalf of the Film Section of the Imperial War Museum, London*. Imperial War Museum, London, 1967.

Zöllner, W. 'Der Film als Quelle der Geschichtsforschung', *Zeitschrift für Geschichtswissenschaft*, 13 (1965), 638–47. On the East German State Film archives at Babelsberg.

### Guides and catalogues

*Audio-visual materials for American studies: a guide to sources of information and materials*. University of Essex, American Arts Documentation Centre, 1973.

Bauer, A. *Deutscher Spielfilm-Almanach 1929–1950*. Berlin, 1950.

*British National Film Catalogue*. British Film Institute, London, 1963- (quarterly with annual cumulation).

Chibnall, B. 'The British National Film Catalogue', *University Vision*, 6 (1971), 35–8.

## Select bibliography

Dickinson, T. 'Concerning a national register of film of historical and social importance', *Bulletin of the Association Internationale des Documentaristes*, 3 (1972), 6–7, 19.

'Filmbestände Verleihkopien von Dokumentar- und Kulturfilmen sowie Wochenschauen 1900–1945', in *Findbücher zu Beständen des Bundesarchivs*, Band 8. Koblenz, 1971.

*Films for historians*. British Universities Film Council, London, rev. ed. 1974 (material for hire).

Gidley, M. and Goldman, D. *Audio-Visual Materials for American Studies*, University of Sussex, Centre for Educational Technology, 1970

Gifford, D. *The British Film Catalogue 1895–1970*. Newton Abbot, 1973.

Gray, D.W.S. See Pratt, K.L. and Gray, D.W.S.

*Interim Distribution Catalogue 1974*. British Film Institute, London, 1974.

*Library of Congress Motion Pictures*, 1912–39, 1940–9, 1950–9, 1960–9. Library of Congress, Washington, 1913–71.

Loy, J.M. *Latin America: Sights and Sounds. A Guide to Motion Pictures and Music for College Courses*. Consortium of Latin American Studies Programs, no. 5. Gainesville, 1973.

*Museum of Modern Art Department of Film, Circulating Programs*. Museum of Modern Art, New York, 1969.

*National Film Archive Catalogue*, part 1, *Silent news films 1895–1933*; part 2, *Silent non-fiction films 1895–1934*; part 3, *Silent fiction films 1895–1930*. British Film Institute, London, 1960–6.

Niver, K. *Motion Pictures from the Library of Congress: paper print collection 1894–1912*. Berkeley: Los Angeles, 1967.

Pratt, K.L. and Gray, D.W.S. *China: an Index to European Visual and Aural Materials*. London, 1973.

*A Survey of History Films for Hire*. Birmingham University, Library Film Service, 1972.

Thorpe, F. 'The Slade Film History Register', *Film and History*, 2/4 (1972), 36–9.

*Verzeichnis der Wissenschaftlichen Filme. Teilverzeichnis G: Geschichte: Erziehungswissenschaft, Publizistik, Sport, Kriminologie*. Institut für den Wissenschaftlichen Film, Göttingen, 1973.

Williams, G.A. *Guide to Sources of Illustrative Material for Use in Teaching History*. Historical Association, London, 1965.

**Some periodicals and serial publications regularly containing articles on film and history**

*Film and History*. The Historians Film Committee, c/o The History Faculty, Newark College of Engineering, Newark, New Jersey 07102, U.S.A.

*History*. The Historical Association, 59a Kennington Park Road, London SE11 4JH

## Select bibliography

*The History Teacher*. California State University, Long Beach, California 90840, U.S.A.

*Journal of Popular Film*. University Hall 101, Bowling Green State University, Bowling Green, Ohio 43403, U.S.A.

*Publikationen zu Wissenschaftlichen Filmen: Sektion Geschichte, Pädagogik, Publizistik*. Institut für den Wissenschaftlichen Film, Nonnenstieg, 72, 34 Göttingen, West Germany

*Sight and Sound*. British Film Institute, 81 Dean Street, London W1V 6AA

*University Vision*. British Universities Film Council, Royalty House, 72 Dean Street, London W1V 5HB

# Appendix: addresses of organisations involved with film and history

British Inter-University History Film Consortium.
　　Executive Secretary, Dr Derek Spring, Department of History, University of Nottingham, Nottingham NG7 2RD
British Universities Film Council.
　　Royalty House, 72 Dean Street, London W1V 5HB
Fédération Internationale des Archives du Film.
　　Secretariat, 74 Galerie Ravenstein, 1000 Bruxelles, Belgium
Historians' Film Committee
　　c/o The History Faculty, Newark College of Engineering, Newark, New Jersey 07102, U.S.A.
Historical Association.
　　59a Kennington Park Road, London SE11 4JH
Imperial War Museum.
　　Film Department, Lambeth Road, London SE1 6HZ
Institut für den Wissenschaftlichen Film.
　　Nonnenstieg 72, 34 Göttingen, West Germany
National Film Archive.
　　81 Dean Street, London W1V 6AA
Slade Film History Register.
　　See British Universities Film Council, above
Stichting Film en Wetenschap.
　　Hengeveldstraat 29, Utrecht, Holland

# Index

# Index

# Index

in Education, 165
National Film Archive, 16–17, 19, 28–30, 33–4, 37–42, 44–6
National Film Collection (U.S.A.), 73
National Film Theatre, 27, 39, 45–6
Negroes, in American films, 72
Netherlands, film material on, 1–2, 25
*Neville Chamberlain*, 136
*New Earth*, 25
*New Society*, 173
newsfilm, 55, 58, 62, 96–102
newsreel, 7–8, 15–16, 18–22, 26–8, 33, 56, 58–60, 62–4, 75, 80–1, 95–119, 124, 127–8, 133, 137, 140, 142, 158, 167; television, 46, 117, 118n, 137
*Nine Days in '26*, 176
Northcliffe, 1st viscount, 97–8
Nottingham University history department, 134–6

O.R.T.F., 16
*October*, 162
*Ohm Krüger*, 22
*Omnibus* (series), 25
Open University, 10–11, 28–30, 135, 142, 144–9, 152–4, 164, 172–3, 175–6, 179
*Opening of the Kiel Canal*, 97–8
*Organisations of Peace, The*, 154
Oxford University, 149

*Panorama* (series), 25
Paramount company, 18, 21, 33, 56, 112, 117
Paramount newsreel, 112–14, 117
Pathé, Charles, 102
Pathé company, 16, 102–6, 112–13, 115
Pathé newsreel, 18, 26, 33, 102–6, 112–13, 117
Paul, Robert, 95, 98–9, 106, 117n
Peckinpah, Sam, 77
Pennebaker, D.A., 57
Pennsylvania University, 146
Pétain, Philippe, 26
Phonofilm, 110
*Picasso Mystery, The*, 25
*Pictorial News Official*, 106
Picture Palace (cinema), 117n
*Plow That Broke the Plains, The*, 25, 61
*Point of Order*, 59
Pontecorvo, Lisa, 7
popular attitudes, reflected in film, 67–71
*Pravda*, on *Tchapaev*, 83
Praz, Mario, 53
Pronay, N., 2, 7, 59–60, 63, 136, 147, 151–3, 159
Public Archives of Canada, 47
Public Record Office, 40

Pudovkin, V.I., 53–4
Purser, Philip, 173

quantitative content analysis, 74–5
Queen Mary College, London, history department, 135–6
*Quo Vadis?*, 36

Reading University history department, 134–6
Rediffusion company, 46
Reed, Carol, 67
Referat für zeitgeschichtliche Filmforschung und Filmdokumentation, 1
Reimers, K.F., 2, 143
Renoir, Jean, 23
*Rescue of Living History, The*, 39
Reuters, 104, 115
Richards, Jeffrey, 130
Rijksvoorlichtingsdienst, 16
*Rise and Fall of the Third Reich, The*, 171
*River, The*, 61
Roberts, J.M., 149
Rochemont, Louis de, 56, 59
Roemer, Michael, 65
*Roman Way, The* (series), 170
*Rome Open City*, 23
Rose, A., 71
Rosen, R., 146, 148
Rossif, Frédéric, 81
Rosten, L., 68
Rotha, Paul, 171
Rothermere, 1st viscount, 110, 112
Rouch, Jean, 82
Rouquier, G., 82
*Rublev*, 82
Russia, film material on; pre-1914, 98, 103; inter-war period, 22–3, 26, 82, 83–94, 113; World War II, 18, 26–7, 30, 136, 153; post-1945, 82

Sadoul, G., 1
*Sailors of Kronstadt, The*, 89
Samaran, C., 1
Samuels, S., 146, 148
Sanger, Gerald, 110, 118n
Schramm, P.E., 1
Schuursma, R.L., 1, 10–11, 151
Scottish Film Council, 47
semiology, 9, 75–6
Serbia, film material on, 101
Service Cinématographique de l'Armée, 19
Seton-Watson, C.I.W., 149
*Settimana Incom.*, 19
Seymour-Ure, C., 108
Shirer, W., 171
Silverstein, N., 53–4

207

# Index

Lightning Source UK Ltd.
Milton Keynes UK
22 October 2009
145297UK00002B/40/P